SPEAK TO ME, BROTHER

Books by Anne Miller Downes

SPEAK TO ME, BROTHER
THE PILGRIM SOUL
THE HIGH HILLS CALLING
THE EAGLE'S SONG
MARY DONOVAN
HEARTWOOD
ANGELS FELL
UNTIL THE SHEARING
SO STANDS THE ROCK

Speak to Me, Brother

BY
ANNE MILLER DOWNES

PEOPLES BOOK CLUB

CHICAGO

COPYRIGHT, 1954, BY
ANNE MILLER DOWNES

PRINTED IN THE
UNITED STATES OF AMERICA

This is a special edition published exclusively for the members of the Peoples Book Club, P. O. Box 6570A, Chicago 80, Illinois. It was originally published by J. B. Lippincott Company.

For

Grace, Carl and Margaret

BOOK I
A Concert Grand Piano
11

BOOK II
Coming of Age
83

BOOK III
The Accounting
215

SPEAK TO ME, BROTHER

Book I: A Concert Grand Piano

CHAPTER I

THE GIRL WAS making her way up the steep side of a ravine toward a country road. To speak of her ascent as climbing would hardly be accurate for with the agility of a chamois she found a foothold on the slightest roughness, stepping lightly over or around boulders, her bare toes seeming to caress lichen and moss.

At one sheltered level she stopped to brush aside leaves that were half covering the delicate hepatica and spring beauty. As she stood for a moment looking down at the fragile texture of the pink and white blossoms there came into her face that half smiling, tender, wondering expression that often can be seen on the countenance of the hardiest woodsman when he suddenly comes on this affirmation that snow and storm and winter are past and spring has arrived.

Adjusting the strap around her books, securing her stockings and shoes, she pressed the awkward bundle hard against her side, then straightened up. One might wonder how she was to proceed, for confronting her was a nearly perpendicular rock; however, without hesitation she raised herself on tiptoes, grasped the slender trunk of a birch and as though weightless sprang to the level above.

Here she became conscious of the man who had been standing there for some time, hardly ten feet from the road, curiously watching her throughout the entire ascent. Her face which had become flushed with the exertion now expressed surprise as she stood before him and, in answer to his gruff, "Well, Valeria, where did *you* come from?" murmured almost inaudibly, "From school, sir."

"You know who I am?"

"Yes, sir." Did she know! Her brother Phil, who was often irreverent, usually spoke of "the great Uncle William." Once, in discussing him she had argued, "There is probably nothing great about him, only rich." Phil had answered, "To the poor, the rich are always great—great monsters, great benefactors or great objects of envy, but always great."

Remembering Phil, there was the glint of a smile in the eyes she raised to look at him. She saw a portly middle-aged man with heavy jowls, a nose too large for even that face, bushy eyebrows and bushy grayish-blond hair. His expansive waistline suggested heavy eating, rich dinners such as she had never known and a sedentary mode of life such as she had not encountered. Still, beneath the heavy eyebrows the eyes held a kindly expression as he stared at her.

He carried his coat over his arm and altogether he looked flushed if not fagged. Forgetting her shyness and embarrassment, she spoke eagerly in a voice now vibrant with the indefinable quality half solicitous, half soothing—something eternally maternal. "You must be tired walking up that hill, I never knew it to be so hot on a spring day. I don't think Mother is expecting you. Why are you walking?"

Didn't she know he owned a beautiful blue automobile? Hadn't its elegance impressed all the neighbors when it was parked in front of their village house at the time of her father's funeral? Hadn't the great Uncle William driven all the way from Cleveland with his wife and chauffeur to place his blue car among the drab blacks in the funeral procession and call on Mother later? A brief call to be sure and Phil had remarked, "How solicitously he asked Mother if Father carried insurance that would tide her over." Now here was the great Uncle

William puffing up the hill like a poor farmer, red-faced and spent and what a mess he was going to see when he reached the new home. Somehow she must warn her mother.

They were standing in the shade at the side of the road. He took out his handkerchief and mopped first his brow, then his entire face even reaching his neck within the confines of a stiff collar. "Unseasonable heat! Open winter—climate must be changing." He added gruffly, "Aren't you going to put on your shoes?"

"No, sir. I like to go barefoot at home."

"Well. You do—huh? How much farther up this hill?"

"Only a quarter of a mile." Then with the eager curiosity of youth, "How did you get here?"

"I drove to the house in the village where I expected to find you. They gave me directions. Drive one mile north on the concrete road—that turned out to be two miles—take the second left, second house up the dirt road. Road! No one in his senses would drive a car up this grade, over those rocks. Road! Almost crumbling off the side into that ravine. One bounce, one skid—must be seventy to a hundred feet down in places. Some of this up-state New York country is mighty primitive. We have good level roads around Cleveland. Now you say another quarter mile."

"They should have said a mile and a half." Her lips curved in a mischievous smile. "Our neighbor, Mr. Waters' man, drives up and down this road every day in his car."

"Car? What kind of a car?"

The smile gave way to laughter. "I think it's a Model T but I've only heard it called Lazy Liz. My brother says it must have been the first one Henry Ford ever made. Anyway it works. Mr. Waters' men drive trucks too. Milk trucks. My brother thinks Henry Ford is a genius. Did you know he brings cars off an assembly line? Phil says they are coming out like popcorn out of a popper and so cheap that pretty soon every farmer can own one. Then they'll have to put in new roads even in back country and farms, even our farm will increase in value."

He was looking sharply at her. "Well, you can tell your brother that may not be all the balderdash it sounds like. My opinion of that Detroit mechanic is he'll be a millionaire or broke in the next few years. He's a born gambler."

With child-like frankness, "How did you make your money, Uncle William?"

He looked startled but answered, "Drygoods and real estate. It's all gambling."

She was leading the way, her slender feet seeking the cool moist earth at the edge of the road. She spoke apologetically, "I'm afraid you'll find the hill from here up the steepest part of the road."

"Well, take it slow. I've got myself into this now so I'll see it through." He added, "Except for your father's funeral, it's a good many years since I've seen any of you or known much about you. Perhaps you can get me caught up." He was looking at her sharply. "You seem to be intelligent; perhaps you can explain the whole situation to me. Why did you leave the village house, only four miles from the city limits and civilization, where you and your father and your grandparents were born? Your mother owned the place. Years ago, I signed off, your Uncle Sam signed off, leaving your father sole owner. No mortgage—unless your father put one on later?"

She looked straight ahead and spoke with great seriousness. "No, sir, there was no mortgage but some people wanted it because it was authentic early American and it was a little small for six children, not enough bedrooms and not enough land and Mother was offered two thousand dollars for it and she needed the money. Mother is very impulsive, you know."

"She is—huh?"

"Yes, sir."

"Then why, if that house wasn't good enough did she bring you all up here? Or have you got a mansion on top of the hill?"

The eyes she turned to him held an alarmed expression. She

must disabuse him of that idea. "Oh, no, sir. We are not on top of the hill. It's not such a big house but it has beautiful farmland and woods. Mother loves land and woods. We owned it and I think—I think it was very cheap, something Father got from a client who was leaving it. There are almost no taxes and no mortgage and—"

"Well, and what?"

She looked at him with an intense expression. "What counted was the food. The farmer on the hill, Mr. Waters, works the land and we get all the milk and eggs and vegetables we can use."

"He rents it? Pays good rent?"

"Oh, no, he doesn't pay rent—only in food." Then with emphasis, "We are getting along very well. You see—"

"See what?"

"Perhaps you never knew that Father had to go to work in the factory office while he studied nights to get his law degree. He had been admitted to the bar only a few years before he died. He and Mother had always intended fixing up this place with all the land and woods, plenty to eat while they educated us. He wanted us all to have college educations. I think Mother is trying to do what he planned." Now there was a glint of laughter in her eyes. "He had promised me a gold ring with my birthstone if I crammed and finished college when I am twenty. He promised Phil, my brother, a gold watch when he finished. Phil wants either to go to Cornell and be a doctor or be a composer. He is a fine musician but Mother says she has taught him all she knows."

They were again resting in the shade. He spoke with harsh bluntness. "Phil is the hunchback?"

The smile left her eyes, giving way to hot anger. She spoke as she might speak to one of her own age. "Phil is not a hunchback. Phil is very handsome."

"Huh? I was given to understand he was a cripple. Don't know as I got a good look at him during the funeral—pretty big crowd there. Seems to me I remember your father borrowing quite a sum of money from me when the boy was a year or two old—had to have expensive treatment, just had a new baby to pay for—must have been you."

Why was the girl so angry? Her eyes were fairly smoldering. Hot temper? She surprised him when she demanded, "Didn't Father pay you back?"

"Every cent, though I didn't ask for the money. I remember very distinctly being told the boy would be a cripple."

The girl's own back seemed to straighten and stiffen as she answered, "I will explain that. Naturally I was a baby and would not know about borrowing money nor what I cost nor exactly what happened to Phil but I have been told. When Phil was a very little boy he cried all the time, night and day and they knew he had pains somewhere and then he couldn't get up and down the way he should and they took him to doctors, then to New York to a great hospital and a noted specialist—I don't remember his name but he said it was tuberculosis of the spine and he could be cured for they had caught it in time and he *was* cured although it took a great deal of time and cost lots of money and kept Father and Mother very poor."

She had poured out the explanation hardly stopping for breath. Before he could speak she went on, "Phil is wonderful. Mother never allowed him to do everything other boys did like baseball or staying too long in the water and he learned not to cry about it. He always laughed. Now he's all right and he's very smart in school and he's very handsome."

"Well."

Now she seemed rather ashamed of her angry outburst. "I guess it makes me mad when people call Phil a cripple. That's one reason we like it on a farm. He must always have good food and plenty of rest and fresh air and then he'll be all right, never have trouble."

He smiled. "Seems you like your brother. You'd fight for him —huh?"

She turned her head away as she answered quietly, "We get along."

"So you're younger than Phil?"

"I'm nearly fifteen."

"You could easily pass for sixteen or seventeen."

He started to walk on. "What about the others? It's the younger girl, Barbara, I'm supposed to be interested in. Twelve or thirteen, I believe?"

"Yes, sir."

"Your Aunt Sophie fell in love with her when she saw her at the funeral. Never stops talking about her. Your aunt's like that. If she sets her heart on a platinum diamond bracelet or anything else, you can argue and stall but you get it for her in the end. A baby or a daughter—not so easy—huh? Not so easy to buy her a baby or a little girl?"

She looked completely perplexed and made no answer. Then as the silence seemed embarrassing, she said, "Barb is very pretty."

As they started up the steep rise, he turned to her with an affectionate smile lighting his heavy countenance. "I make my guess it'll be a gold wedding band you'll get before you're twenty. It was you that I noticed at the funeral. Must have got those eyes from your mother's side. No lovers yet? They don't wait out here in the country."

Her eyes were following the movement of her bare toes as a crimson flush started in her face spreading down even to her throat; yet there was laughter in her eyes and she sighed with happy relief. Evidently he had not seen the youth with rolled up trousers, shoes and socks strung over his shoulder, hand clasped in hers as they slipped and slid and splashed their way up the stream now swollen by spring freshets. The boy had cut back through the fields to the village apparently just in time. Now as Uncle William repeated his question with his insistent "huh?" she shook her head demurely. "No, sir."

Was it a lie? How could she tell? A friend? Of course Jim

17

was only a friend. She knew quite well what her Uncle William meant by lovers and that wasn't so about Jim, and she repeated, "No, sir." Then with sudden courage, "Would you mind if I ran ahead and told Mother you are coming? I'll send one of the twins to meet you. I'm awfully late."

"You'll do nothing of the kind. I'll take the scolding if there is any. I'm enjoying getting acquainted with you. Tell me about your schooling. Are you bright, up in your class? Cramming? Poring over your books at night? Not out with the boys? You keep a hired girl?"

Hired girl! Her eyes were brimful of laughter for she could fairly hear Phil answer that one. He would swing out his long, thin arm in that funny way and bow in her direction. She could hear him say, "Of course we keep a hired girl. Here she is, named Val, our drudge, our woman of all work." Once when her father was still alive, her English teacher, Robert Loring, planning extra work for her and Phil, had suggested Valeria come to his house in the evening. She had been too embarrassed to offer excuses but Phil had answered, "Val's rather busy evenings, even mornings and noontime. You see she has a baby named Miriam that she's always taken care of, still a troublesome brat, twin boys to haul out of bed mornings, dress and feed and get back into bed before midnight, a nearly useless older brother and a mother suffering from arthritis, often confined to a chair or bed." Oh, how funny Phil could be. She was startled when breaking through her thoughts came the "huh?"

"Oh, no. We can't afford a hired girl." Then she repeated with emphasis, "We're getting along very well. We love it up here on the farm."

"Where did you get that name? Who ever heard it before? Valeria."

She laughed. "Mother says that she and Father had a pact. She was to name the first boy and Father was to name the first girl. She named Phil for her father, Philip Ainsworth, and Father named me Valeria."

"For what ancestor? Never heard it in our family. None of the Macraes went much beyond Mary, Elizabeth, Hannah or Emily."

"I never heard where he got it. I really think he just liked it."

"Sounds exactly like him—full of notions. Ambitious even as a little boy. Might have become anything with that ambition. You want to learn a lesson from that, Val. Your father married before he was twenty-one, girl without a cent, poor college professor's daughter. Brought a grand piano with her, then six children." He seemed very earnest about this. "You must have sense when you grow up. People don't have such families these days. You have to think about what you can afford. Ought to give children a chance, advantages, education, not just breed like rabbits. Six children!"

"Really seven. One baby, Constance, died."

"Yes, I think I heard of that."

"Did you?" She spoke absently, thinking Phil would have replied, "How did you, our great Uncle William, ever hear of that trivial event, the death of an eight-months-old baby?" They walked on the level in silence and for a moment she was lost in memory of the baby and how she cried that day as she helped Phil put the cradle in the attic, quietly and stealthily so Mother would not see them doing it.

He stopped to rest and she spoke almost as she would to a child, "We're almost there."

They rounded a bend in the road and came upon the house. Before them was the place she had been bragging about. He stood staring at it.

She hoped he was seeing the row of wonderful sugar maples on each side of the road, the two magnificent elms—oh, such beauties—standing where the lawn should be. She hoped he would notice the great pines and hemlocks, dark and rich and so inviting on the hill or the wide fertile fields across which the afternoon sun was sending such a beautiful light.

She glanced at him nervously and saw his eyes were fastened

on the old house with its center doorway, its row of eyebrow windows and slanting roof. The paint was peeling off and the side verandah sagged at one end. Then he gazed at the fence or at what was left of it. Then there were the sheds and the barn. Once that barn had been red. Should she tell him how happy they had been when they found the roof didn't leak? It was the only roof that *didn't* leak when they moved in.

The great Uncle William's silence was so depressing that she spoke with unusual pride. "Phil and I, as soon as we can, will be bringing in some money. Then we're going to fix everything."

Still silent, he only stared at the place. They went through what should have been a gate and then the twins came shouting as they raced across the grass followed by two barking dogs. "Val, Val, where have you been? Miri cut her head open."

They had been taught to come home from school and change into play clothes but, exaggerating the heat, they had nearly stripped. They were in rags and tatters, dirt smeared on faces, arms, and feet, caked on knees. Soberly she introduced them. "This is Mark and this is Andrew. This is your Uncle William."

There was a moment of cold silence and the most deadly sort of appraisal. The two boys stared at the man and their only motion was the digging of bare toes into the dirt. Uncle William cleared his throat and said, "Well, one blue eyes, one brown. Which is which?"

Valeria repeated the introduction. Mark with the brown eyes. Andy with blue, and a little smaller but quite as strong.

Again, "Well, twins, huh?"

Another awkward silence, then Valeria laid a hand on one shoulder as she whispered, "Run tell Mother that Uncle William is here from Cleveland."

They were off shouting, the dogs after them. She turned with a forced smile to the big man. "Won't you come in?"

They walked down the dirt path and she noticed he tested the railing before using it to help him mount the paintless steps.

CHAPTER II

VALERIA'S HAND was on the doorknob and, with all the hostess-courtesy her mother had taught her, she was starting to say "Come right in," when the words were lost in a bellow from inside. "Hold there—no entrance! Go around back."

Through the few inches of opening, she saw two saw horses and heavy planks on which she could just discern two pairs of shoes, two trouser legs, all liberally spattered with paint. Phil's voice—and what a charming voice it was compared to the gruff voice she had been listening to for the last half hour—Phil's voice, clear, resonant, gay, calling, "We're painting the ceiling, Val, only about a square yard more and we'll move into the parlor tomorrow. Jake's down helping." Then in his high clear tenor he sang lustily his version of one of their Christian Endeavor hymns. "Paint me and I shall be whiter than snow."

Now above Phil's voice came a shouting from somewhere in the rear, "Mommie, Mommie, we're to tell you that Uncle William's here from Cleveland."

She heard Phil's ejaculation, "Great Scott!" as she turned to the portly gentleman standing behind her. Her face was flushed but she drew herself up with dignity. "We'll have to go around to the back if you don't mind. There are only two doors."

She glanced at his fine, highly polished black shoes, then led the way along the well-trodden dirt path circling the house. Once as the passage was uncomfortably narrowed between tumbled packing boxes, she apologized, "You see we're not entirely settled yet. We're going to chop these up for kindling wood."

He muttered, "Thrifty lot, aren't you?"

The door opened directly into the kitchen, a large sunny room which extended across the entire width of the house. Here was surprising order and neatness. At one end was a sealed fireplace, its age established by the row of old closets and warming ovens. However, in front of it stood a modern range and nearby a new sink with a shining faucet.

At the other end of the room was a bay with three windows composed of tiny panes of glass. He looked at the large cleanly scrubbed oval table.

Valeria must give her mother time, so with the air of a Newport hostess showing a guest about a mansion, she explained, "This is our kitchen. We eat here because what would have been our dining room is Mother's room. She has arthritis but just now she's been laid up with sciatica, a terrible pain in her hip and leg and it's hard for her to go up and down stairs. Someday, when Phil and I can get around to it, we plan to put an addition on at this side—a new dining room downstairs looking right out into the flower garden, we'll have a flower garden then —and over the fields to the woods and hills. Then upstairs we'll have a new bedroom and even an extra bathroom."

"You have a bathroom?"

"Oh, yes, upstairs; but Mother has a lavatory of her own. We have just put in both. We have just finished putting in electricity too. You see it's very convenient. Really it's wonderful and we are getting along very well."

She walked slowly across the room and placed her hand on a doorknob. For a moment she lost her composure and spoke nervously, "I can show you the parlor but I'm afraid we can't sit there because everything's heaped up and covered ready for Phil and Jake to paint and paper. You could look in. It's really a large room, though just now—"

He walked over and looked in. True the furniture was piled up; might be chairs, tables, sofa; packing boxes might contain books but no one could be prepared for that monster of a grand, yes, a concert grand piano, sheathed in gray canvas. An elephant in that low-ceilinged room could not have been less appropriate or more uncomfortable looking. He muttered, "What? That piano!"

Valeria whispered, "Mother couldn't live without her piano. It was Grandfather Ainsworth's. He was a musician." Then she added, "Mother loves music and woods."

He turned away and walked toward a cushioned armchair near the bay. "I'll sit here."

Valeria followed him, her face flushing with embarrassment. She said in a low voice, "When Mother comes in, that's the only chair she can rest in."

"What about this?" He was reaching for a baby's highchair and Valeria was laughing when another door opened and Mother walked in. Louise Ainsworth Macrae. He had always wondered about her. His wife, Sophie, hated her thoroughly. He knew how it always worked. Any man could tell you. You met a man, liked him, found him mighty congenial but if the wives didn't hit it off there would be no dinner parties, no bridge, no visits or return visits. On the other hand when the wives did hit it off you dined with some milksop, stifling your yawns through evening after evening.

Now, even before they spoke, he wondered; his eyes narrowed as he watched her with his sharpest expression. She was thin, almost emaciated, bony, the skin stretched tight over the cheekbones, the lustrous dark eyes that Valeria had inherited were sunken. The pretty features—yes, Valeria had that fine nose and chin. She wore a warm-looking dark red wool—dress?—no, it must be called a robe.

She held out a slender hand, "This is a great surprise, William."

He took her hand. "You had no telephone or I'd have called when I reached the village."

She smiled. "No, we have no telephone. Sometimes it's inconvenient, then sometimes I'm not sure that it isn't a great blessing."

She turned to the armchair and held the arms as she slowly lowered herself into it. "Can you find a chair? Had you come some few days from now, we would have been more settled. As it is we reek with the smell of paint."

Valeria had chosen for him the stoutest of the odd chairs and he sat down.

The sun was just above the rim of hills ready to sink out of view but now a beautiful golden light seemed to fill the room. Valeria had disappeared but within minutes she was back, changed into a gingham dress and began busying herself at the stove and sink.

The polite pleasantries dispensed with, the inquiries concerning health and business superficially disposed of, Mrs. Macrae asked, "What are your plans, William? Where is your car? What about the night?"

He had rooms engaged at the Inn in the village but he would like, if he were welcome, to take supper with them. He cleared his throat, then abruptly, "I'd like a chance for a talk alone with you. I haven't driven from Cleveland—though I did stop in New York for some business—didn't come for nothing."

She smiled and said smoothly, "No—no?—" with a rising inflection.

"My car is down at the foot of the hill. I'll have to get some word to the chauffeur. Chap can go back to the Inn for supper."

"We would have been glad to take care of him. We always have plenty." She was smiling pleasantly. "But if you wish to send word, Mark and Andy will run down."

"Fine, fine." Then in his frank, brusque way, "What about his coming back for me? Nine o'clock not too late?"

"Oh, say ten or ten-thirty. I usually read or sew until near midnight."

The boys were dispatched, repeating the instructions. Valeria called, "Round up Barb and Miri, then come right back and wash up. Do you know where they are?"

Mark shrugged one shoulder. "Oh, Miri's around showing her busted head to everyone."

Uncle William turned to the mother with concern but she was still smiling calmly. "A scratch which bled a little. It has been cleaned and bandaged."

When they sat down to supper, Uncle William seemed impressed. The whole place appeared to be run like the proverbial well-oiled machine. How did Valeria, going so swiftly and quietly from stove to sink, manage to prepare such a supper? How had she slipped upstairs to superintend washing, lay out clean shirts and small pants, consult with Phil? Without fussing, Phil moved the mother's armchair to the head of the table and took his place at the opposite end. The youngest, the little girl, Miriam, sat by her mother; across the table Barbara sat between the twins Mark and Andy. Now that he could get a good look at the girl he didn't wonder Sophie had fallen in love with her. She was exquisite, with blond curls rippling over her forehead and big blue eyes glancing at him. Here as with Miriam and Andy was evidence of Macrae blood.

He found it difficult to look at Phil. He'd better remember not to call him a cripple when talking to the mother; nevertheless, in spite of all Valeria might say, a glance would tell one there was something wrong. True, there was not a great hump on the back; in fact the spine appeared to be straight but stiff. His shoulders were hunched up rather high, no slope, a square effect and he held his head a trifle to one side as though his neck had stiffened in that position.

Now he could remember his brother John's letters telling him about the trouble with the first-born son. He remembered John had called it Pott's disease, described the pain like neuralgia and there was some paralysis—not hopeless because the child was only two or three years old but it would require long, expensive treatment. The boy would die or be a complete cripple without such care and he, Uncle William sent the money by return mail, a loan, that was understood, then more money.

He remembered John's description of the little boy who, on sunny days was strapped to a board which they hooked on to the outside of the sanitarium in the Adirondacks—must have fresh air, sunshine and especial food and care. He remembered how uncomfortable he thought that must be, hooked and tied; but John had written that a child didn't mind inaction as an adult would. Children were adaptable. Yes, he was beginning to remember the details now. He remembered feeling a little small in taking John's money, paid in slow installments, but he, William, was a believer that "business is business," "you make your bed and you lie in it," "to lose a friend lend him money." After that all intercourse between the families came to a dead stop. Better go their separate ways; as Sophie said, they had nothing in common.

Again he glanced at the boy. Guess you would call him handsome; old-looking for his years too. It was not only the crippled look about his shoulders and head, the pallor of his long thin face, the satirical curve to his lips or even the piercing brilliance of his dark eyes—no, there was something else. Uncle William was used to dealing with all sorts of men. Some were plain dumb, some sharp, trustworthy and untrustworthy, honest men, crooks, one soon got their number. The one kind that a blunt Westerner couldn't tolerate was the fellow whose thoughts one couldn't fathom. Never knew what he was really thinking. Well, there was the mother and there was the son. No way of fathoming what was in those minds hidden beneath the pleasant smiles and easy talk.

Here was brother John's family. Never had he felt more out of place and ill at ease. Then, just as he was lifting his fork to appease his appetite, there came the blessing.

He laid the fork down quickly as all heads were bowed and Louise Macrae leaned forward, placed her elbows on the table, rested her forehead in her hands and prayed. This was no mumble of "God bless this food to our use and us to Thy service" such as his father had blurted out in one breath; this was a prayer. This was a prayer for food, raiment, house, strength to be honest, to be good, even to be cheerful. Everyone was mentioned by name even to the last—the uncle who had come to "break bread" with them. "If it is pleasing in Thy sight, may he enjoy length of days, prosperity and peace of heart. Amen."

If to himself he was ejaculating, "Holy Mackerel!" they did not know, for instantly when the prayer was ended, there was eager passing of such creamed potatoes, cold ham, sweet home pickles, then such chocolate cake and preserves and cups of fragrant tea, such emptying of mugs of milk as did a hungry man good both to see and enjoy.

Even before they left the table, the new, highly prized electric lights were exhibited. One would have thought electricity had been discovered recently and solely for their enjoyment. One light over the table and one over the sink and the twins had to be stopped from turning them on and off.

There was a bustle of washing and wiping and putting away dishes, the gathering of school books and Valeria's disappearing up the narrow stairs to the rooms above. Phil had vanished earlier and in course of time the mother resumed her place in the armchair near the bay and he took the seat opposite her.

Of all the hard tasks that had fallen to his lot, this was the toughest. Then he thought of Sophie. He couldn't go back and confess defeat to Sophie.

Time slipped by in desultory talk of school grades, petty illnesses. When he tried to pin her down to price of property, expenses of clothing and caring for six children, he got nowhere. Her head was bent over some mending; darning long stockings, socks, a trouser rip. Only occasionally he found the dusky dark eyes beneath the fine straight brows meeting his and then he saw something of the glittering brightness of Phil's eyes and never once did he have the remotest idea what the woman was really thinking of.

Expenses? "We are all doing very well, William."

He did not dream that stretched out on the floor in the bedroom above, Valeria and Phil lay with heads close to an old stovepipe hole, listening, trying to catch every word.

Valeria had told her brother, "We really got very well acquainted. I liked him. He's a good sport. I bet he's come to offer either a regular income to Mother or to pay for your college education."

"You're an imbecile, Val. I'll bet you my last cent he's come to get, not give."

"*Get*! Get from *us*? What could *he* get from *us*?"

"Wait and see."

Below, Uncle William's eyes traveled from sink to stove, up to the ceiling and then to the freshly painted walls. "It must have cost you plenty to fix this up—electric wiring and bathrooms. Or was it in good condition inside?"

"It was a shambles, William." She seemed to be speaking frankly now. "Perhaps one of our great sources of happiness just now is the results from our own hard work." She enumerated the accomplishments but not the cost. "Piping in water from the hill, a wonderful supply that they promise will never run dry; then the electric wiring and the bathroom, new range and sink. Imagine! There was a wooden sink, actually rotting, and an ancient iron pump. Everything had to be torn out and we needed a good plumber for that. Then, after replacing parts of floors, we could start painting and papering. Our neighbor, Mr. Waters, has a hired man, Jake, who is devoted to Phil and he is helping." She left the impression that he was helping as a friend, not mentioning that she paid him by the hour. "We plan to have the interior finished by the end of the summer and then, next spring, we'll paint the outside and perhaps make a lawn." She looked up, her eyes penetrating and in them something of a mocking smile. "You know, William, it is quite wonderful to find right at one's hand, projects, creative work for young people. Let them think it out and enjoy the thrill of accomplishment. Why, Mark and Andy did the job of replacing the bricks in the parlor fireplace. Jake taught them. Then keeping the kindling ready, cleaning and so forth will always be their job. Don't you see it will be *their* fireplace?"

He was gazing soberly about the room. There was even more mockery in her smile as she continued, "You would laugh to see them strut around when something is finished. You see, they feel like veteran builders, contractors, architects, painters, carpenters and even plasterers. They have learned a lot."

He stared at her, his eyes narrowed. He had always wondered about her, always thought of her as one of those parlor ornaments, the kind he detested and Sophie hated; always find them in college circles, smug, "cultured," conceited and superior, politic. Their bread and butter depended on playing the political game right with superiors, presidents, deans and rich alumnae. He couldn't stand the type. He had thought of her as encumbering the world—and his brother John—with a concert grand piano and six children.

He was silent and she seemed absorbed in placing a patch beneath the trouser rip. Still, he remembered that in spite of the encumbrances, John had finally got out of the factory office, entered at the bar and was practicing law. Must have been *her* project. A married man can't do it alone. His wife has to be the architect.

She broke abruptly into his thoughts. "Do you ever see your brother Sam? I'm afraid John lost track of him."

He cleared his throat uncomfortably. "There's always one black sheep in every family, so they say. Guess it's true. Sam was our black sheep, just no good."

"Tell me about him."

"Nothing much to tell and not worth telling—the black sheep."

"Still, I remember he was very good looking, very blond with blue eyes. I always fancied Barbara and Miriam look like him."

"Barbara?" He looked startled. "Perhaps when he was a little boy. Now he's an old man, no one you'd want around."

"No—no?" She rearranged the patch. "I remember John saying you and Sam were rivals for Sophie."

"Oh, that! Guess he did bring her to the house. She soon found out what he was like and dropped him. Regular Jekyll and Hyde. One night at a dance up at her school, the next night, or three or four, at some low dive."

"Yes—yes? And then you married her and became manager of her father's big department store and made a fortune in real estate besides. You must have worked hard, William?" There was something suggestive of sympathetic understanding, even admiration, in her voice.

"You work and pay dear for all you get in this world, Louise."

"I'm sure of that, William. Then what happened to Sam?"

"Disappeared. My father was a hard man, honest, poor, but one of the old-time strict kind. I saw him horsewhip Sam once, out in the barn. Sam was sixteen, a big fellow too, he'd got a girl in trouble."

"You say he disappeared?"

"Worse. Married one of those women and took her with him. Understand there was a baby born, a girl. Must be about Valeria's age. Sam joined the army, guess that life suited them both for a while. Then I believe she left him. The last I heard he was down in Mexico with the daughter."

"What is the daughter's name?"

He looked annoyed. Now why would Louise Ainsworth Macrae want to know that? He answered, "Calls her Jess, if I remember."

She repeated as though thinking it a pretty name, "Jessie Macrae." Then she added, "John always wondered about Sam. I think John was fond of him."

"John? He was the youngest—different. Never saw three boys so different. Children can be so different you'd never believe they could have come from the same parents—huh?"

"Yes, that's true, William."

This was getting him nowhere. He hadn't come here to bring

up the painful subject of Sam. He moved uneasily in his chair, scowling. Then at last the opening came.

Louise Macrae said with disarming sweetness, "Now, tell me about Sophie. Except on that day of John's funeral when I really did not see anyone—now I can't remember who was there —except on that day, I haven't seen her since my marriage. I remember you both came on. She was so good-looking. I think she graduated from the Haverhill School, didn't she?"

"Oh, yes, she was well educated, what they call a finishing school, not your college stuff but all a girl who will never have to work needs to know."

She had laid aside her mending and now she held a paper seemingly to shield her eyes from the ceiling light.

She replied, "Yes—yes?" Something annoying about the way she said No, No? or yes, yes? Something more annoying to talk to her half in the dark, her penetrating cavernous dark eyes peering out of the shadow.

Sophie. Now he knew how to go ahead. He told her of Sophie's life, very prominent socially, chairman of committees of this and that in the city, heading charity drives, president of the woman's society in one of the largest churches, strong on organization support for symphony concerts. That ought to please this woman who loved music so much she would ruin the parlor with that elephant of a piano.

Now he got down to the point, about Barbara. He kept lowering his voice and Mother's answers were inaudible to the eager ears straining above.

Only once they heard their mother's voice distinctly. "I agree with all you say, William, and I sympathize deeply with your loneliness and your dread of facing old age. I can appreciate all the hazards in adopting a strange child and somehow although Sophie and I have never been friends, I feel that she would give care and love and advantages to any child and certain pleasures such as I shall not be able to give."

Then the ears above lost the rest. Below, Louise leaned far

over and spoke in a low tone. "I am going to be frank with you, William. I don't wish to go into tiresome, boring details about myself—about my physical condition—but I have reason to believe my years are numbered. My only prayer for myself is that I may live to guide the children until they grow up to independence."

She did not explain to him how she had tried to plan and calculate. Up here their expenses had been reduced to the minimum. They had a good house, plenty of food and the simple clothing needed for school. There was some money left from John's insurance and the sale of the house and this must stretch over years. And she might advertise for music pupils if her health permitted.

Twice he cleared his throat but he seemed unable to find exactly the right words.

She relieved him by speaking frankly. "You ask to take Barbara for a long visit this summer to your place on the lake. You have more than that in mind, William."

He blurted out, "We would like to adopt her. We would give her every advantage. She would be provided for, for life."

"No." Her voice trailed off as though sudden pain and weariness had overtaken her. "No, I would never consent to that. Adopt her? No. The truth is I am thinking of Valeria. She is frightfully overworked and that will not diminish over the years."

He seized on the argument. "Yes, it would be only fair to relieve Valeria of one burden."

"I know." She sighed deeply. Then she smiled. "Valeria doesn't call her sister a burden. I have never seen a girl with a stronger maternal instinct. I hope she marries young."

"A pretty girl like Valeria? She'll be able to pick and choose." He leaned over, his face flushed with eagerness and not a little triumph. Apparently it was all going to be easier than he had expected. "Well, let's drop the question of adoption for the time being." Then, as he afterwards told Sophie, he put his big foot in it all. He spoke like a philanthrophist bestowing manna on the poor and needy. "When I come to take the little girl home with me, Louise, I'll draw you a check."

Drawing herself back against the cushion of the chair, her eyes blazed yet her voice rose hardly above a whisper. "You cannot *buy* anything here, William. You had actually persuaded me to believe it meant Barbara's welfare, freedom for Valeria and great happiness and pleasure for you and Sophie. You may understand you can neither adopt or buy her."

He felt sick and in his own blunt way he apologized and told her how he felt.

They talked on and on and on. She told him how different two sisters could be. Valeria, the born mother, sometimes too serious for her age. Barbara, the fly-away, light-hearted, gay. But they adored each other and got along beautifully together. When he rose to go the ears straining above heard her ask, "You must have Phil go down the road with you. There are no street lights until you reach the village."

They heard his hasty, "No, no, I prefer to go alone. I know the way, need the walk to cool down." Then, "When shall I come for her?"

They were arranging a date. Then there was the door closed. Then silence.

Valeria's face was buried in her arms. Phil raised himself and reaching out his thin hand laid it on her head. He felt her whole body quiver and shake with the sobs she was stifling.

He whispered, "What are you crying about, Val? Rich uncle suddenly wants our pretty Barbara. She'll get everything money can buy."

She raised her head. "She can't send Barb away. There's something black and wicked in this. I can feel it. I'll hate Mother if she does it. I'll hate her. She is doing something wicked."

"Don't, Val. Please don't talk like that. You can't hate Mother. She's not herself. Haven't you seen what I've seen?

She's never been the same since Father died. It's the way she sold the house, the way she's done everything."

She lay still for some time, her body first quivering then stiffening under his caressing hand.

Finally she straightened up. "You've won, Phil."

"The bet? Sure, I knew he hadn't come to *give*. He came to *get*."

CHAPTER III

"It's a low-down trick, Val—eavesdropping."

Valeria and Phil were walking down the road, the long jaunt to the high school in the village. They had dropped back, leaving Barbara to go ahead with her younger schoolmates.

"I'm not ashamed. I was eaten up with curiosity to find out what brought him here. I was sure it was to give Mother a regular income or send you through college. That's not *mean* eavesdropping."

"I think we ought to make a clean breast of the thing and tell Mother all we heard. Then we could talk about it and argue with her."

"I'll do nothing of the kind. In the first place arguing with Mother gets you nowhere. In the second place I'm not always honorable like you. I keep some things to myself—even lie about them."

"Like wading up the brook with Jim when Mother thinks you're 'conferring with your teacher?' "

Her face reddened. "How did you know that?"

"Don't get so flustered. I saw the picture like a vision in the new paint I was putting on the ceiling." His eyes were sharp as he watched her. "The hem of your skirt was wet, little girl. You're a simpleton. I also notice the silly, moony expression on Jim's face when he watches you in school."

"You're too smart. You see more than there is to see. Besides, you're always honorable, Phil. You're good."

He laughed, a short, mocking laugh, "Thanks. I'll treasure that. You forget which of us thought the old fellow was a good sport, come to endow us with his extra dollars, give us an income and play the part of Santa Claus? Which one of us thought only evil—that he had come to get, not give?"

"You always win an argument but you might learn not to crow."

"Well—huh? That's an idea."

He had imitated his Uncle William perfectly.

"You'd better stop that—huh?—or you'll get the habit and be saying it when you shouldn't."

"Kind of effective—hate to drop it."

"Phil," she spoke seriously, "what burned me up was the way Mother acted this morning. She was so cheerful and sweet and innocent. You'd never dream she had just done something so wicked."

He shrugged. "She hasn't done anything yet. Besides, what's so wicked when you come to think it over? Allowing a niece to visit an adoring rich aunt and uncle? Nothing wicked about that. She'll break the news gently to us, in time. At that we were acting too this morning, hypocrites all around. Bad thing to start. I think we'd better own up."

"I won't. I didn't do it in a dishonorable way. I was hoping for something awfully good."

They were nearing the school grounds. She tossed her head and was turning away when his thin fingers reached out suddenly and fastened on her arm. He was smiling in that pleasant baffling way his mother had. "Believe me, I'm not good. 'As a man thinketh so is he.' That makes me a bona fide son of Satan. I—"

She interrupted, "I don't believe in Satan."

"Now you listen. I know you don't believe in Satan or sin or evil, yet you're calling Mother wicked before she's done anything. All proving only that you're a girl. Also proving you're an innocent imbecile. Now you listen to this elderly statesman. Don't you go getting in love with Jim Ferris."

She was angry. "I'm not. He's just a friend."

His fingers tightened as she tried to pull away, asking angrily, "What's the matter with Jim?"

"Nothing. Absolutely nothing. At least nothing that you could understand. He's one of the nicest boys in town, one of the very nicest."

"He's a friend just like Louise or Flora or Jane—"

"Not exactly. Watch your step, little girl. Remember I won my bet last night."

She walked off, the color and anger and agitation slowly receding. However, her brows were puckered as she entered the schoolroom door. She thought, "Phil's wonderful. He's so good but he's as hard to argue with or understand as Mother. What a mess I'm in, that Latin and my English essay only outlined."

During the chapel quarter hour she planned. Latin came at the end of the morning so she would use her recess to prepare that. What could she do about English? The class came directly after assembly. Her favorite class, her favorite subject, her favorite teacher. She was proud of her high marks in composition, the only marks that averaged far above Phil's. She had a brilliant idea. She had chosen as her subject, "A Walk in the Ravine." It had been selected long before Jim Ferris had entered that loved place. All that she intended to write was clear in her mind, the source of the stream from the high hills, trickling down into this deep cut until, in spring, it became a torrent rushing over the rocks—the wooded slopes, the treasure house of flowers and berries and mosses, the animal life, insects, mammals and fish, the coolness when the fields were hot.

As she entered the classroom door she was smiling but was quite unconscious of her heightened color and the brilliance of her eyes. *If* (it was only one chance in fifteen, the number in her class), if he should call on her, she would bluff it, hold up her outline and read, fill in the words after school and get the paper in on the right day. It was exciting, sort of a challenge.

Doctor Robert Loring. Without question he was the most popular member of the faculty, perhaps the most popular person in the school. The boys would have so voted because on the baseball field he was one of them, playing, as Phil said, "For all he's worth." He was good at tennis and basketball. Perhaps the girls would have voted for him because he was young and good-looking; it was known that he had come directly from his university to teach in their school.

The hum of conversation ceased, the faces were turned toward the door as he walked in with his easy stride, and placed his papers on the desk. Yes, Valeria thought, it was an easy stride, not the mincing step and air of importance of many of the teachers but the air of one who tramped the hills. He had come down through the woods one day and stopped to call on Mother and often Valeria noticed telltale mud on the sides of his shoes. She liked that. She liked his hands, the way he opened a book, the sensitive way his fingers turned the pages. She liked the way he treated a boy who had not done his required reading. He would smile at him and say, "How much you've missed." However, if by any chance she found herself near him in a hall or if, as once happened, he walked across the school grounds with her, she scarcely raised her eyes, became stupidly tongue-tied.

Now, after his pleasant "Good Morning," his eyes traveled across the rows of students. Was it the unusual brilliance of Valeria's eyes, the agitation apparent in her face that attracted his attention? The blow fell. He said, "We will have time to hear two of these short essays, then discuss the form. You may read yours, Valeria."

She rose, clutching the single paper in her hand. Her heart seemed to be throbbing in her throat, her cheeks were burning. She looked directly into his eyes; fine eyes, gray-blue in color, sometimes penetrating, sometimes full of laughter but now definitely sympathetic, almost affectionate as they looked into hers. Not in words but in a flash of deep understanding she felt he was so honest, so direct, so clean.

She bent her head over the paper for a few seconds before she looked up and spoke in a low tone. "I am not prepared. I have nothing but my outline." She saw the smiling eyes become cooly penetrating. He turned to another pupil.

Up in the little house on the hill, the mother still seemed "sweet, cheerful and innocent" as she kept an eye on three children who had been scrubbed and dressed by Valeria and now impatiently kicked and squirmed and wiggled as they waited for Jake and the Model T. Every day, the car arrived apparently loaded to capacity with Mr. Waters' two children and another picked up from a small cottage tucked over the hill. Always with a prayer that the brakes would hold, Mrs. Macrae watched Jake slow down, heave it around, backing into the mud of their driveway, then with the authority and seriousness of a general deploying troops for battle, allocate the spots where Mark and Andy must stand and the lap on which Miriam must sit.

To look at those six clean, eager child faces, some serious, all excited, all living in the moment only, sometimes brought a tightening of Mrs. Macrae's throat.

To no one but Jake would such a cargo be entrusted. If by any chance there was a breakdown or a tire popped, he merely stopped, ordered them down with, "Now hoof it, kids. No dillydallying on the road." However, there had been only two such incidents.

On this spring morning when the car was packed, Jake jumped down and strode up the path toward Mrs. Macrae who was standing in the doorway. He stood six feet two, a heavy man with a long angular face, an easy smile, deep-set eyes of a dark blue that surprised one for they never seemed designed for his burned brown skin. A plain, homely young man, he swung his large hands as he walked and Mrs. Macrae was remembering what Mr. Waters once remarked: "Some men are good for nothing. Jake's one of these fellows who's good for everything."

They exchanged good mornings. His voice was surprisingly low, his grammar not too secure. "I'm thinking, Mrs. Macrae, that Phil oughtn't to be reaching up at those ceilings. Mr.

Waters says there's nothing pressing today and after I deliver the kids, I'll come back and get the rough done."

She thanked him and stood watching as he folded his long legs into the space left for him in the car. It spit and choked and churned but somehow, although sounding as if it were likely to explode at any moment, made the first steep grade, then went merrily out of sight.

She stood for some time, supported by the door jamb on one side, her stout cane on the other. The eyes that had followed the car turned first to the fine maples bordering the road. What a wonderful place to be! Beyond those maples the ground fell off sharply toward the ravine. She strained to hear the murmur of the stream and pictured vividly the rushing water, the rocks, the wild flowers, the mosses, shrubs, birds and fascinating insects. No human habitation in sight. A wonderful place to be . . .

She looked again at the maples as she thought of what they might mean to different people. It was back in March that their real friendship with Jake had its beginning. One day he made his way through the snow to the kitchen door and in answer to their cordial welcome came in and sat awkwardly on the edge of a chair. They had known him only as Mr. Waters' hired man and the trustworthy chap who took the little ones to school.

Bluntly he stated the purpose of his visit. "I wondered what you planned to do about tapping those maples."

Louise didn't understand. "Tapping the maples? Is there something wrong with our maple trees?"

"About sapping time. If you want I'll take charge. These two husky boys are big enough to help, learn how."

To her many questions, while the twins, an eager audience, stood near, he answered, "Still winter? No, by the middle of March we can tap on the south side. I'm going to do all the maples back on the ridge."

Then came days when the boys watched and learned, when their mother listened to the ring of the hammer driving the metal spikes; when there came that first strange drop, drop, drop as the sap began plopping into the bottom of the tin buckets; then the steady music of the flow as buckets were emptied into big pans. Sometimes the buckets would overflow and Jake taught the boys to drink that new sap coming from some deep springs of nature. The boys would rush home to tell Mother how a whole barrel of sap was needed to make a gallon of syrup and a gallon of syrup made eight pounds of sugar and how Jake considered their trees almost the best in the hill and how on one big giant of a tree that stood alone and got plenty of sun he would hang four buckets. By the first of April there were roaring fires as the sap was boiled at night and old Grandfather Waters told the boys that in his youth it was quite a common sight to see five or six hundred pounds of maple sugar piled up in the country store for then, in this upstate country, that was the only sugar the homemaker used; and Louise, always worrying about whether she had been wise or reckless in bringing her family up on this hill, would go to sleep in peace sure that this was a rich experience for her children. Now as she stood looking at the maples she saw much more than their beauty.

She knew the city. She had lived in the city. She scarcely remembered her mother who had died before her school years. Her father had been a professor of choral work, trained the Glee Club, taught organ and piano in a large city university and what they called home was an old-fashioned apartment not too far from the college in the very heart of the noisy, dusty, crowded thoroughfares where strangers passed strangers, where no one ever seemed to hear the cry that must have risen from thousands of human hearts—"Speak to me, Brother."

Her father had said that, one day when they were caught in a crowd of pushing, hurrying humanity. She remembered him vividly as he looked that morning: shoulders bent, hair prematurely gray, his sensitive musician's face showing the nervous strain under which most musicians work and live. He had said to her, "Watch these faces, Louise, not one in a hundred evidences any peace of mind. Lonely faces. I can hear the cry from many a heart, 'Speak to me, Brother,' I should like to set their cry to music." Then he had added, "If my quartette sells we'll get a summer in the mountains. Perhaps there will be a ravine, perhaps the smell of balsam."

The quartette did not sell. However, he managed to send her away to the less expensive schools but always to one where music was important. Did he dream of her as a concert pianist? Afterwards she often wondered, but he died when she was in her freshman year at college and scarcely a month later she met John Macrae.

Sixteen years. Yes, sixteen years of such a depth of love and fruition as is given to few. There should be no lonely, only child. They would allocate the money from her small inheritance to pay for babies; John had his regular exacting work in the factory office and out of that they could save to help him achieve his ambition to enter the bar. And to what a paradise he had brought her—the small house on the elm-lined village street. The country walks and what she always called, "Father's ravine." Up on the high hills there was the smell of balsam and the fragrant needles underfoot as she and John walked hand in hand through the templed woods in early summer evenings, Paradise. The strange brothers who never came to see them but signed off all rights to the property, leaving them feeling like a king and queen, sole owners of a kingdom they would not have exchanged for a city mansion.

That second baby was so beautiful and John named her Valeria and John had said, "Now I have two of you, almost exactly alike, same dark eyes, thick brown hair, same little nose and chin, same little hands and feet." Then the little boy ill and they thanked God that rich brother William advanced the money for his cure. They paid back every cent, for John was doing well, working in the office, studying nights, passing examinations and no one dreaming that he was working too hard. There was Barbara, a second daughter, then the death of a baby, the arrival of handsome twin boys, then later came the exquisite little girl Miriam—another Macrae with John's blue eyes and blond hair.

Six of them, and it was all still Paradise. Sometimes she and John stole away and climbed the road to wander over this tumbled down place on the hill which had been, as John said, "Sort of dumped in my lap." Sell it for the price of the land? No, they loved the deep wooded hills and Mr. Waters wanted the fields, and there was the ravine. "Someday, when we get on our feet, we'll fix this up, Louise. We'll build on back a studio big enough for your father's piano." It was always spoken of as her "father's piano" and they always joked that it took up more room than all six children together.

Paradise turned overnight into a black hell. No, no... She reached out her hand and steadied herself by touching the wall as she made her way to the kitchen and sank into her cushioned chair. The sciatica was better, oh, much better but she was lame and unsure on her feet. The doctor had said arthritis was creeping up and down her spine, stiffening her aching legs.

Useless? She was alone and in her fear and loneliness she cried out, "Dear God, if I had only been left my health!" For a moment she let the tears come, then wiped them away. "Useless? I am here. That's what matters. *I am here.* I can watch over them, guide them, love them. They need me. I am here. That's all that matters."

She was thinking of a great man whose exploits she had followed with breathless interest, a great Norwegian. Perhaps in her heart she belonged to the people of the far north countries. This man, Fridtjof Nansen. She remembered one of his exploits. Landing from a sea which was a grinding, seething mass of moving iceblocks, with no bases to fall back on, he determined to cross Greenland. He had said, "If we know there are no bases, if we know there is nothing behind us, then we must go forward."

"That's it. If one knows there are no bases to fall back on, then one goes ahead. I must go forward without fear."

She had slept little through the night after that amazing visit with William and then there had been breakfast and watching the children until they got off to school. She rested her head against the pillow.

Now she heard Jake moving into the parlor. How good to have that rough kind fellow helping Phil out. How good. Yes, she would remember there were no bases left behind. She would look steadily forward. And as Jake worked, she slept.

* * *

Valeria was not thinking of it as either father's or grandfather's ravine. It was *her* ravine. As she and Jim reached the crossroad, she hesitated, looked up the long steep dirt road. She ought to go straight home. Long since Phil would be there, changed into work clothes and likely toiling like mad on the parlor ceiling. Barbara lingering in the village with some friends. Mark and Andy and Miri back from school and Mother left alone to look after them.

Phil never had to walk up the long hill. One of the big dairymen came back from the city about the time Phil's last class ended and it was understood that when he rattled the cans and whistled, Phil was to leave promptly and ride home.

Now Jim watched her as she stood looking down at her brown oxfords, hesitating. He was a nice looking boy, neither handsome nor plain. Fairly tall, well built, a pleasant smiling face and nice manners. He belonged to a nice family. In fact everything about Jim Ferris was nice. He had a nice mother, a father who was generally acknowledged to be the leading physician of the district. They lived in a comfortable colonial style house with nice grounds. Dr. Ferris had inherited the home and as the hospital was situated between the village and the city he preferred to stay in the old house rather than to move into town.

He expected his only son to go leisurely through college and medical school and inherit his practice.

They were not rich though they were far from poor. Just perfectly comfortable. The doctor drove one of the new expensive cars but he also kept ready a splendid span of horses and Jim had his own saddle horse which he usually used when he went out to the country club to play tennis or golf. He played both games fairly well.

For months his eyes had been following Valeria whenever she appeared in hallway or classroom and for weeks he had managed to join her, sometimes walking part way up the dirt road and twice pushing up through the ravine. Only yesterday had they taken off shoes and stockings and waded, for at last her shyness had worn off and she found herself talking, laughing and absolutely free with this new friend.

He reached for her hand, drawing her toward him. "Come on. If we only had bathing suits that pool is deep enough for a swim."

The idea made her laugh. She was following him down a grassy path. They found a boulder, sat down and removed their shoes and stockings.

"You have the prettiest feet and ankles I've ever seen, Val."

She had learned no smooth way to accept compliments, so she ignored this one and said, "I got my skirt wet yesterday and Phil noticed and guessed I had been wading in the brook."

"Did you tell him to mind his own business?"

"He thinks I am his business."

"It was when you slipped you wet your skirt. Now hold tight to my hand and I won't let you slip."

It was such fun and oh, so beautiful. The afternoon sun sifting down through the tree branches. The exquisite color of the budding leaves, the moist earth, the minnows and water spiders and sometimes in the deeper pools trout darting through the clear water.

Had anyone asked what they talked about, she might truthfully have said, "Nothing." Only once was there something of moment. He spoke casually, "Did I tell you that I'm off Cornell—going to Harvard."

"No. Why? I thought your father said Cornell was so wonderful."

"It's what Mother always wanted—Harvard."

They had to climb around the deep pool. At first he held her hand tightly and then, when they were on safe ground, he dropped his shoes and socks and drew her into his arms.

She scarcely breathed. He pushed back the hair from her forehead and looked into her eyes. "Val, will you be my girl?"

Her heart was throbbing, choking her and she could not speak.

"Val, will you? Will you be my girl? Promise me."

"I guess I am your girl, Jim. I'm certainly no one else's girl. I never had a boy friend before."

"I mean forever and ever, Val. I just dream about you day and night. I never get your face out of my mind. If you were old enough I'd dare Mother and Father and throw up college and get a job and we'd get married. If you were only a little older."

Once he raised his head and smiled, "Your lips are the sweetest thing in the world, Val."

So were his. The lustrous beauty of her eyes was raised to his eyes as he urged, "Promise me, Val. Promise me you won't go with other fellows when I'm in college. Promise you'll wait for me."

There was wonder in her voice. "I promise, Jim. I'm sure I'd never want to go with anyone in all the world but you."

They lingered at the parting place. She climbed the bank up the same path where Uncle William had watched her only a day ago. She stopped and put on shoes and stockings. She examined her skirt. It was dry.

CHAPTER IV

ONLY A DAY AGO. Hadn't Minerva sprung forth from Jupiter's brow completely armed? Something entire, perfect? Valeria walked slowly up the hill, her eyes filled with wonder and a light that rivaled the golden glow in the western sky.

There had been no vacuous hours in her young life; no empty days to be filled with dreams or girlish romances, no idle hero worship. At eight years old, a shy little girl, though the dearly loved favorite of her father, she had been a little mother. Often Louise had said to John, "She bathes and dresses the baby every day. She was born a mother. When the twins get to raising Cain, as they do about once an hour, she can handle them better than I."

He had answered, "She mustn't be imposed upon, Louise. I want her well educated, college surely, and her music. It won't be long before we can afford a good hired girl. She must have friends and more playtime. I don't want to see too much of this little mother business." Louise had agreed, but agreement changed nothing.

After they had moved into the house on the hill, one day Louise was resting in the easy chair, talking to Phil. "It is such a blessing to have one thoroughly practical member of the family. I wavered this way and that and couldn't decide about the dining room but just like that"—she snapped her fingers—"Valeria settled the question—a downstairs bedroom and lavatory. A girl who can prop her Latin textbook on a shelf above the sink and learn her conjugations while she washes dishes simply astonishes me."

Phil's lips curled as he walked away. There was a mocking smile in his eyes. "Val's rather pretty, Mother."

She looked after him. Often she was a little startled by the turn of this son's mind. "Now what do you mean by that remark, Phil? I hope, in a few years, we can buy her pretty clothes and she can have more social life and, although your father would have said 'college,' if the right young man comes along I'd prefer to see her married." There was earnest conviction in her voice as she finished, "Some girls are born for careers but Val is born to be a mother."

He had been standing in the middle of the room, his back turned, listening intently. Now he turned again, came to her chair and looked down into her face. This mother—impractical, impulsive, cultured, talented, courageously hiding her grief, her hunger for the presence of the strong man on whose love and wisdom she had depended. She was gentle. Even the boys shouting, quarreling, yelling at each other in their play, instinctively lowered their voices when they came to her side and said, "Mother."

They loved her. Would that love prove to be the weakness that might turn Valeria into a slave to save her, to take her place as the mother of this entire family?

She looked up at him. "You say Val is rather pretty. Val is a beautiful girl, Phil. In a few years we must plan what to do for her."

He repeated, "In a few years. In the meantime, Val is doing something for us—it might get to be a bad habit."

She laughed, "Oh, Phil, you do say such ridiculous things. Val is a happy, healthy, capable girl. When the right man comes along she'll marry and still be happy, healthy and capable, I am sure. What are you worrying about?"

He shrugged. "About Val, that's all. I'm glad to learn you have such a nice idea of her future." He laughed rather shortly. "Now we've got Val disposed of, here are the samples of wall paper."

"I'll number what I like best, then perhaps we'll vote on the final choice."

"Another nice idea," and he went back to his work.

His mother looked after him, frowning. Not understanding, she knew her remarks had displeased him.

Now the parlor was painted and papered and they were impatiently awaiting Valeria. It was Andy who saw her coming up the path, slowly, lingering at each step as though reluctant to come in. He ran to her. "We're all waiting for you, Val."

She smiled at him, leaned down and putting her arm about his shoulder, hugged him close, then kissed his forehead.

"You're awfully late, Val. It's almost supper time and Jake's got to go."

"Well, why doesn't he go?" She was back to the practical.

"Search me. He's waiting for you."

"Then let's run."

Noisily they burst into the kitchen, then hurried to the parlor. They all watched as she looked from ceiling to walls and were delighted by such a radiant smile, such happy laughter, such brilliant glowing eyes. Mother was saying, "All I can think of is a tornado as I watch Jake work. I'm sure no three men could accomplish more. Then Phil pitched in and Mark and Andy cleaned up the rubbish. This is Friday, so I promised they can all stay up tonight and perhaps we'll get the floor clean and the rug laid and really have a parlor before Sunday."

Jake was smiling broadly, his eyes on Valeria's face. "Perhaps I'll run down tonight, won't have time tomorrow."

It was Valeria who thought quickly, "Could you stay for supper, Jake? We'd love to have you."

"Thanks. I'd better go up and make peace with Ben. He's had charge of all the milking."

She urged, "That's over now. Let Andy run up and tell Mr. Waters."

He looked singularly awkward and confused. Finally he said, "I might risk it."

"Good. I'll hurry supper," and she ran quickly up the stairs to her room.

"Let's wash up, Jake." Phil led the way to the kitchen sink. As they scrubbed, Phil laughed, "Val's a winner."

He saw Jake's face turn a deep red as he dried his hands and arms. His answer surprised Phil. Slowly in his low, drawling voice he said, "Val's a nice girl, Phil."

Phil replied lightly, "Bet your life, she is." Then they gave the sink over to Val who came in barefoot, a washed-out gingham dress hanging limply on her slender figure.

Jake may have felt as out of place as Uncle William had but he responded, as they heaped both food and praise on him, with a wide happy smile. When Miriam spoke with pride, "We have company every night now," he nodded, "Yes, I saw the car and the man at the foot of the hill."

Louise Macrae smiled to herself. The entire countryside would know of the visit, every movement, how late the man stayed, the exact rooms at the Inn where the chauffeur ate, on and on. It was like living in a goldfish bowl, although they could not see a human habitation from their place.

Without watching she saw every movement of the strong work hands, every expression on the plain face of their guest. There was a sweet light in her face as she looked about the table. She pondered, what is a gentleman anyway? Something in the heart that expresses itself in consideration, in manners that are good manners because they manifest unselfish thought for others? Why are bad manners accepted when combined with an evening dress or tuxedo and the owner called a gentleman? She would trust Jake with son or daughter, any child, any animal, or her bank book.

They were all excited about the "new" room and when the meal was over, as Valeria took care of the dishes, the others hurried back to the parlor floor, cleaned it, rubbed the furniture, laid the rug and began setting the tables and chairs in place.

Perhaps it was the unconsciously realized feeling of permanency that gave such impetus to their work. Professor Ainsworth's few fine etchings were hung only after many trials and serious debate. Because the parlor was on the darker side of the house they had chosen a paper with a soft leafy, yellow design on a white background. The narrow black frames of the etchings stood out sharply, picking up the black of the ebony piano which stood as nearly in a corner as its size allowed, contrasting with the rich coloring of books on the shelves opposite. In the curve of the piano they put the small mahogany sofa. Louise said, "Valeria, we'll get new covers for those armchairs—none of that mustard and horrid red—some old gold or soft dull blue or a touch of mauve." Most of the furniture consisted of old pieces, beautiful and cherished, from the house in the village. They set one armchair by the fireplace, a low cushioned chair for Mother opposite. The great cabinets containing her father's music, manuscripts and books were still in unpacked crates in the barn. Only the music for immediate use was laid on a settee.

They were almost breathless as Phil and Jake and Valeria moved the quaint desk with its high glassed in shelves to a place between the windows. It seemed a miracle, for it fitted exactly.

All day Saturday there was cleaning and more arranging but they slept late Sunday morning, no one calling them no matter how high the sun had risen or how many times Valeria had to make more toast or boil more eggs. And no one passing could have dreamed how pretty was the interior of the house with the peeling paint and tumbled down fence.

As they ate a late Sunday dinner there came a steady downpour of rain from the clouds which had been gathering overhead all morning, a cold rain such as a northern May or June can use to return a taste of winter. Mark and Andy brought their kindling from the shed and soon a fine fire was blazing on the hearth. Hardly had Mother settled in her chair, her knitting needles catching the light from the fire as she worked on the endless sweaters, woolen for winter, cotton for summer (and how efficiently they saved expensive shirts!) when Jake was seen striding around toward the rear, a rough coat held over his head.

He stood in the kitchen door—"Only wanted to speak with Phil a moment"—but Mother called, "Jake, if anyone has earned the right to enjoy this room and this fire, you are he. Now, just wipe your feet and come in for a few minutes at least."

Valeria, sitting at the desk, her head bent over her schoolbooks, looked up and smiled. "Jake, take off your boots and come in."

"I'll take off my boots." He looked sheepishly shy and happy.

He sat awkwardly on a straight backed chair as Phil asked, "What's on your mind, Jake?"

"I won't be able to get off daytimes, work too heavy, but I thought evenings the light is good till near nine. I'd like to start on that side piazza. If you'd see your way to ordering the lumber, I'd put in new props and a new floor. Val says she don't like cement around much so the kids could haul in stones from the fields and I'd do a foundation and steps and a stone walk. Look mighty pretty; and if you'd lay in paint I'd get the whole house scraped—and—"

They were deep in the discussion, Mother looking a little worried as they estimated the cost, when they saw a horse and rider making their way through the mud. A handsome saddle horse and on it, hardly recognizable under the raincoat and dripping visor, was Jim Ferris.

Valeria heard Phil's low whistle as he passed her and went out to the shed to meet him.

She had swung around, her back to them all, her head bent over her book as color burned from forehead to neck. Greetings were exchanged, the horse tied and there was laughter as Phil said, "Wipe your boots there, Boy, we don't allow even water on our clean floors." Mother was holding out her hand. "What a nice surprise, Jim."

Valeria's heart pounded. She glanced up, meeting his eyes for a fleeting second, managing "Hello" as casually as she could. Would she ever be able to "handle" situations with that wonderful ease with which her mother continued, "This is our friend and helper, Jake Young," then "Phil's friend, Jim Ferris."

They shook hands. No, they hadn't met though each insisted he knew the other well, by sight. Mark rose and gave his chair to Jim. Then Mother whose eyes were keen and bright, "Isn't this delightful? Without planning it, we are having a real housewarming. I think it would be nice with the cold rain outside and our fire here, to have our first tea. Barbara, go to my room and bring out the little drop-leaf table by my bed, Valeria will make tea and Mark will fill plates with cookies."

Valeria, standing by the kitchen sink, both hands clutching the edge, was staring at the faucet with unseeing eyes when Mark nudged her. "Val, listen, what plate will I use? Look Val, the cookie jar is almost empty."

What cups would she use? The everyday ill-assorted ones? Take down the few precious old ones? Had Mother counted ten? Oh, Mother was so impulsive! Had she imagined she was in her father's apartment, serving tea to one old gentleman or perhaps a student?

For a moment tears of chagrin stood in Val's eyes. Then she angrily wiped them away. How nice it must be to sit in an easy chair and say, "Valeria will produce a tea party," not remembering that one can't bake while one is scrubbing and settling furniture. She would have had cakes and pastries ready, had she had time and warning.

Mark was leaning on her arm, "I say, look, Val, the jar is empty. Have you got some cookies somewhere?"

Valeria turned to him, laying her arm around his shoulders.

"You listen to me, Mark. I was going to bake this afternoon when I finished my lessons. That's all the cookies there are. Promise me that you will hold back, not eat one or let Andy or Miri or Barb eat one until after they have been passed *three* times to our guests? Promise?"

"Gee! I'm hungry."

"Promise, darling, and I'll make you a chocolate cake later for supper."

"I promise."

She took down the precious cups, boiled the water, set up the little table, and Mother charmingly, graciously served the tea. However, Mark in rapid succession made three trips offering the cookies, then dashed for the kitchen commanding Barbara, Andy and Miri to follow. No guest had a chance at a second cookie. The tea almost choked Valeria but she kept busy as a waitress, finally clearing the little table.

Jake rose and Mother thanked him again and told him to go ahead with his plans. Phil went out with him and three were left, Mother chatting pleasantly, Jim smiling pleasantly and Valeria sitting stiffly in a corner of the little sofa. This was not the ravine.

To Mrs. Macrae's questions, Jim explained that he was entering Harvard in the fall. He asked, "Phil will make Cornell or some school of music? Easy for him."

Curious how Mother's voice could so suddenly trail off into a tired note. "We haven't made all our decisions yet."

Phil returned with that mocking smile in his eyes. Only some dire necessity could remove Mother from that armchair. He could not produce the necessity so he turned the talk to horses. Jim's was a beauty. The kids loved a chance to ride one of Mr. Waters' old nags. Jim said eagerly that he'd come up soon and teach them to ride his horse.

It was all very cozy but finally Jim got to his feet. He politely thanked Mrs. Macrae for letting him join the housewarming party. "So long, Phil, see you tomorrow morning."

Phil remained seated and Valeria rose. "Where did you leave your raincoat, Jim?"

"In the shed." She led the way through the kitchen where the empty cookie plate sat on the table, and a frightfully noisy game was in progress. When they went into the shed, she carefully closed the kitchen door after them. There was a long interval of time before the horse and rider came into view again, heading for the road.

In the parlor Phil watched his mother with an amused smile in his eyes. She sat still, resting her head on one hand, looking tired.

She glanced up. "Jim didn't come to see you?"

"You've guessed it."

"What does this mean, Phil?"

"It means you are to insist that Val come home every afternoon direct from school. You must do that."

"What a ridiculous statement. I am delighted to see that my pretty daughter has attracted the admiration of a boy like Jim."

His lip curled. "Val's a little girl, Mother. She takes things seriously like a child but she doesn't get over things like a child."

"Then what she needs is experience. Jim is a fine chap, looks it, acts it, the son of our doctor, one of our best families. A friendship like that is what I would have planned for her had I had the ways and means."

He was silent.

"She's been seeing him? Where?" She looked perplexed.

"Ask her."

"I shall not embarrass her."

They could hear Valeria now in the kitchen, ordering the children out of her way as she prepared to bake cookies and the promised chocolate cake.

"Phil, when there is a good opportunity, when the others are out of the way, perhaps tonight? I must talk with you."

The boys built up the fire before they went to bed, leaving Mother in her armchair. Long after Barbara and Valeria had retired, Phil came quietly down and took his place in the opposite chair. For some time there was silence.

"Phil, I don't know where to begin. Sometimes it is hard to state in words truths one holds deep in one's heart."

There was an appealing look in the eyes she raised to his. "You see, my son, whether we will it or not, you are the man, the head of this family."

"Sort of a broken reed but the best that offers at the moment?" He was coughing.

"I don't like that cough, dear. Jake was right. You have been doing too much strenuous physical work. That reaching up was bad for you."

"Go on, Mother. I'm to be the head of the family."

"Don't make it hard for me. I know you don't mean to but sometimes you seem to return sarcasm to my words to you."

"I don't mean to."

"I'm sure you don't." She spoke slowly, sometimes pausing between sentences. "Perhaps I was not wise in using up so much money to fix up the house but Phil, it matters so much, oh, more than you can ever imagine, to young people, to live in attractive surroundings. To girls it means more than words can tell. Why, this afternoon, I felt all was repaid when I saw that young man in this room. Girls like Barbara—and she's growing up fast—and Valeria and then Miriam, must have a pretty home, cultured atmosphere. I express myself poorly, I know, but I feel how vital it is."

He sat with eyes fixed steadily on her face but he did not help her. She went on. "Perhaps I spoke impulsively this afternoon when I told Jake to go ahead but I do want the house painted, the walks and lawns made and a pretty home for us all.

"We could not stay in the village for although there was some land, there was no one to plow and tend crops. Here, I saw the low taxes, the larger house with its extra bedrooms. When Mr. Waters said he would supply us with all the milk we could use, with butter and eggs and fresh vegetables in summer in return for the use of the fields, I saw a great saving." Her brows met in a worried frown. "I didn't dream, Phil, how the money would melt away. So many things to buy, sugar, flour, coffee, tea, oh, dozens of items mounting up every week. Then I get a new pair of shoes for the boys—if they could only go barefoot to school and church—and before I get them paid for they need new ones. There are all our clothes, mounting up to large bills even though I make our dresses and underclothes. There is the dentist bill, the drug store, the doctor, books, pads, pencils—and always the unexpected items.

"Perhaps I was wrong in using so much of the insurance money to make this a comfortable home. Perhaps we could have got along without the new paper but I did so long to see you all in a proper home. Now, I must conserve what is left. I shall have to count every penny."

She stopped as though exhausted. There was a crispness in his voice. "Mother, don't try to lead up to telling me that college or further study of music is out of the question for me. I've known that a long time. Before I tell you what I've planned, tell me about this Uncle William business."

Carefully, she repeated almost their entire interview, her promise to allow Barbara to make the long visit.

"You had, sort of subconsciously, an idea that he might come across with more than a summer for Barb?"

She frowned. "I don't know what I thought, Phil. I was a little impetuous but I'll keep my promise. It will give Valeria a freer summer. Barbara is of so little help around the house."

He smiled. "You know, Mother, I've been thinking that you might get well if you'd stop worrying yourself to death. I've known for a year past that I had neither the money to go nor the strength to work my way through college. Now cheer up. I've got a job and I start work the day I get my diploma. In fact I was offered two jobs. Mr. Smart at the factory said I could come into the office and with a little night work in bookkeeping and stenography soon have my father's old place. Then Mr. Haskell in the bank said I could start in, at the bottom to be sure, but with a chance to work up there. I chose the bank. There you are—a weekly wage, sugar, flour, dresses, and perhaps college for Val a year from now and we'll tell Uncle William to go to the devil."

The result was unexpected. His mother buried her face in her hands and her emaciated body shook with her crying.

He went to her, knelt, stroked her head. "It's good news, Mother. Don't you see, Mother, you're not alone? I'm in it with you." He laughed, "The funny thing is—" He stopped abruptly, then finished, "I want it just this way."

She dried her eyes and smiled. "I see why Valeria always says you're wonderful, Phil. I haven't known you as intimately as she has. Just like magic you've made the path seem clear ahead."

She added, "You always liked mathematics?"

He looked puzzled then laughed. "Mathematics? I'll probably be learning how to fill an inkwell without spilling, never was good at mechanics."

He rose. She did not see the curl to his lips or the feverish brilliance of his eyes as he said, "No one knows anyone, Mother."

"Oh, Phil, how often my father said that." Then, remembering the morning on the crowded New York street, she described it all to him. "My father could hear that cry from each lonely heart, 'Speak to me, Brother.' He wanted to set it to music. He was so talented and so unsuccessful."

He stood with his back to her. He repeated, "Talented and *un*successful. Do you mind if I go to bed now? I guess everything's settled. Can I help you?"

"No, Valeria fixed my bed and my thermos. I'll sit awhile till the fire burns out. Good night and thank you, Phil."

"Good night, Mother." He went rather swiftly up the narrow stairway.

CHAPTER V

VALERIA, working with her mother, managed to get the last stitches in Barbara's traveling dress just in time. It was a dimity, a soft brown with white polka dots. "It won't show the dust. Now turn slowly, Barbara. Yes, the skirt hangs perfectly. With a white hat and your white bag and shoes, it's a pretty costume."

Barbara twisted this way and that, her blond curls shaken back as she studied her reflection in the long mirror. "But why can I take only one dress and my best nightgown besides?"

Mother sighed. "I wouldn't deprive your Aunt Sophie of the pleasure of buying a summer outfit for you. She requested that in her letter. I enjoyed buying the material and making this one. What fun you will both have!"

Valeria who had been picking up the scraps, now removed the dress to give it a last pressing, ready for the morning journey. Louise's eyes rested thoughtfully on the two girls, Valeria with lips set hard, testing the iron as she smoothed and pressed, Barbara, less than two years younger, with her beautiful blond curls, her pretty face and—yes, their mother thought, as pretty a figure as could be dreamed of by any girl. Throughout the weeks when they had all known of and discussed this great event, Barbara had carried her head high. She of all the family had been chosen. Separation from her brothers and sisters or even from her mother meant nothing to her for she had never experienced it for a day or night. She felt herself very "special" and surely she was to be very special.

The arrangements were complete. Uncle William, staying at the Inn, had engaged a man at the station to drive him up and down. He had not changed his opinion of the rocky road but he had expressed astonishment and great admiration for the changes, both interior and exterior, to the house.

"Now you begin to look prosperous and well set up, Louise. I always say never go to the bank to borrow or meet a man to do business in an old suit of clothes. Look prosperous and soon you find you are prosperous." When told that Phil had already accepted a "position" in the bank, he looked pleased. "Fine. Many a bank president never saw the inside of a college. Some of the heads of our largest business corporations never finished high school. It's the ambition, guts that count. Guts! A man with brains, not afraid of hard work, is bound to get somewhere. I worked hard to get where I am." He did not look toward Phil when he delivered that speech. The quality of the smile in Phil's eyes might have been found disconcerting. "Now sharp at eight in the morning. I'm always punctual."

So, sharp at eight in the morning breakfast was out of the way, all were dressed and ready. Little Miriam's eyes were wide with wonder but two small boys looked on with unsmiling faces. Once Mark had come into her bedroom as Valeria spread the quilt. His arms tightened about her waist. She saw tears in the brown eyes. "Val, how long will Barb be gone?"

"I don't know, dear." She smoothed his hair.

"Will Miri have to sleep all alone?"

"She'll soon get used to it."

"I'm glad you're not going."

"So am I. Now run along and no tears. We must all be happy. You see Barb's happy."

Whether Barbara was happy or unhappy was a moot question. After kissing each one she looked back at the group gathered in front of the piazza and suddenly she began to suck in her lips and take steps toward them. "Mommie, can't someone come with me?"

They were all neatly dressed for school. Phil turned quickly away and walked toward the house. Mother looked at Valeria. "You go to the Inn with her, Val."

"I'll get my books." When she reached the door, Phil handed her the strapped bundle.

"Naturally, your job, Slavey. Don't absentmindedly get into Uncle William's car."

"No danger," she answered tartly and ran down the walk.

Uncle William sat in front with the driver, the two sisters in the back seat of the station carriage. "For all the world like two captive slave girls. Oh, for a knight on a white horse to rescue them."

His mother was annoyed. "Don't talk such nonsense, Phil. We are all going to miss Barbara but I feel sure this visit may lead to a pleasanter relationship with our relatives and advantage to you all."

"I'll gamble it's leading to something."

The carriage had disappeared and now, getting his own books, he walked alone down the long steep hill.

On the following evening, Mr. Waters stopped on his way from the village to hand Mrs. Macrae a telegram. "Arrived safe. Advise install telephone at once."

Mark seemed puzzled at all the laughter. "We do need a telephone. Lots of farmers have them."

Phil nodded in agreement. "And a chef, two maids, a gardener, a laundress, not to speak of an endowment."

"What's an endowment?"

Phil left a patient explanation to Valeria.

A week later they received the first letter from Barbara. They were astonished at the pretty, legible handwriting on the dainty pink notepaper. It was Miriam who discovered, "It's got a smell."

"Perfumed, dear. Many ladies use scented notepaper."

"How do you get to be a lady, Mother?"

Phil groaned, "Cut it, Mother. Don't go into that. Read the epistle to the underworld."

She read,

"Dearest Mommie: It is wonderful here. The lake is wonderful and I have a blue bathing suit and slippers and cap to match my eyes. It is wonderful here. We have parties and long rides and ice cream and we go to a big store and buy things. I have different clothes for every day. Tell Miri I have a wonderful room, all pink and white all to myself. This is important. I am not to be called an ugly name like Barb. My name now is Bobbie Macrae.

I'm sending kisses and love from
                              Bobbie Macrae."

Mother laid the letter down and even she didn't find words to break the long silence. The two boys sat with solemn faces as Miriam leaned over and smelled the paper again. Still no one spoke. Phil walked out and Valeria returned to her work. Mark lingered near his mother. "Why did Barb change her name?"

Mother smiled cheerfully. "Barb wasn't a pretty name. Bobbie is much prettier."

"I like Barb better."

"We'll get used to Bobbie." Mother's voice had a weak, trailing off quality and presently she laid a thin hand across her eyes.

The last days of June and now schools were closing. Phil had received the highest honor marks in his class but when his mother expressed her pride, he turned the praises off with light banter. "It's not honor marks that get you anywhere, Mother. It's guts. What a powerful word g-u-t-s! If I can acquire guts instead of scholarship I may get to be a bank president. You see I take the great Uncle William's words to heart."

He was sitting at the grand piano and without waiting for a reply he struck the chords of a Chopin Prelude. His long bony fingers seemed to find the deepest vibrations of the splendid instrument. A tormented soul could find relief in those first magnificent chords, in the sensitivity expressed in the repeated pianissimo that followed, dying off into something which from his fingers sounded almost like a sigh.

His mother sat with bent head. "Beautiful, Phil."

He played two more Preludes, then rose abruptly.

"Phil, I often worry about this. I sometimes wonder if I made a great mistake in not pursuing your musical education. You have inherited your grandfather's talent. You are certainly the most talented of all my children. Even as a child you sang and played as though it were a natural expression."

"Why the worry?"

"I think now you should have followed a musical career. But —to be a concert pianist requires not only long years but long daily practice, five, six, seven hours and I feared for your back. Then to compose or teach is so hazardous, sometimes so heartbreaking."

"You were sure I would be talented and *un*successful like Grandfather Ainsworth?"

"I'm seldom sure of anything. I sometimes think it would be nice if we had princes or dukes or some kind of wealthy patrons as they did in olden times to support talented musicians."

"When Mozart, surely one of the divinities of music, wrote Oxen Waltzes to stave off the butcher? Played before kings and queens, even the Pope giving him some order of merit, playing his own compositions before he was fourteen, when his wealthy patron made him *sit with the servants?* One of those servants finally kicked him out. The father of six children, they gave him pennies for his compositions. When he made a concert tour he pawned his silver to pay expenses and when he died at thirty-five there was a rainstorm and they left the poor young body by the road and no one to this day knows what became of it. That was in the day of wealthy patrons and princes. Gosh, Mother, I've read that life until I've felt as though I lived it. Then take Franz Schubert. Some thick-headed biographer wrote that the way Schubert existed is a matter of mystery. His health finally broke under the strain of turning out hundreds of compositions on almost no food a day. He had only thirty-one years on earth.

When I think of Beethoven's mighty head having to bow before wealthy patrons it makes me shudder."

His mother's eyes searched his face as he talked with an eloquence that astonished her. How little she knew the depths of this son. He finished, "No thanks. Wealthy princes or American millionaires are not the answer."

"The government? Washington?"

"Every tinpan alley sharper with political influence would be endowed. And who is to judge talent or genius? I don't think there is an answer. It seems to be the way the good Lord ordered it—a little screwy like much of His work," he laughed—"only I don't think all of it is *His* work."

"I sometimes wonder just what you do believe. Without my deep faith in God's goodness and love and care, I could not have faced many of the difficulties of life. I can't tell you how often prayers have been answered. I mean prayers for help, not for material things."

He stood in front of her looking down into her face, a gentle smile softening his often too sharp expression.

"I'm sure you would not pray for a new hat."

"No, I wouldn't. You do believe in prayer, Phil? You do *believe?*"

"Yes, Mother, don't worry about me. I believe in God—some power started the whole shebang going, all the worlds we catch glimpses of on a starry night. When? How? I leave all that where every philosopher I have ever read leaves it—we know nothing. About the Gospels, I think that is the greatest story ever written and I think the history of the early apostles and the martyrs the greatest story of faith ever written. Only I go you and Val one better. I believe in the Devil. I think he is in man."

"Phil! What preposterous things you say."

"You asked for it. If I ever could write a book I'd prove it by man's history. The history of man is the history of sin, of Satan."

"You shock me. Think of those very martyrs you spoke of. Think of all the good people who have lived on earth."

"I've thought a lot about them. That's the battle. They were winners. Some—perhaps most—lose the battle and others end in a draw, about fifty-fifty."

She gazed into space for a long time, then sighed, "You are a thinker like your Grandfather Ainsworth. Sometimes you startle me. When you played that Prelude today, it was played so exactly as he played it that I felt almost as though it must be his fingers on the keys. Isn't that strange?"

"Glad you told me." Then he laughed. "Now I'll tell you something; sometimes when I read one of his marked books I stop and say 'this is funny,' if I were marking this page, those are the exact words I'd underline. Poor old fellow. So he heard the human cry for brotherhood and wanted to set it to music and never did. Speak to me, Brother. I'm glad you told me that."

Her smile was tremulous. "Perhaps *you* will, Phil.

"Your father always said, 'Give Phil all you can, Louise, according to his strength, then after he finishes college he'll choose his own career.'"

"Which you did. So why the worry?"

"Because I can't see you as a banker, even a bank president." She laughed as she joined even for a moment in his ridicule of Uncle William.

"Stop worrying about everything, Mother. Oh, ye of little faith."

She smiled, "You certainly use Bible quotations for your own purposes."

He changed the subject abruptly. "You splurged, I see. Bought Val one new summer dress and *white shoes!*"

"A girl has a right to one pretty dress."

"A girl with a beau?" He was smiling and his mother noticed there was tenderness rather than the sarcastic curl on his lips.

"He seems such a nice boy, a desirable friendship for a girl like Valeria."

He stood looking down at her as her deft fingers hemmed some sheer material.

"If Uncle William wants to find ambition and guts he ought to come in contact with a certain mother of three girls." He was going through the door when he turned with a smile. "I, possessing neither ambition nor guts, liked it the way it has been for the past two years. I liked the bare feet, half-naked kids, the noisy rabble, the solidarity, all for one, one for all, a no-account underworld but like Carlyle's wife, 'wholly our own.'"

She could not reply for he was gone.

Only two days left of school, examinations over, and Valeria in her much-washed gingham sat on the big rock near the pool dangling bare feet in the cool clear water. Summer had taken full possession of their ravine. Above were dense masses of shrub and undergrowth while the trees in full leaf formed a splendid wall. A garden must have walls and this was her garden of love. She watched the minnows playing tag, the gay water spiders skimming over the surface while the trout now sunned themselves in the warmth of shallows, now darted into the depths of the pool.

Hardly had they been seated when Jim took from his coat lapel his high school fraternity pin and carefully fastened it onto the flimsy gingham, directly over her heart. "You'll wear it always, Val?"

She hardly breathed. "Yes."

"You know it makes you my girl?"

She nodded.

"Forever and ever?" laughing now.

"That's a long time."

"Not too long for us."

Had some iconoclastic elder called it "necking" or "spooning" she would have been as shocked as though he had called the beautiful cross in their church pulpit "a piece of brass." In some miraculous manner, surely a gift direct from God, she was entering into womanhood and love simultaneously. As she leaned against his shoulder, his arms around her, hands clasped or fingers playing with fingers, every touch surcharged with magic, only the glow in her eyes could express her happiness. Sometimes when he stretched out on the mossy bank and pulled her down into his arms she lay realizing only the ecstasy of living, of being young and alive and in love. And Jim went so far and no farther. Mother's confidence in Jim, her satisfaction in having so fine a young man as her daughter's first beau was not misplaced. As Phil had sneeringly said, "Jim's a nice boy, one of the nicest boys in the village." Perhaps as a doctor's son Jim knew all there was to know. At any rate he knew that kisses and hugs were—harmless? Surely.

"Val, there's something else I want, not to give you, Pop would blow up if I gave it to you but I can lend it to you for the summer. I want to give you Nell." His saddle horse? She fairly gasped, "Oh, Jim, you can't do that. I don't even know how to ride."

"Remember I promised Mark and Andy I'd teach them? I'm going to bring her up day after tomorrow and teach you and the kids then I'm going to lend her to you for the summer."

"For the summer! What would you do without her?"

"Gosh, I hate to tell you this! I won't be here. Without even consulting me, my mother has engaged passage and is taking me for one of those educational gallops around Europe. I expect I'll have to inspect every cathedral and walk endless miles through every art gallery from London to Munich."

Her lips opened, then closed without emitting the words of shock and disappointment. Her eyes widened as she stared straight ahead. "That will be wonderful for you."

"Oh, no, darling. Anything but. It's a dastardly trick and I told both old parties it was a trick, then Mom had to confess. They have been 'watching with apprehension,' their own words, my—what they call my infatuation for you. This trip is medicine pure and simple. They aren't fooling me. Pop's hipped on the subject of preventive medicine, like the Chinese. He gave me lectures on life when I didn't know what he meant. Gosh, I've got some progressive parents, Val. I got madder and madder and told them off about you. I said we were engaged and Mom threw a fit. I am a mere baby, still on the bottle, in her eyes!"

There was a little of the weak, trailing off of her mother's voice in Valeria's now. "I guess we are awfully young, Jim. I don't feel young though. I guess I'm not really young."

"It's the very devil to be an only son, Val. The old parties living under our roof watch me and train me as though I were a prize dog getting primed for a blue ribbon test. When I see Mark and Andy I have to laugh. I had to learn good manners, correct speech, sit down or get up or bark or shake hands just like a dog. Mom's as stubborn as a mule and she doted on making me a perfect gentleman."

Val smiled weakly. "I think you are a perfect gentleman, Jim."

The sun had long since left the stream and was filtering through the higher branches of the trees.

"I must go, Jim."

They walked slowly toward the zigzag path that led up to the road. "Val, darling, we have a few more days. You *will* come to the school dance with me on Friday?"

She nodded. "I'll have to walk down with Phil because I'm to help with the music."

"And please, darling, change your mind about the dance at the Country Club Saturday night. I want to take you. That will be my last dance."

She looked strangely nervous and indecisive. "I've never been to anything like that, Jim. City people and all. I've never seen anything like that."

"I'll take care of you, Val. We're going to do everything together for the rest of our lives so we may as well begin."

He was holding her close in his arms, then he raised his head and smiled his pleasant smile. "When I get to college I'll be more on my own. I'll plan to have you out for everything, dances, football games, everything. You know I've told you, Val, that when I'm twenty-one I'll come into my grandfather's money. It isn't a wonderful fortune but it will make me independent of Pop and he's a miser."

Her eyes were searching his hungrily. "Oh, Jim, sometimes four years in college and all that Medical School and hospital work seem like ages and ages and ages. You're going to meet so many girls."

"Quit that. You're going to meet men too. You promised me. You'll wear that frat pin all your life or until I get you a college one?"

"I promise, Jim."

"I'll be up day after tomorrow with Nell. Now say you'll come to both dances with me?"

She nodded. "I promise, Jim."

She made her way up the path, up the road and turned reluctantly toward the house. Her head was bent. The years ahead loomed like ages and ages but even while her lips quivered tremulously her eyes shone for there were these precious days directly ahead.

CHAPTER VI

LOUISE HAD ATTENDED the graduation exercises in the morning and now she was resting before serving as one of the chaperones at the school dance, for was not this the first important function of its kind to take place in her family? She insisted that the sciatica was troubling her very little and about the crippling arthritis she never complained and seldom spoke. More than once, in answer to Valeria's inquiries, she had smiled. "No matter what troubles come to you in life, Val, never allow yourself to become one of these whining women. Whining. Organ recitals. Shed your tears in private but hold your head up and smile before others."

With frank admiration, Valeria for days had been watching her mother's ingenuity. She had taken from her closet a sheer black evening dress, laughing. "This is the *pièce de resistance* of every poor college professor's wife or daughter or for that matter of every poor gentlewoman in the world—a conservative black evening dress." Now she cleverly hemmed it up to daytime length, filled in the V neck and with a white band about her throat, her hair beautifully brushed and coiled at her neck she appeared distinguished yet simple and unpretentious as she walked down the aisle of the auditorium. For the dance she had dropped the hem, opened the conservative V and would feel quite well dressed as she took her place in the line of seated mothers.

Through all the preparations her mind seemed intent on Valeria's appearance. With her daughter seated before her own mirror she braided the long dark hair and wound it about her head. "Don't pull it back so tight from your forehead, dear. You have curly hair, something to be grateful for, so fluff out the curls. You'll carry your white shoes down the road but be sure to put them on the minute you get there. Now stand up and turn around."

Her first party dress! A simple white wash muslin with a bit of narrow lace edging the round neck and finishing the puffed sleeves, and Mother's narrow gold chain and tiny locket, something treasured from her childhood, now the girl's only ornament. This was a party dress?

Louise Macrae stood back and looked at her. It was quite all she could afford for it must do for these occasions and for Sundays through all the long summer. Above the dress the young, amazingly pretty face with dark lustrous eyes looked so solemn that her mother laughed. "Smile, Val, don't forget to smile. Why, you look as serious as though you were going to court rather than to a dance. Now remember, don't forget to smile."

Phil with a large bundle of music under his arm, looked her over. "All right, Val, you'll do. Let's get going. Don't forget you promised to spell me once in a while if Ernie's cornet, two intervals off key and Ben's fiddle always flat and Guy's drum racing me, all start breaking my ear drums. Everybody depends on the piano to keep the beat."

Louise's laugh was gay. "Never mind, you'll have fun."

They did have fun. No one had to remind Valeria to smile for on this night there was such happiness as one might treasure in one's heart for life. As early as they were, Jim was there waiting. "Every waltz and most every twostep, Val, and the Virginia reel at the end and the grand march and I take you home."

True, many of the well-to-do girls wore silk dresses and dancing slippers whereas Valeria's shoes were stout canvas pumps useful for the street and church but Phil kept the beat and the orchestra outdid itself with simple waltzes and Sousa twosteps and around and around she glided lightly in Jim's arms. Sure, everybody saw and everybody talked and they were blissfully unconcerned.

Sitting at the end of the line of mothers, Mrs. Ferris pressed her lips hard together as with unsmiling intentness she watched the girl. Mrs. Ferris had fashionable connections in New York, in Boston and elsewhere and she had ambitions both social and financial for her only son.

Sometime in the evening, Dr. Ferris dropped in and for a few minutes took the seat beside Mrs. Macrae. He praised Phil, his musical talent, his scholarship, and finished his remarks with, "Val's growing up fast, prettiest girl in the room." She did not dream that, as he sat down by his wife, he continued "Guess you're right, Mama, prettiest girl and prettiest menace, might wreck a boy's whole career. By next week when the ship sails that will be taken care of."

Phil had gone out for some deep breaths of fresh air and a rest for his ears, while Valeria took his place at the piano. The moon had risen and although the tall elms were in full leaf the light filtered through and lay in silver patches on the grass. He was enjoying the quiet, the feel of the soft green beneath his feet when a figure turned in from the street. As the man approached he saw it was Robert Loring. They exchanged greetings, then they spoke of the fine weather, the large graduating class.

Doctor Loring looked toward the lighted building. "I *am* late. The orchestra seems to be functioning without its leader."

Phil laughed. "Val is spelling me."

"You seem to be a remarkably talented family. Are you all musicians?"

"In various degrees." He spoke of his grandfather, his mother's love of music, her training. He laughed. "We begin with music and reading then painfully learn to add the practical things of life."

Loring walked with him to the end of the green, then they retraced their steps. Nearing the door, Phil stopped to listen.

"Sounds as though Val's piano and Guy's drum were fighting a battle for leadership; guess I'd better get back on the job."

As they lingered on the steps Doctor Loring said quite casually, "Phil, I want to say to you and your mother that Valeria has an unusual talent in writing. I would like to see it cultivated. You both will make college?"

Phil turned away, his lips twisting. "Eventually, I hope."

The older man spoke earnestly. "If at any time I can be of any assistance to either of you or to your brothers, it would be my pleasure to help."

"Thank you." Phil's foot was on the doorstep, then he turned with his most engaging smile. "I never thought of it before as a special talent. When the kids were little, Val used to tell them a story nearly every night to get the mob quiet. She made them up out of whole cloth and what amused me was the fact that they were never fairy tales. She always made up stories about real boys and girls. She'd keep one story going for a week."

"That interests me. In the work she has done for me she has shown that feeling for the drama in real life. I would like to keep in touch with her."

Phil still smiled as he made his way to the piano, noticing that Dr. Loring went directly to his mother and took the seat beside her.

On Saturday morning, Mother rested and Valeria brought her breakfast on a tray. The girl had been up at dawn practicing the new way to wear her hair. The morning cleaning was hardly finished when Jim rode in with the two boys racing by his side. Mark, sometimes Andy and often Valeria mounted and absorbed every item of Jim's instructions. They relaxed, held the reins correctly, learned to sit straight but "go with the horse." They "went with the horse" until they were all in a state of intoxication, waiting for turns and fairly panting with excitement as each graduated to the road, up the hill, out of sight, then back with wide, triumphant grins.

Jim stayed for lunch and then it came out that he was to leave the horse with Valeria for the summer. At first Mother tried to laugh it off. Jim's horse? Thinking, "a useless saddle horse to feed and care for?" she asked smilingly, "I think your father will have something to say about that, young man."

"It happens to be *my* horse. A family friend gave her to me."

Mark and Andy could not eat. They would fix up one of the stalls in the barn, take out all the crates, scrub it and polish it like the parlor floor. Feed? They would go to the village and sell papers. They would work for Mr. Waters. What wouldn't they do!

She would think it over. But she couldn't take time to think it over. Jim was leaving Nell and he was leaving town Sunday morning.

He left the horse and went home on foot. Under Phil's sarcastic directions, the boys moved and cleaned and scrubbed and prepared the stall and begged Jake for feed until they could earn money. Sometime that late afternoon their mother sat with bent head, tapping her fingers on the arm of the chair as she did when she was troubled.

When alone with her daughter, she asked, "Why do you look so nervous and solemn, Val?"

Valeria dropped down in the chair near her. "I don't want to go to that dance tonight, Mother, and I don't know how to get out of it. It won't be like last night. They will be city people, wealthy people. I won't know anyone."

The fingers tapped nervously. "I understand, Val." She was silent a moment. "Then why do you go?"

"I promised Jim. It's his last dance."

"You must learn to make your own decisions, Val."

The girl looked at the floor; no use trying to explain. She looked up as her mother spoke earnestly. "I regret, dear, that I won't be there to help you but why not take it as a challenge? Say to yourself—here I am among strangers but among Jim's friends. I will try to make them my friends. You see, dear?

You lack social experience but not good manners. There won't be many more attractive girls there. Hold your head high, enter into all the fun, enjoy yourself and smile. Remember to smile. If anything goes a little wrong, keep smiling. Take happiness with you, keep it with you. The party will be just what you make it. I think it will be a splendid experience for you and I am sure you will come out all right. Don't, if some trivial thing upsets you, draw your lips down and look like a judge sentencing a criminal, as you can—but remember to smile."

Val sighed. After supper, she obeyed instructions and stretched out on her bed to rest, then at eight rose and put on the white muslin dress and canvas pumps, the locket and gold chain.

At nearly nine, Jim drove up in one of his father's buggies. He seemed angry, explaining, "Pop's in one of his miser moods. Went off in his car before I could get it. Left me this *brute* and old buggy." He was wearing white trousers, a navy dress coat and low white shoes. He gallantly helped her in and they drove off as Louise breathed a prayer.

In some ways Valeria was difficult. Barbara would have taken this dance lightly and gaily. It didn't help to hear Phil remark, as he settled to his book, "A lamb to the slaughter."

"She needs experience, Phil."

"She'll get it if I know that crowd."

She got it. At the foot of the wide steps Jim helped her out of the buggy and an attendant, looking a trifle astonished at the outfit, led the horse away.

The wide verandah circling half the building was ablaze with light and filled with what seemed like crowds of girls and women and handsomely outfitted men, young and old. Already the orchestra could be heard and couples were drifting in to the dance floor. Beyond, in another room, white coated waiters were preparing tables for the supper and setting out rows of glasses near the punch bowls.

Jim said, "The ladies' room is down that corridor by the red curtains. I'll be waiting for you here."

Why should she go to the ladies' room? She had brought no wrap, neither powder puff nor rouge: nothing but her handkerchief which she was clutching tightly in her hand. Nevertheless she went. She must learn.

No one paid the slightest attention to her. Girls in lovely evening clothes—oh such dresses, chiffon, lace, rustling taffeta cut low, only tiny straps over their pretty shoulders—were crowded before mirrors as they rouged and powdered. Maids in black dresses with frilled caps and aprons were receiving wraps, running here and there. Valeria stood alone.

How long should she stay in the ladies' room? Slowly, shyly, she walked out. Her heart leaped with joy and relief when she saw Jim. The orchestra was playing a waltz, he drew her into his arms and they glided off. Now she could smile. He looked down into her eyes, "Everything all right?"

"Oh, yes." Then her eyes glowed. "Isn't the music wonderful, Jim? I'd like to play with an orchestra like that. I guess I could spend the whole night just watching that man at the piano. Phil would love it."

She wondered as they danced around and around why the music didn't stop and then she was to learn that it wouldn't stop much throughout the entire evening. Then someone touched Jim's shoulder and she learned about cutting in. Abruptly he left her and she looked in amazement at the little red-headed man who held her tightly. "Bill Waterman." Should she say, "Val Macrae?" The moment was lost and she said nothing. He was rather dumb also and he jerked rather than glided through the waltz. Then Jim was back, and what a relief!

At last the music stopped and Jim led her to the punch bowl. Around them were men, men and more men. Jim introduced her to this one and that. Far across the room the ladies and girls were gathered in groups, their escorts bringing drinks. Jim said, "Want to sit down awhile?" She looked across the room. How had she got isolated in this group of men? Must she cross that empty floor all alone?

She remembered to smile. "Yes, I'll sit down awhile."

"I'll bring you a drink."

"Hold your head high and smile." She remembered as she crossed the room but she hadn't counted on coming to the first group and seeing Jim's mother, Mrs. Ferris. Valeria smiled and Mrs. Ferris returned the greeting with a slight nod then looked away, talking vivaciously with a friend.

There were a few vacant chairs way down toward the door but she couldn't walk past all those women and laughing girls. She stood back near the wall and oh, how well she knew now why she should not have come. Her heavy canvas shoes! Had they been dangling on a cord from the chandelier she could not have been more conscious of them and of her cotton dress, her childish chain and locket.

She saw girls she knew, the ones who had worn silk dresses the night before at the school house, not real friends and they paid no attention to her now. While she was standing, waiting, she glanced up and saw Mrs. Ferris look steadily at her canvas shoes, then slowly up, up, scrutinizing her dress but the eyes turned away before reaching her face.

Jim came with the drinks. Timidly she asked, "What's in it, Jim? It tastes like liquor."

"Good? Just fruit and a little champagne. Won't hurt you." She drank it thankfully because her throat was dry. He went off with the glasses. She saw girls stop him, laughing and chatting. She saw his ease with men. The orchestra tuned up and his arms were around her. Twice young men to whom he had introduced her cut in and she managed to talk a little and smile at them but always Jim was back.

Now she was becoming painfully, frighteningly conscious of something else. Women and girls were looking at her with cold, appraising stares. She was becoming conspicuous dancing half hour after half hour with Jim Ferris or his few best friends. Her little cotton dress, her canvas shoes and only Jim. "Smile, Val, smile." The smile was freezing on her face. She could feel it stiffen. She clenched her teeth and held her head high and smiled.

Sometime between twelve and one o'clock there was supper. Jim led her to the long table. It was sort of a scramble, the men reaching, the waiters rushing here and there. Jim filled two plates and found chairs. Her fork moved the chicken salad but she was afraid of choking and she could swallow only a little.

"I'll get ice cream."

That was easier. It slid down cool and refreshing. He brought coffee and nothing in the world could have made her say, "I still take milk in the morning with the children and cambric tea at supper." She drank the coffee.

It was during the next dance that the red-headed little man cut in again. The music stopped, then the orchestra burst forth merrily into exciting, unusual music. The little fellow exclaimed "Polka," seemingly with great glee. "Come. I'm part Polish. I'll show you how to dance this as it should be danced."

She drew back, resisting his pull on her arm. "But I don't know how to dance a polka."

"I'll teach you."

She herself was startled by the agony in her cry, "Oh, please don't. I don't want to learn here."

"Now watch!" and to the amusement of the ladies sitting along the wall, he pranced off by himself. "One, two, three and a hop!" The hop was grotesque—a jerk as though a wooden puppet were being pulled by strings. While he was illustrating, she looked around, now almost hysterical with fear of ridicule. Where, oh where was Jim? She could not see him but she did see the door opening on the wide piazza. When the little man's back was turned she fled; through the door, down the steps, over the paved way, on until she reached the lawn and the sheltering trees. She stopped, looking back at the lighted building, the gay dance seen through the many windows, the lilting music fainter.

She stood alone in the darkness under the big trees, breathing deeply. The cool evening air was good. She mopped her face with her crumpled handkerchief. Not far off she could hear men's voices, perhaps the chauffeurs.

She had no sense of time; it might have been five minutes, ten minutes, hours or ages. She was frightened. What had she done now? What would Jim think? Was he looking for her? Must she go back? How could she walk into that door? Alone? Those women had been watching, laughing.

She was miles from home. What should she do?

Then she saw Jim. He hurried out of the door, walked quickly up and down the piazza. She wanted to call but she was afraid she would cry. He must have gone back in one of the other doors.

It was as though her feet were leaden and she could not force them to move. Again Jim, standing in the doorway, looking up and down the piazza. A friend joined him. "She's probably in the ladies' room."

"No, I sent Judy to look."

The friend laughed and went in. Then she called, "Jim, Jim."

He came running. With his arms around her, "What is it, Val? The drink or the chicken made you sick?"

Smile, Val, smile. Quite casually she answered, "I just needed a little fresh air, I guess."

"Why didn't you tell me?"

She wound her arms about his neck. "Jim, do you care an awful lot about staying until the end?"

"Oh, that's the fun, Val. They asked me to lead the grand march. You'll have loads of fun."

They walked back and entered the door. Some women smiled knowingly, some frowned. They discouraged young couples going off by themselves in the woods. So, she had been enticing Jim!

There were only two waltzes, then the reel, then the march.

79

"Just watch me, Val, out of the corner of your eye. Do on your side whatever I do on mine."

She held her head high and the smile felt like an ice mask on her face. Once she caught sight of Mrs. Ferris and heard her companion say, "A brazen hussy—bold. What an air."

She stood at the head of the long line of couples with Jim. As if in a nightmare she watched and went all through it.

Then in his arms, holding her far too tightly, there was the last short waltz as the orchestra played "Good Night, Ladies."

Was she supposed to go to that ladies' room again for her wrap and for final powdering! She had no wrap but she went. Now, instead of receiving no attention, she was stared at avidly.

Jim was waiting. The attendant held the horse and she was helped into the buggy.

Now there was a moon and the beauty of shifting light over the fields and highway as they jogged home but Jim had to watch out, for the horse shied as cars passed. "This is the worst brute in Pop's stable. Shies at shadows and won't stand."

The last failing meant that when they finally reached home he must hold the horse with one hand as they stood in the road. With his free arm he held her close and never had his kisses been so sweet.

"Until fall, sweetheart."

Her head was on his shoulder.

"I'll write to you, Val. You'll write long letters?"

"To where?"

"I'll get an address to you. I suppose it'll be some express company or Mom's bank."

He was gone. She stepped on to the walk, then stood a long time looking at the moonlight and shadows across the field. It must be nearly three o'clock in the morning. Never before had she been out alone in the night and for a few moments she was engrossed in savoring the experience. The night breezes seemed to be sighing through the tree tops and she thought how Beethoven would have set that sound to heavenly music. Over by the fence the aspens quivered and made a sound out of all proportion to their size. She knew how the little leaves were fastened to their stems and why they could flutter and turn and twist and whisper when the elms and maples were silent.

From the back their shepherd dog came running, wagging his tail vigorously but he did not bark. She held his head hard against her knees and rubbed his ears. "Good, Shep, be quiet."

Up on the hills the moonlight lay on the hemlocks and pine, leaving the shadows black beneath. Home. Their home. She must be like Mother for she loved this solitude. It was like strong arms holding one safe. Her faith was childlike. Here the beautiful earth, up there the stars and above God watching over them all. And she didn't have to smile. Tears streamed down her face and she was almost blinded as she reached the door, gently pushed Shep back, turned the knob and entered.

Instantly Mother called, "I've been listening for you, dear. Was it all you expected?"

"Yes, Mother. I'm tired. I'll go right to bed."

"Yes. I'll wait until morning to hear. Good night, dear."

"Good night."

She slipped off her shoes and crept upstairs but she heard Phil cough, a wide awake cough. She slipped into her room and closed the door. Her hands fumbled with the catch on the little chain but she finally got it off, then her dress and at last was in her nightgown. She pulled the covers over her head and buried her face in the pillow and cried. Her whole body trembled with her smothered sobbing. Oh, how she loved Jim. She knew Jim loved her, so why did she feel so sure that they had said good-bye forever?

It was June of the long days. Already the light was changing and soon the sunlight would be creeping into her window but this was her only chance to cry. In the morning it would be "Smile, Val, smile" again, for Mother and Phil must never know. Not in all her life would she let them know how poor and ashamed and frightened she had felt or how she longed to run away and hide herself from everybody's eyes, especially from Mother's and Phil's eyes.

They would always speak of that summer as "The summer we had Nell, Jim Ferris' saddle horse. Remember the fun?" It was also the summer Phil started in the bank. And the summer Miriam fell out of the apple tree and broke her leg. Valeria would remember it as the summer she received some postals from Jim, from Paris and Venice and Rome, but never a return address.

His mother arranged their home coming so late that they landed at Boston and he went directly to college. Mark rode Nell home when Dr. Ferris demanded her return, pleasantly of course and with excuses about his own saddle horse being lame. Valeria would always remember Mark's face when he came into the house after his long walk up the hill. One would have thought he had attended Nell's funeral. She hurried out of the kitchen before anyone could see her face when Mark said almost casually that Dr. Ferris had told him they were renting the big house and moving into the city, more convenient for him, and with Jim to be away for years ahead it would be lonesome for Mrs. Ferris. She remembered walking up through the deep woods until she could come back and smile naturally. She remembered when they heard that Dr. Ferris was selling his stable and Mark inquired about the price of Nell. It was the last time in their lives she saw Mark cry. She found him out in the stall, with Andy patting his shoulder.

They would remember that a world war started at the end of that summer. Also they would remember it as the summer when Barbara did not return because Aunt Sophie had entered her in a splendid private school and who could deny her, Bobbie Macrae, such advantages?

There was so much to remember.

Book II: Coming of Age

CHAPTER VII

"They call it 'coming of age.'"

They all laughed as they sat around the supper table one Sunday evening.

Phil was in his merriest mood. "You see how it works. On Saturday night, you are still a child, with only a school book knowledge of government but wake up on Sunday morning and you find yourself a man, twenty-one years old with a complete knowledge of world affairs, good judgement, ready to decide the fate and welfare of millions of fellow citizens; in other words able to vote."

It had always been considered a happy coincidence that Phil and Miriam's birthdays fell on the same date. Now the pretty blue-eyed girl looked up and tossed her blond curls, "I'm come of age too, I'm entering my teens."

Phil turned to her sternly. "You're a child. You're twelve today."

"Tomorrow I'll be going on thirteen."

"And you're still a brat. You shirk doing dishes, you leave your room a mess, you get ink on your dresses, you tear your stockings climbing fences and trees, you ask for help every night with your arithmetic, you spell John—J-H-O-N—and kitten—K-I-T-I-N. Not to speak of what you do to your grammar; you still have to be driven to bed at night and hauled out every morning. You're saucy and pretty fresh. You're still a brat."

A tall handsome lad rose laughing, "Don't mind him, Miri. I'm helping Val tonight."

That was Mark—already looking like a man, graduated from high school, athletic. His mother's adoring eyes were not the only ones that followed him as he cleared away the plates now scraped clean of the delicious creamed chicken, the lettuce covered with thick slices of tomatoes. An empty platter had been heaped with hot biscuits. Carefully he crumbed the table, then returned to Valeria.

"You carry it, Mark."

It had been quite a question what to do about candles. Together, Phil's and Miri's years came to thirty-three and Valeria had said there would be no room left for frosting so Mark had bought one big candle and one tiny one and now lighted both and set the four tiered cake before Phil as Mother poured hot chocolate into their best cups.

And there were presents. Mother had knitted Phil a gray wool sweater, one with buttons and button holes that he could wear like an extra vest under his jacket, there was a penknife from the boys, with nail file and screw driver and he wondered how on earth the boys had managed that much money. There was a necktie from Valeria and a pretty dress and hair ribbons for Miriam. Just as they seemed surfeited with cream-filled cake and chocolate and happiness Phil reached into his pocket and taking out a little box pushed it across the table to Miriam.

All eyes were on her as she untied the blue ribbon, looked at a little white box, opened it and gasped, "A gold ring. Oh, Phil!" She flew around the table and almost smothered him with kisses, then she almost cried with happiness as she tried it on and found it fitted her middle finger. There was a beautiful stone and she looked up, "What is it, Phil?"

"A garnet and it's a real one. You see, little brat, it fits your middle finger now and if you don't lose it in the woods it will graduate to your fourth finger and then when you are really in your teens it will look swell on a pinky."

Mother's eyes narrowed as she watched Phil's face. How characteristic, the sharp tongue and the loving, sacrificing heart. It was she who wanted to cry.

When they gathered in the parlor that evening, Phil played for them. They were all musical, even little Miriam whom Mother pronounced "not bad" if she would practice regularly. She wouldn't. Mark and Andy each did "fairly well"; Valeria was "good" but Phil was their musician. On that birthday night, he seated himself at the piano and did "requests." Chopin—two preludes, Polonaise op, 3; Beethoven—the Waldstein in C; some Schubert—a fantasia, two Moments Musicaux. He astonished them, for no coaxing could ever persuade him and they loved his voice, by singing two favorite Schubert songs; then, just when his mother, noticing his pallor and the tenseness of his neck and head, was both longing to hear more and wishing he would stop before exhaustion, he sat still a moment, head bent over the keys. There came the first thrilling notes of the Appassionata.

Professor Ainsworth's grand piano was meant for a concert hall and now the walls of the room seemed inadequate to contain the volume of sound as with passionate eloquence he played as they had never heard him play before.

As the last notes died away, he rose, stood a moment looking from face to face; his lip curled in his most sarcastic smile as he bowed, "Thank you for listening to my birthday concert," and turning abruptly, he went up to his room. They heard the door close.

Mother's hands were gripped so tight about the arms of her chair that the knuckles gleamed white. "We have a big day before us tomorrow, an important day. Go right up, Miriam, and don't have to be told again to get into bed. Mark and Andy— right away. Val will help me." As though they had been awed into silence, they all departed.

She was in bed. "An extra pillow, Val, I'll put out the light when I begin to feel sleepy."

Valeria lingered. "Mother. Phil is so wonderful. He ought to have been a great concert artist."

"I don't know, dear. I don't know. Sometimes I feel there have been some terrible mistakes made about Phil. I don't know. Perhaps—perhaps what seems to us the greatest mistake was surely God's will, not ours, in making him—not strong. I simply don't know. I can't think it out. He looked absolutely ill when he rose from that piano. As white as a ghost. I simply don't know."

Still Valeria lingered. Her voice was almost a whisper. "Mother, if I tell you something will you never, never breathe to Phil that you know?"

"I promise, dear."

"He hasn't told me but I found out. It must be in his spare time at the bank or when he goes up early and closes his door but I accidentally saw them. Phil is writing songs and piano and orchestral pieces and he is sending them to a publisher in New York and using a city address."

Mother's face grew white and pinched as Valeria spoke; her eyes held in them the strange glittering brightness that could come into Phil's. She grasped Valeria's hand and held it tightly. "You must never speak of that again. Understand, Val? You are trespassing on another's soul. I don't understand Phil. I understood my father but not this son. Sometimes I feel that he is older than I. Sometimes I feel that his soul is a battleground. I don't understand but I shall never trespass."

Valeria stood with eyes staring widely. She whispered, "I won't trespass again, Mother."

As she passed Phil's door she lingered, seeing the light in the crack by the floor. She longed to call "Good night" but she went on into her own room.

Now she understood something that had always mystified her. Now she knew why Phil had never twitted or joked or spoken a word; why Mother had acted as though she had not noticed when it was all over between her and Jim. Slowly she unbraided her hair. Now she understood their code of honor. They were too sensitive and honorable to trespass.

She had not told her mother because she wanted to be a tell-tale. It was because she was so unhappy about it. Phil doing something so wonderful and not taking her into his confidence. She was deeply hurt. Why didn't he tell her? Why didn't he tell her anything any more? They were drifting apart. When she tried to cross the gulf that was widening between them, he treated her with cold sarcasm. Mother didn't understand. How she would like to hear Phil answer that one—God, in His wisdom making a little boy a cripple! She got into bed. Perhaps it was she who couldn't understand anyone. Funny, how happy they had all been at the table celebrating the birthdays, laughing, seeming so close—and now! She couldn't understand . . .

Hours passed but Louise was sleepless. Once she reached out for the bottle of sleeping tablets, then pushed it back. No, she would be drowsy in the morning and she could not afford that luxury tomorrow.

At first she thought only of Phil. Clearly she remembered the night when she let him know she was at her wits' end to get ready money for their daily living. He did not discuss it with her; he told her he already *had* a position in the bank. Only a year later he casually told her he *had* procured a better position in a large bank in the city; he *had* arranged with a friend to share a room through the week nights, coming home for Sundays.

Room with a friend? This was important. Surely she must be allowed to know something about a man with whom her son shared a bedroom.

She had asked, "A friend, Phil?"

"Yes, Mother, a friend. He is one of two sons and three older daughters—two married with swarms of children. They are Italians. Father, mother and the older ones hardly speak English.

Marino, my friend, is a violinist, teaches, plays in orchestras when he gets a chance and composes.

"Now set your mind at rest. I couldn't be in more interesting, congenial surroundings and I needn't pay a dollar for the privilege of living with them if I couldn't. In other words, they like me. I like them."

He was coughing. "What's more, Mr. Martin who rightfully investigates the homes and manner of life of his bank family, watching out for those who may be living beyond their means and thus subjected to temptation—Mr. Martin approves."

Then, most astonishing, he *had* bought a second-hand "flivver" and could come home or go where he wished to go and take her on important errands, free from dependence on trolleys or trains. Now, was he waiting, working, striving as her father had done, until he could announce that he *had* published his own compositions?

A secretive nature? Not exactly. Wouldn't the psychologists explain the strong, dominant masculine personality, thwarted and frustrated by the pity, the coddling, the love given to the crippled child? Why did he always laugh with that twisted curl of his lip when one spoke of "regretting that he had given up all thought of college"? When had he given up the dream of being either a doctor or a composer or concert pianist? Hadn't that dream sustained him through those gruelling years when he had pushed himself through class after class, winning high honors in so few years of schooling? How had he accustomed himself to seeing pity, nothing but pity in human eyes? How had he felt when he *watched* boys playing baseball, tennis, football? When he saw Mark and Andy outstanding in both athletics and scholarship and wearing sweaters bearing the big school letter?

What an astonishing evening it had been! That he was a talented, a thoroughly competent musician she had long known. But that playing tonight! Surely only some greatness of soul could produce such an interpretation of great music. Never before had he let himself go as he had tonight. And his singing! Often, sometimes nightly, they all sang familiar songs or hymns and his clear tenor always led but seldom could they persuade him to sing alone as he had tonight. How frightfully tired and ill he looked when he rose from the instrument. What a strange evening. They had been so happy at the table. How charming he was when he surprised them all with the beautiful gold ring for Miriam.

What was in Phil's mind? Was he, as she wanted to think, the nominal head of her family, devoted to sisters and brothers, handing her those neatly folded dollars that, with Valeria's help, had covered all their expenses? How he had goaded or praised or advised those two handsome boys through school! "Sure you can be on the team and take the extra language too. You're no weakling." Often she had watched the light, sometimes almost a glitter, in his eyes when the twins triumphed over the seemingly impossible. How had he managed to save that money for their tuition? It was he who had planned how they could help by working through four years until they should get their engineering degrees at Cornell. They could wait on table, tutor, clean rooms if necessary. Do anything and everything to earn a dollar. Jovially he vanquished their misgivings. "Once in and you'll never give up without that degree. Then the world's your oyster and you'll have tools to open it and find the pearls and no one, no one on earth can take those tools away from you."

Those two boys would never let Phil down. Never. Tomorrow, they were starting for college and Phil had gotten the day off and was driving them; but what was in Phil's mind and heart? Was it possible that in spite of her love, a son could be a stranger to his mother? And Valeria? Why this estrangement? Once the brother and sister had been such happy, easy companions. What had happened there?

She must sleep. Through all the years she had known one source of help, a source that had never failed. She laid her hand over her burning eyes and prayed. Into God's love and care she would entrust the lives and future of her children. Why He had taken from her side that husband who had been such a tower of strength and wisdom, she could not question. She accepted His will. She prayed for strength to stay with her children. She prayed for the lovely daughter out in Cleveland, for each and for all and a sweet peace came into her soul and even as she prayed she slept.

CHAPTER VIII

NOT THAT ANY KIND of weather would have mattered, but it did add to their happiness to wake up to a fall day of glorious sunshine and the dry, cool air that one drew deeply into the lungs with keen pleasure. In spite of Mother's haste in dressing, Valeria was already preparing oatmeal, cakes and maple syrup (the special treat), chocolate for Miriam and the boys and coffee for Mother and Phil.

"When did you and Andy get up?" She turned laughingly to Mark who stood near the sink watching her.

"With the dawn." He had come in from the barn and sheds. "Val, I'm sure there's enough wood cut and kindlings to last you until Thanksgiving. Anyway, in case you need us, Phil says he could bring us home for a Sunday."

She looked into his face. "Since when have I become a weakling? Can't I swing an axe or a hatchet?"

He looked serious. "And you're not to mow the lawn nor allow Phil to touch it. Jake has a boy who likes to do it."

She laughed. "For what Jake will pay him. Do you think I'm both a weakling and a simpleton?"

"I know you're a mule when someone tries to manage you."

They heard Phil coming down the stairs whistling a gay, popular tune. If his color was bad his spirits were good. "All aboard. Fuel up, boys, the express leaves on the minute."

The prayer was a little long this morning but they restrained their desire to squirm and were soon emptying oatmeal dishes, heaping up the pancakes on their plates, then finishing off with doughnuts.

Dressed in their new suits, each carrying his own suitcase, they kissed their mother, Valeria and Miriam, and with Phil at the wheel went off gaily waving their caps as they disappeared down the road.

Valeria's eyes were shining as she turned to her mother. "I can hardly believe it. At last! Mark and Andy off to college! Isn't it wonderful to see a dream come true?"

"Yes, it's wonderful," and Louise's face seemed to catch some of the radiance in her daughter's eyes. "As you say, a dream come true." Then she added with forced brightness, "Perhaps you could follow their courses in nightwork, Val? Then with a year or so get a degree? From some college?"

Valeria's laugh was contagious. "Me? Engineering? Not for me."

"I didn't mean engineering."

"I'm all right, Mother, forget it."

She settled a large manila envelope securely under her arm and with a cheerful "good bye" started up the hill. She wore a navy wool coat over a wool dress, her stout oxfords but no hat. She still dressed her hair in the pretty way, the braid wound neatly about her head with the curls fluffed out softly over her forehead. Beneath the curls one noticed the firm chin, the mouth set perhaps in a too unyielding line, the beauty of her dark eyes.

She had purposely started early that morning; now, half way up the hill she left the road and made her way through pine and hemlock to the top of a sharp declivity, one of the prettiest places in the ravine where large rocks, apparently tossed helter-skelter, caused the water to form cascades, whirling eddies and make music as it tumbled and spun to the narrow stream below.

From the bosom of her dress she took out a letter, opened the single page and read and reread, the eager glow in her eyes belying the set of her lips.

A war had been fought and won—surely one of the most momentous wars in all history—called the World War and no one dreamed that it would later receive the numerical I. No, it was the war to end all wars and America was victorious and people did not dream that no one was ever to be victorious in war again.

When Phil had appeared at his draft board they had brushed him off lightly—no use to them. Couldn't he do clerical work? They smiled at him and sent him home. He too had smiled when he told the family, "I'm of no use to my country" and even Mother had not suspected the humiliation and sense of impotence that festered in his heart. The war would produce plenty of cripples but it didn't start with them. Robert Loring had been at the front for two years, but Jake was forced to remain on the farm.

Jim had graduated from Harvard in time to go to France as an officer. One day she had been astonished to receive an envelope postmarked London. He must have been on leave. Opening it eagerly she found a snapshot of him in his uniform. Under the picture were two words, "Remember me?"

Long ago Phil had remarked to his mother, "Val may be a child in years but she doesn't take things as a child and she doesn't forget as a child." It seemed to Val an eternity since those first casual notes had come from Cambridge, inviting her to come out for a dance. The unyielding line had grown more settled on her lips as she told herself, "In the first place, I can't go with neither clothes nor money. And in the second place I don't want to go." As to the first reason she knew that had she, with tearful eyes, discussed the matter with her mother, that resourceful person would have managed somehow to put together a party dress; and had she talked to Phil, he, in some miraculous way, would have managed to find money for expenses. Was it her knowledge of their struggle to meet the unavoidable bills that deterred her? Needless luxury for her when the others were fighting for necessities? Was it her feeling of just not belonging in Jim's fashionable set? Her lack of smart, light talk? Fear that she would be awkward and dumb at such a dance, not even knowing the new steps?

Long after such invitations had ceased to come, she laughingly told Phil of her refusals. He turned to her and said sharply, "Why didn't you go? Why didn't you let me know?"

"Because I didn't want to go."

More sharply, "Why didn't you want to go?"

For a moment there had been a slight quivering of her lips, a moment of weakness that later she would feel ashamed of. She raised her eyes, filled with tears. "Oh, Phil, why couldn't I have been that kind of girl? I mean a girl who looks pretty, goes with boys? I wonder how it would seem to be gay and smart and sophisticated." Then forcing a smile, "I thought I'd like trying to be silly but I guess I needn't try. I'm silly enough."

Phil's eyes narrowed. "Val, you probably don't realize that when you were a little girl you were painfully shy. You hid in the kitchen or ran to the barn if Mother asked you to play for company. Then, when only the family was around you played beautifully. You got almost sick when you had to recite in public. In school, I noticed that you turned white as a sheet when Dr. Loring walked with you or singled you out for special notice. That shyness is sort of a disease and living here on the hill with so little contact with the city or the outside world doesn't help."

With tears still in her eyes, she began to laugh. He couldn't know she was remembering that night of the dance at Jim's golf club when the woman said, "Bold, brazen," as she, Val, held her head high and smiled and smiled and smiled.

"What are you laughing at?"

"I think the cure for shyness is worse than the disease."

His penetrating eyes had studied her for some minutes before he spoke gently. "I don't know the answer, Val—how to get you out of this trap we've sprung on you."

Her face flushed. "Guess I sounded like a cry-baby. I'm strong and well."

"You need to be."

She had laughed. "Well, I am."

She was remembering Phil's calling her shyness a disease as she reread the letter from Jim. Fortunately she had been at the postbox when it arrived. Seeing the New York postmark and Jim's handwriting, she slipped it into her pocket, not opening it until she was in the privacy of her room. Now, in the shelter of her loved ravine, she pondered. Of course, Mother and Phil thought it was long since "all over" between her and Jim. Surely she also knew that. Yet there was something of the old sweetness in her heart, something of the old excitement because his letter proved that he remembered.

He told her that "Mom" had been in Boston several winters and now "Mom" had taken an apartment in New York where he was returning to his medical education, interrupted by the war.

She knew every word by heart but she read it again, lingeringly, especially the ending.

"I am more or less on my own now, Val; have come into what the lawyers called 'a modest competence.' It's modest all right for New York and Pop is still a miser. What I want to know is whether that rickety little Inn is still in existence. If it is, I'm coming up to see you. It's a lifetime since we walked in the ravine but I haven't forgotten one of those days. Why won't you send me a picture? You teaching in that little one room school on the hill! I can't imagine that. Do you go barefoot to school? This is the longest letter I have ever written. You see I am thinking about you. I suppose you are what people call 'my childhood sweetheart.' I warn you. War doesn't turn youths into children. It turns them into something else again. I'm coming to see you, Val, when I get some days off. If you must teach, why don't you get a job in New York then we could have some fun. Hope you can read this scrawl. You remember I always got D in writing.

So long until I see you,
Jim"

So long! No one here in the tree shadows with the rushing

waters below, could see the hurt look in her eyes and the twisting of her lips. So long! She folded the letter, put it back in her dress and retraced her steps to the road.

Her job? There were only seven youngsters now in the little school and when the new road was made and the big central school finished, this little old schoolhouse would be closed. In the first winter after her graduation from high school the teacher had been taken ill and they had asked her to continue the term. She had been such a success that the parents had requested her to continue until the new plans materialized.

The money earned might be a pittance but it had helped in buying shoes and other necessities—and she loved the early walk. Coming out every morning neatly dressed, meeting the bright faces of the children. How she loved them! For hours every day they were wholly her own. She was mother, father, brother and sister to them. She planned for every hour, corrected smudged papers in the evenings, visited their parents, played with them in the school yard. She loved them.

Next year? Had she only been able to save her money she could have gone to a normal college and prepared to be a real teacher. Next year? She saw no future at present but every night she prayed and perhaps something, some way would be opened for her. Oh, if Mother were only well and strong, she could leave home.

So long! When they had been in love, when they had been "engaged" and "for life," when they had sat on the big rock, their bare feet dangling in the cool water, when they had climbed the little path, he had not left her with "so long!"

She was approaching the Waters' place and she dropped her eyes, seemingly intent on the stones and ruts for somehow Jake always found himself working near the road when she passed. She would look up, smile "Good morning" and hurry by, knowing his eyes would follow her until she was out of sight over the hill. The children came from nearby and there was no reason for his services now, toting them in the flivver.

Jake. Of course as Mother often remarked, he was the "salt of the earth." There were few days when Valeria did not see him for he also often managed to be overseeing work on their fields in the afternoon when she was coming home. Overseeing was now Jake's job for Mr. Waters had made him the acting head of what was fast becoming one of the finest dairy farms in the state. More and more fields had been bought and now men came from far away to see the herds of Guernseys, Jerseys and Holsteins and the four-thousand-dollar bull. And Mr. Waters was president of some state dairy organization and, as he said, "Jake runs the place" while he was in Albany or traveling, speaking, organizing and looking after the political interests of dairymen generally.

What hadn't Jake accomplished in these years! No more insecure grammar. He was always Phil's friend, coming shyly but persistently to the house to borrow books or report to Phil who had found it great fun to engineer him through a correspondence course. Sometimes Phil would hand him a half-dozen selected books and laugh. "Jake, when you finish these, you'll be an educated man."

Always to see Phil? Valeria knew too well what was in his eyes and she was not surprised one night when, walking alone through the pines on the hill, she met him coming toward her.

She found a shy man can become a bold man when for too long a time his heart has been eaten with the hunger of love.

With his strong hands he held her arms and looked into her eyes. "I may not be much on the social scale, Val, but I'm superintendent of this place and it's going to grow bigger and bigger and I'll always have plenty of money to take care of you and a family."

She cried out, "Oh, Jake, don't spoil our friendship."

His hold only tightened on her arms. "Val, I can't live here every day seeing you and loving you the way I do. I can't stand it. I'll love you and take care of you as long as I live. I'll take care of your whole family. They will be as much my care as our own family. I can't see you wasting your life on children not yours. That's not for a beautiful, healthy young woman like you, Val."

She managed a feeble smile. "Why, Jake, I love teaching."

"Because you haven't known what it is to have your own children and your own home. Since I first saw you, just a girl with pigtails hanging down her back, I've loved you and it's been hard for me to see you work. I've wanted to come down nights and help you in that kitchen."

He pleaded, "I could take care of your mother, Val. It's been too tough on Phil. He needs help. Can't you see how he's gradually going under?"

"What do you mean, Jake? Going under!"

"Sometimes outsiders see more than those close to you."

"I don't like what you say."

"I say the truth, Val. When I say I love you and will take care of you as long as I live and will look after your family as though it were my own, I mean what I say."

Her head suddenly drooped as though a weakness had come into both back and neck. "Oh, Jake. If I only loved you."

"You would learn to, Val."

She raised troubled eyes to his. "No, Jake. A person doesn't have to learn to love."

His hands dropped from her arms. "It isn't still Jim?"

She was silent, biting hard on her lips.

He turned his head away. "I wouldn't stoop to say anything against him. Perhaps there is nothing to say against him but I will say what I think. He's no rock on which you ought to build your life, Val."

Again she made a weak attempt to smile. "I'm not building my life on anyone, Jake. You have that all wrong. I am quite independent and I want to stay so."

Now his eyes searched her face. "I don't know you all through, Val. I guess no one can know another until after years together as man and wife, but if it's no one else that keeps you away from me, I'll wait." Then almost pathetically, "You won't let my speaking turn you against me?"

Her eyes filled with tears as she looked into his eyes. "No, Jake. You are my very best friend outside of my family."

"I'll wait, Val."

He turned abruptly and walked away and she couldn't explain why after he was out of sight she laid her head against the tree trunk and cried.

Was this the way life was? Must she hurt Jake as Jim had hurt her? Didn't anything ever come out right after you were grown up? And what did he mean by saying Phil was going under? If anyone but Jake had said that!

She would never speak of what happened up there in the woods. Jake was proud. She remembered the night he told them that his name was Alfred. "My name is Alfred Young. They got to calling me Jake when I first came to the farm. I didn't mind. But my name is Alfred Young. My people were Welsh immigrants. They were poor and my father was a miner. He got a job in the mill at the village but his lungs were already affected and he didn't live long. My mother stayed in her few rooms until she died and because I had good work up here I could give her everything she wanted, good food and good clothes for church. They were poor, but good honest people."

Phil had replied warmly, "Don't call your people immigrants in that tone of voice, Jake. We are all immigrants in America, all from some foreign country, melting into one kind. Nothing like it has ever been seen in the world. Also," with Phil's most charming smile, "the Welsh happen to be one of the finest strains in our melting pot. No criminal gangs from Wales. Your Welshmen brought us one of our greatest riches—a heritage of Welsh music and Welsh singers. I never heard of better blood. I'd be proud to be Welsh." Then Phil joked, "Shall we call you Alfred?"

"No, stick to Jake." Yes, Jake was proud.

Valeria had other admirers. A certain young lawyer sat near

them in church and she found that when she raised her eyes from her hymn book she was sure to meet his. Then he found excuses for walking home with her and getting acquainted with the family and the three brothers had a holiday teasing her. Every dispute or argument ended with hilarious laughter and, "We'll get Val to consult the law."

None of them guessed that on the way up the hill one Sunday night he told her how much he loved her and asked for an engagement. She had "regretted" her lack of interest with dignity and courtesy but he still came to call and still "hoped." His name was Conrad Whiting but Mark called him "Conrad Willing," and mimicked his speech, his manners, appraised his prospects. When Valeria begged them, "Please don't all run away when he calls," they reversed their habits and crowded the parlor, "sitting him out" until Valeria wondered how a girl ever did get married with three riotous brothers around. But not one of them ever spoke of Jim Ferris. Even Mother never mentioned his name.

She loved not only the morning walk to school, she loved the hour when she stood at the door and with gay good byes the children ran through the yard off to their homes. She gathered her papers, closed windows and doors and had that delightful walk down the hill in the beauty of the late afternoon.

On this fall day, she was ready to leave when a man's voice spoke to her from the doorway. She was startled but smiled when she recognized one of the school district trustees.

He was very kind and praised her work but said he must remind her that the school would close at the end of the term and none but normal school or college graduates could be hired for the Central School.

"Yes, I know that, Mr. Deering."

He sat on the edge of her desk. "But the point is we know you are the best teacher we have ever had in this school, Miss Macrae."

"Thank you. I have loved my work."

"Why don't you plan to go to normal school? We'll have a position waiting for you."

She smiled brightly, "Perhaps I will."

He shook hands and departed, saying, "I regret having to tell you this. I only wish we could transfer you."

Walking down the hill, her lips formed the firm line. How old she was! Nearly twenty. They would miss her meager salary. She would miss being able to help. How, instead of scraping together enough money to send her to school, could they be sure of enough to keep Mark and Andy in college? Suppose the boys were unable to find work enough to pay their way?

She stopped on the road and stared into space, hating to face a thought that came back and came back as often as she thrust it out of her mind.

She *could* help them. There was one way a girl with a pretty face could help. She could marry Jake. For years Jake had been saving money and he had told Phil of the sum he had in the bank. Jake had not only a good salary but an interest in the dairy. He had asked for that and Mr. Waters seemed glad to give it to him. Mr. Waters could not do without Jake.

Her feet dragged over the stones and ruts. Would it be right to marry without love? To marry for money? Would she learn to love him as he thought? Though she liked him so well, she did not like to have him touch her. Oh, if she had never known Jim. She could close her eyes and feel the magic sweetness when Jim's fingers played with hers.

Was this something one could *think* out? She tried, but all she could do was feel. Why did thinking about it make her feel as though fingers of ice were clutching at her heart?

She would pray. Harder than she had ever prayed in her life she would ask God to give her some sign to tell her what would be right.

As she came over the crest of the hill she looked down at the white house with the dark green shutters. They had completely forgotten the shambles of a place into which Mother had moved —perhaps dumped was the word—six children and a concert grand piano. Capable hands and strong young bodies could create wonders. True, that addition for dining room, extra bedrooms and bath had never materialized beyond the confines of their dreams, but there were stone paths, a good driveway, a flower garden to which new beds were added each year and that most beautiful adjunct of cottage or mansion—an extensive, beautifully kept tree-lawn. Along the fences bordering the fields were walls of lilac, elderberry, and all the lavish beauty Nature offered. Beyond the fences the Jersey herd moved here and there in the rich pastures.

Long ago Jake had brought men and with stones and cement reinforced the foundations of the good barn. They had laid a floor across the great beams and now one could mount the ladder and enter, not the modern studio that Louise and John had once visualized, but one of the children's own making.

Reverently she and Phil had unpacked the crates and sorted all Grandfather Ainsworth's manuscripts and notes, laying them on the new, built-in shelves. There was a plank table, an electric light and a little wood-burning stove. Some day they would manage a new coat of red paint—some day. Perhaps it was good to be always unfinished, good for ambition. Perhaps dreams were essential to the joy of living. And many of their dreams had come true.

She began to hurry, her eyes widening in astonishment. What was going on in front of the place? There was Mother leaning on her cane talking to a group of four men. There were two cars and, now she saw clearly, young men with a surveyor's instrument, walking off with tapes, shouting directions to each other.

"It's the new road, dear. It isn't *going* to be built. It is *being* built." Mother introduced her daughter. She looked frail as she leaned on her cane and there was a distressed expression in her face. "It's the maples, Val. They tell me some of these must come down."

The men paced and counted and shook their heads sadly. "We're putting in posts and a heavy chain all the way up from the highway. We can't come one foot nearer the edge on the ravine side. We're sorry but there's no way out. We have to have the road width and a ditch and drainage on this side."

Another man said, "What gets me is why there's never been an accident on this road. They tell me Waters takes his milk trucks up and down every day. Must be some drivers!"

Mother's voice was pleasant but there was sadness in her face. "My son drives up and down; in fact all the neighbors do. You see we know the road. Those maples!" Her smile was pathetic. "They are such beautiful trees and Nature takes so many years to grow them. And living with them—they are like dear old friends."

"Only two, Mrs. Macrae. You're lucky we won't have to touch those big ones by your gate. Often we have to clean out long lines of elms."

"I suppose it is progress."

"Building this road is years overdue. There'll be two lanes. We'll keep one side usable most of the time while we're working." He added cheerfully, "A good road almost doubles the value of your property."

Mother smiled as she turned away. "I know." As she limped up the walk with Valeria she slipped her arm into her daughter's and leaned heavily against her. "I never was very practical. I realize this is progress. The next time Uncle William brings Barbara for a visit, how pleased he will be to find he can drive to our door. How he has damned that old road." She sighed, "I never was decently practical. To see the ravine fenced off and those two beautiful maples cut down to make a ditch for drainage! There will be traffic also. The man said they were making a diagonal cut to another main road. Traffic!"

She stopped on the walk. Her eyes rested on the house, swept across the lawn then focused far away on the wooded hills. She was unconscious of the daughter's arm on which she leaned. She was thinking of her husband and their walks up into this wild place. Now she had two young sons in college. They were such little boys when he died. And that sick boy, their first-born, now a grown man and a banker! Aloud she said, "How time passes. How inevitable the changes are."

Valeria did not reply to her mother's remarks. She hardly heard her last words for her eyes were also fixed on the distant hills. She was watching a small group emerging from the woods, finding her very own private path which led steeply down to the old stone wall forming the boundary between their lawn and the pasture where the cows grazed.

Often in her high school days she had wanted to join such a group, but relentlessly her home duties had forbidden her to take the time. Leading the group she recognized Robert Loring, taller than the students, setting the pace with his light, easy stride. He called these expeditions "nature walks."

For a moment her face flushed and her eyes shone with excitement as she thought that she would love to tell him that she with her baby classes tried to do just what he was doing with older students, teach eyes to see and ears to hear.

Had she been alone, Valeria would have fled tongue-tied into the house but secure in the protection of her mother's social ease, she waited.

Seeing them, he sent his students on toward the road and vaulted over the stone wall.

He was shaking hands, holding Valeria's in a quick, warm clasp. "I was trespassing. I apologize. The truth is I was lost until we found a trail which we followed. What's the penalty?"

Charmingly, Louise Macrae offered a cup of tea. No, he must join his students and go on. However he stopped to ask about the twins and their start for college. They spoke of the new road and the loss of the maples, then he turned, looking into

Valeria's eyes, his own smiling and yet penetrating. "May I come up some evening and talk shop with you, Valeria?"

Her cheeks flushing with pleasure and surprise, she asked, "Shop?"

"You're teaching?"

"Oh, my babies!"

It was Louise who found the right words of thanks and a cordial invitation to stop any evening. However it was Valeria's eyes that followed him as he went quickly down the path and joined his group.

As they continued their walk toward the house, Valeria said, "Mother, what is it that makes a person, even wearing corduroy trousers and muddy shoes, appear distinguished-looking?"

"I expect it's a combination of many qualities—perhaps good breeding and character to start with. Doctor Loring appears to possess both. How lucky you all were that he liked our village and decided to remain here."

Standing in the doorway, she looked at the loved maples. She spoke cheerfully. "It's all right, dear. Why, I've read of whole villages being wiped out to make place for a reservoir. That must be heartbreaking. We should be thankful that only two maples must come down. I'll drop a card to Phil, warning him about the construction. What an eventful day! The boys off to college and the new road started!"

Valeria answered, "Yes," rather absently. She was thinking, "He would think me a simpleton if he *did* come to call some evening and we sat in the parlor with Mother but I'd love to show him some of my secret places, that field filled with pink lady slippers, my fringed gentians and where the arbutus grows so thick you can hardly walk without stepping on it."

CHAPTER IX

THE BANK WHERE Phil was doing so well occupied a corner site in the busiest, noisiest part of a rapidly growing industrial city. Like many of the edifices erected in that period for the exchange of money it was built (at least in outward appearance) like a Greek temple. Surfaced with brick and stone there were Ionic columns resting on a platform from which one descended wide steps to the street. Inside were Vermont marble walls and brass fixtures which were always highly polished.

Here one might always find courtesy and honesty. The men behind the cages or sitting at the desks in the several enclosures at the side knew that their president, Ezra Martin, on all occasions reiterated his watchword, "Courtesy and honesty." Not a quick smile which he called "a mere crack in the face" but a pleasantly genial, sympathetic countenance, a fatherly interest, must be bestowed on every client whether it be a rich man manipulating the buying and selling of stocks or the timid widow seeking advice concerning a meager insurance or the poor who week by week deposited small savings sure of the safety of their hard-earned dollars.

The beauty of the building, the responsibility of their calling seemed to bestow a special dignity on both officers and petty clerks, even on the elderly man in gray uniform who guarded the brass gates that opened on a winding stairway and the vaults in the basement.

When the clock told each one that his moment had arrived for luncheon and a breath of fresh air, some who were the favored sons of officers or directors walked some three blocks up the street to a famous club and lunched with others of the elite and wealth of the town. Some who counted their dollars scrupulously because of the needs of wife and children sought out restaurants where meals could be purchased at moderate prices. A few for reasons which might be classified as miscellaneous slipped around the narrow streets and found a sandwich and coffee at a counter patronized by truck drivers and all sorts of workmen. Philip Ainsworth Macrae belonged in the last class.

Standing behind the metal grill work or sitting at his desk under that gilded dome, one could not but admire his handsome face, his head slightly thrust forward and always a little to one side, his pleasant smile, his brilliant eyes and his remarkable mind, discerning, quick and accurate in arriving at solutions of all kinds of financial problems. In his carefully pressed navy suit and spotless white shirts (Valeria always had that bundle wrapped and tied on his return to town Monday mornings) he looked what Ezra Martin appreciated, an aristocrat, a young man the banker would have been proud to call a relative, a young man whose growing friendship with his son was gratifying.

This son, Hal Martin, two years older than Phil and a college graduate, was being trained to do the same line of work in which Phil was proving his ability. As one would expect, the father visualized Hal learning thoroughly all phases of banking from A to Z and at some far off time, stepping into his shoes.

The president's son. Behind his back the men called him "Sunny Boy" and smiled. The appelation suited him. He was short in stature, round-faced, smiling.

Through the years there may have been some jealousy on the part of older men, especially Smythe and Murphy, the two most trusted men on the premises, as Ezra Martin pushed Phil up and up into positions of confidence. It was realized that Ezra Martin had known the young man's father, saying publicly, "Your father was a friend of my brother's. Tom has often said he had the makings of as brilliant a lawyer as the city boasts. Never one better than John Macrae." Phil also said publicly that he owed his chance to his father's reputation.

When Valeria asked, "What is Hal like?" Phil replied, "A pretty boy, a Mama's pet, adored and spoiled. I'm afraid the only son may turn out to be a Papa's problem."

"Do you get along?"

"Marvelously. Give us a year or two more and I'll have to keep a weather eye open or we'll be chums. I have to think up excuses to get out of free lunches. It works fine. I cover up for him and he tells the old man how hard I work for the bank and I get a little more money."

"But you don't like Hal? What do you have to cover up?"

Phil laughed, "Like Hal? I find him interesting because I'm discovering that behind his cherubic face and sunny smile is a diabolically clever mind. The two oldest men in the bank, Smythe and Murphy, fine men too, know how he breaks rules and don't do anything about it, so why should I?"

"What kind of rules?"

"Would you like to know something about a bank, Val? How does Mother feel when she takes her small amount of money and puts it in the bank?"

"She feels safe."

"What makes it safe? Some grand old man, the very soul of honor and dignity, like Ezra Martin, is president. Back of him there is a board of directors, citizens of sorts who like to be called bankers. If they are smart and conscientious, even though they are lawyers or doctors or business men or this and that, they are supposed to watch and know what goes on. Sometimes they do and sometimes they enjoy the honor without too much work. Then there are bank examiners who come in by twos and inspect everything. Then there are the men employed, carefully chosen. Then there is a bonding company which insures the bank in case of trouble. Then there are rules."

Valeria was listening intently. "What kind of rules?"

"All kinds. Here's a few. Employees are not permitted to carry accounts in the bank. They can't draw checks on the bank. They are not allowed to trade on the stock market. Those three rules our sunny boy breaks and Smythe ought to know it. Ezra Martin doesn't know it."

"Do you really know it?"

"Couldn't prove it but I suspect it. There are other more intricate things. You're never supposed to erase a mistake. You should cross it out and let the original stand. I've seen erasures on Hal's books. I've seen Murphy allow Hal to handle the complete transaction regarding certified checks, I've seen him make 'change' for himself. I saw him take a book away one night."

"Don't the examiners see that?"

"Examiners don't exactly look for defalcation—only the solvency of banks."

"Phil, I couldn't work in a bank. I would be scared to death. Think of all those thousands of people who put their money into the keeping of strangers, poor people to whom it means so much."

"It's because men like Ezra Martin and most of the men in banks are so honest and truthworthy that it is safe."

"You don't hate this work, Phil?"

"I hate doing what I don't want to do but I'm darned lucky to find a job that I can handle physically. It's confining but not physically exhausting. I can stick it until we all get on our feet."

Valeria looked long into space. Phil was an artist, a musician, a scholar. He was a square peg in a round hole, but it was something to work for a man he admired and respected as much as he did this Ezra Martin. "It's too bad Hal isn't like his father."

Phil smiled, "Sometimes I find myself worrying about him as though I were that papa. I carefully conceal my opinion that he'll never be worthy of tying his father's shoestrings. It must be hard to have only one son and try to tailor him into being something he is not fitted for."

"I'm glad you like Mr. Martin."

"He's a grand old man, really not so old but his hair is white and he carries a great responsibility and knows it and feels it.

He is the very essence of honor and he's taught me things, outside of the routine work, that I never dreamed of."

"Such as?"

"Well, this is rather subtle but it's important. You must think of the money you handle as merchandise, not money as we think of bills and change. You count, check, file as merchandise belonging to hundreds of individuals, perhaps a widow's insurance, perhaps a poor man's savings scraped together after years of work, always merchandise put into your hands for safe keeping. The teller doesn't look at the bills with thoughts of what they would buy but simply as merchandise which he handles for others."

Val was interested. "I can understand that. If you had a five dollar bill in your hand and thought of it as the amount Billy's shoes would cost, you might be tempted to use it for Billy."

They both laughed.

There were many other points about his bank which Phil had not mentioned.

Ezra Martin scrutinized the habits of the men he employed when they were out of his sight. He found that Phil roomed in a good Italian home with a young son, a violinist who taught in the conservatory and played occasionally in the opera house. Ezra Martin, as was his duty, learned their habits. The young men neither drank nor smoked nor ran with women; instead they sat night after night, when the violinist was off duty, fussing over sheets of music or playing the piano. On Sundays, Phil drove to his home in his little flivver which was parked in front of the Italian's house all week long. No fault to find with that.

That Phil's overcoat was well worn and that he ate lunches around somewhere in the alleys, Ezra Martin knew. Probably saving every cent to send those brothers through college and help his mother with that large family. All of this was Ezra Martin's business. Good for a young man to have serious obligations and take them seriously. If there were any largess due it had better come from that rich uncle of his out in Cleveland. Might raise his salary a trifle at New Year's?

On this November day there was a cold wind from the north and Phil pulled on his shabby coat when his lunch hour was due. He did not saunter out the front door as the fashionable young men were wont to do but slid quietly out of a side door, walked down a side street into a still narrower street and took his place on an empty stool at his usual lunch counter. When the man behind the counter turned to him he gave his order, "Ham sandwich and coffee."

He was sitting at the end of the counter where he commanded a good view of the door and he was rather amused as he watched a young woman trying to park a cute little car, black with gay red wheels, in too small a space behind a huge truck loaded with bales of cotton. Phil looked at the bales and thought, "Probably destined for our mills."

The girl couldn't make it and now she jumped out of the car and stood in the doorway. "Who's driving that truck?"

A big fellow drinking beer laughed. "What's eating you?"

She was smiling coquettishly. "You lummox! You've taken up the space of three cars. If you'd move up a few feet, I could get in. Everything's full on the block."

"Anything to oblige a lady," and to the amusement of the others, the big fellow went out, moved his truck forward: then smiling at the "lady" jumped into her car and neatly parked it.

They came back laughing together and she climbed up on the stool beside him. "What will you have, lady?"

She slanted flirtatious blue eyes toward his. "Treating me?"

"My treat." He patted her arm.

She studied the menu on the wall. "Hamburger, coffee and apple pie."

"After my own heart. Two of each," he told the waiter.

Now Phil was looking at the girl. Curious! He felt that he had seen her before. More than that he felt as though he had known her. That was impossible for as far as he could remember he had never in his life seen hair of that color, or more accurately with that lack of color. He had not heard of platinum blondes and he wondered if her hair had been prematurely white and she had colored it yellow. He thought that she could have been pretty had she been a different kind of person. Kind of person? There was a coarse freedom about the way she moved, something that classified her as did the too heavily rouged cheeks, the scarlet lips and the dark circles under her almost beautiful eyes. Curious that one could call a face with such sharply cut, small features, coarse.

She wore a loosely fitting black coat, doubtless designed to conceal the fact that she was pregnant. Somehow it gave her the appearance of being one of those women with small pinched features, trunks like little barrels, and thin, really skinny ankles. She carried a black patent-leather handbag decorated with large brass initials J.M.

A young salesman was sitting next to Phil. Now he leaned over to whisper, "Watch me break this up. Watch."

Phil glanced at his watch. Ezra Martin doted on punctuality. Yes, he had time and he wanted to watch this show. Quite an entertaining interlude in a banker's dull day.

The lunch had been paid for and now the flirtatious eyes surveyed the salesman who began casually, "A peach of a car you have there. Seen much of the country? Can it climb hills?"

She shrugged. "Hills? It's from California, over the Rockies —all the way round from Mexico. Did you say hills?"

"*You* driving?"

"Sure."

"Some car! Some driving! Got a telephone number?"

"No. Never had one, never expect to have one."

The truck driver gulped his coffee and avoiding the eyes in the smiling faces down the row of lunchers went out to his truck, started the motor, edged out and drove away.

Phil glanced again at his watch. He would have to go, sorry he couldn't stay to see the end of the play.

He was setting his coffee cup down when he nearly dropped it. In her rather pleasant high-pitched voice she turned again to the salesman. "You ought to know people and places around here. Know a village called Clayton?"

"Sure."

"Know a family named Macrae who lives there?"

Keeping his face turned away and hurrying to the door, Phil stood at the entrance long enough to hear the salesman's answer. "Sure. I sell hotel furniture and do business with an Inn out there. I'm busy this afternoon but if you wait until evening I'll guide you."

He did not hear the answer. He hurried down the street, slipped through the side door and was in his place one minute before the end of his lunch time. For a few moments he saw black marks rather than figures on the paper before him. Those initials, J.M.—from Mexico. That something one calls "family resemblance"—Uncle William's answer so long ago to Mother's questions about Sam's daughter—the name clear in his memory —Jessie Macrae. Uncle William's words which he and Valeria had overheard. "There's always a black sheep in every family. Sam's our black sheep."

It was well he possessed enormous powers of concentration. He needed all he could muster for that afternoon's business.

Closing time came at last and he hurried to his rooming place, got into his Ford and headed straight north.

It was cosy in the kitchen with the extra warmth from the range and the brightness of the electric lights. Consciousness of the cold November drizzle outside only added to their feeling of warmth and security.

Miriam had set her own and Valeria's plates on either side of Mother and now she looked down at the long empty table. "It's funny without any boys."

Mother was pouring a little hot tea into Miriam's mug of milk. "The road will soon be finished if we can get more dry weather. These rainy days hold the work back."

"I wish Phil would give up his room in the city and drive home every night."

"It's convenient for him to be able to walk to his work—less physical strain. When the heavy snows come, it would be impossible for him to drive so I expect it's wise for him to keep a place in the city."

Valeria agreed. "He said a fellow takes his life in his hands getting up here even though one lane is finished. The lane is narrow and they've dug deep holes ready for the fence posts and what with the holes and the piles of stone and dirt and the big machines and the stuff the workmen leave around the driving is frightful. The milk trucks still go way around over the hills to the other road."

Soon they were rehearsing the exciting plans for Thanksgiving, only ten days off. Not only would there be the thrill of having the boys home from college but Aunt Sophie had written that Bobbie had expressed a desire to spend an old-fashioned Thanksgiving on the farm. She and Uncle William were completely tied up with engagements but they would put Bobbie on the night train and Phil must meet her with his car at the station in the city. Letters had gone back and forth and the details had been worked out. Miriam would come in and sleep with Valeria, leaving her room to Bobbie. Mother had spent money for new curtains and a fresh cretonne cover for the bed. Valeria was wondering what else they could do to make the room attractive when she stopped, listening, as the dog barked. "There's someone in the shed." She rose answering a knock at the door. "Oh Jake. You out in the rain?"

He dropped his coat on a chair as Mrs. Macrae urged, "Pull up here and have a cup of tea." Mother's voice and smile were unusually cordial.

He took the chair by Miriam who looked up at him with an affectionate smile. "We were just wishing for a boy."

The others laughed and Jake looked shy and happy. " 'Fraid

it's a good many years since I wore boys' clothes." He glanced at Valeria. "Thought there might be some little chore a two-hundred-pounder could be used for. Phil said that blind on your window banged in the night." He put his hand in his pocket and brought out some iron fixtures. "The nails had rusted so I brought these."

Louise Macrae said, warmly, "When I think back to those years when you painted and papered and mended and made walks and driveways, I can never cease to be grateful and wonder how we could have managed without you. Many times I've thanked God for sending us such a friend in our need."

Jake looked sheepish as his eyes rested on the tablecloth. She would never have guessed his thoughts. He wished he could hand back all those dollars she had paid him. He had needed them then for his father's debts and for his mother's support, for her medicines and doctors and her church. He had needed every extra cent then but now—if he could only give them back to her. Again his eyes followed Valeria who had taken the dishes to the sink. He would have slaved at the bottom of a coal mine or on a frozen mountain top for the bliss of seeing her every day.

The wind was coming up. One could hear the high branches of the trees moaning as the gale whipped them together.

Louise asked, "The rain has stopped?"

"Hardly a drizzle, but it's a black, mean night; ice forming on the trees and the road treacherous with water and ice patches that couldn't be seen in the darkness."

They asked about the road. No, he told them, the milk trucks wouldn't risk using it until it was all finished and clear.

Even as he spoke they saw first a flash of light on the window, then as Jake rose to look out, the light moved into their driveway, up the ramp and into their barn. Jake hurried out the door exclaiming, "It's Phil."

The four of them came back, Miriam dancing and chattering in excitement, Valeria questioning, Jake helping pull off the shabby coat. Only Louise Macrae was silent. She saw the pallor of Phil's face, the glittering brightness of his eyes and the shaking of his hands. She went to a cupboard, poured brandy into a glass, added some water and returned. "Drink that." He looked up at her but he did not reach for it. She held it to his lips and he drained the contents at one gulp. He laughed, "My hands were the only things that gave out—kind of got paralyzed —could see every hole, every spot of ice. Kind of enjoyed it— would have been fun—only my hands." He smiled at Valeria, "Would it be too much trouble to make some hot chocolate? Thought I'd get here in time for supper—had to go slow."

Nothing was too much trouble and soon Valeria was making hot, milky chocolate and scrambling eggs while questions were asked and answered. When Jake showed him the fixtures and explained his errand, Phil's eyes brightened. "Miri, you take Jake up and he'll get the blind fixed before it breaks off."

When they were gone, he pushed back his plate and in a low voice he rehearsed the events of his luncheon hour. Val and Mother sat in silence gazing at him, astonishment registered in their faces. He finished, "We need a telephone badly. I had to warn you. She may stop at the Inn overnight but they'll tell her where to find us and she might come up in the morning. I didn't want her barging in on you, Mother, after the girls had gone to school."

"Better to have let her barge in than to have risked your life, Phil."

He laughed. "It wasn't bad when I left the city and I was afraid she might come tonight. I tell you I wouldn't have missed the ride. I enjoyed every minute with the wind howling, sometimes feeling it blowing the car. It's fun to be out on such a night with an engine stuck in a piece of tin doing all the physical work, you furnishing the owl's eyes. I was almost at the top of the hill when my hands suddenly seemed to go numb. They're all right now."

They could hear hammering above. Phil suggested, "You'd better send Miri to bed. I've got a hunch that she might not have money enough to stay at the Inn. She got her lunch for free and somehow I felt that she needed it. They wouldn't know in the village how bad the road is."

They sent Miriam to bed and Jake, pronouncing the blind fast and firm, was going toward the door when Phil urged, "Don't go, Jake."

"You need sleep yourself."

"I'm wide awake. You go down and shake up that furnace and feed it plenty of coal."

When Jake returned from the cellar, they lighted the parlor, Mother established herself in her low chair, Valeria took her school papers to the desk and Jake and Phil discussed the road, the weather, the farm, business and the Thanksgiving plans. Jake said, "I'll take the good car and be your chauffeur when you meet the train. Show Bobbie Macrae there's something worth seeing this side of Cleveland."

Valeria looked up. "If you drive in, may I come with you?"

"Of course, but we'll have to start before daylight. They drop the sleeper off and we'll have to be on hand—then probably wait, no telling how long, until her highness sees fit to dress and come off."

They all laughed and Jake rose. When they reached the kitchen Phil put on his coat. He went out with Jake.

As they made their way down the drive, they looked up at the sky. The wind had shifted toward the west. The clouds were breaking and although the wind was still whistling through the tree tops, there was something exhilarating in the pure, rain-washed air that promised clearing. Phil walked out to the newly opened road and stood looking down the hill, listening intently. "Thought I heard something like a motor. Must have been the wind growling in the ravine."

Jake turned away with a pleasant "Good night." He had, with bent head bucking the gale, progressed some few rods when he heard Phil's voice sharp and a bit panicky. "Jake, Jake. Come back." Jake came running. "What's up?"

"Listen. Don't you hear it?"

They both stood holding their breath, as they listened. "Good Lord, I think you're right. None of our boys are out. No one sick on the hill so it wouldn't be the doctor. No fool but you would try that road tonight."

Phil spoke quietly, "A fool or a stranger. Do you mind walking down a bit?" They walked along the level until the long straight stretch of road was in view. They stopped again as they both heard the motor and saw—what? Phil spoke nervously. "*One* light? Gosh, you need two lights tonight."

Jake added, "The fool's weaving like the devil—must be drunk."

"No, skidding, Jake. I nearly turned around once."

They stood fascinated, watching, Jake saying, "There's nothing we can do but wait and see who it is," even as he wondered what was the matter with Phil, for he heard his hard breathing and felt his nervousness. Then when the car was within a couple of hundred feet of them, they stared with horrified eyes as the light suddenly hit the treetops. The crash followed almost instantly and Phil called in panic, "She's in that hole. Run, Jake."

Jake ran with Phil close behind him. The car light was out and even above the howling of the wind they could hear the car hurtling over the bank into the ravine. Both were breathing a prayer that the trees would stop it.

Jake, with his long legs and superior strength, reached the scene first. The car had been stopped by a large beech but two wheels were dangling in mid air. He climbed over the back and wrenched open the door and saw a girl lying in a heap on the floor partly under the wheel. He knew the rules about not moving the body until the doctor arrived but no rules applied in this place and this hour of night. "She may be dead and she may be unconscious but we've got to get her out and up to the house for help. When I lift her, you hold her legs."

Gently Jake slid her out and they laid her on the ground.

"Feel her pulse, Phil, while I get this door off." With almost superhuman strength Jake wrenched at the door until he had it loose. Carefully he slid the body over and on it. Then he straightened up.

"If you could steady it, I could hoist it onto my shoulder."

"No." Again there was panic in Phil's voice. "I'll take one end. Let's get going."

Jake lifted the burden, steadied it and slowly, Phil trying to conceal his panting as they edged their way up the incline, they reached the road. Jake said, "Lay her down. We'll rest," but Phil almost shrieked, "No, go on. We mustn't let her die. She's my cousin."

Then as though answering Jake's atstonished silence, he panted, "I'll explain later."

Valeria, who had gone to the shed door wondering why Phil had gone out and where he was, heard the voices and now came toward them. Jake called, "Come, take hold, Val." As she reached them, "Help Phil."

Mother who thought she had heard a crashing sound above the wind, now stood in the open front door. As they reached her, she spoke quietly, "Put her on my bed. Flat. Take off the pillow. Get the brandy and my ammonia bottle, Val, and get hot water boiling. Unbutton her coat, Phil, get her throat free." Mother's fingers were on the girl's wrist. "She's only unconscious." When Phil unbuttoned the coat and flung it open Mother staggered back and would have fallen had not Jake's arm supported her. She murmured in a horror stricken voice, "The girl's pregnant. She looks as though she were near her time."

They administered restoratives. Although she had not opened her eyes the girl was stirring, moving her head from side to side as though in pain. Suddenly she called out in her clear high-pitched voice. "You devil, you've taken me over the Rockies. Get on with you!"

Phil shocked them by laughing. He knew she was speaking to the cute black car with the red wheels.

She opened her eyes and looked at him.

CHAPTER X

THE THIN FINGERS pressed against her forehead seemed to quiet the girl as Louise leaned over and asked gently, "My son thinks you are Jessie Macrae—are you?"

"Who are *you*?"

Mother smiled at the instinctive wariness. "I am Mrs. John Macrae, your Aunt Louise. Your car skidded off the road and you were brought to the home of your cousins."

The girl's eyes turned to Phil. "You the hunchback?"

Phil laughed aloud, then abruptly walked out of the room, meeting Valeria who was carrying an old-fashioned crockery basin filled with water. She knelt beside the low bed and began to clean away the blood which was now matting the blond hair, smearing the coverlet and trickling down the face. "Jake, when I raise her head, slip that cloth under." And presently, "Jake, hand me the scissors from that workbasket." And again, "Jake, empty that and bring me clean water. It's not a deep cut. We can clean and bandage it."

The girl tried to pull away her head as Valeria held clumps of short blond hair and cut close to the roots.

"What in hell are you doing? Damn you, cutting my hair."

Valeria's eyes flashed angrily. "I'm taking care of a nasty cut. And you're not in hell either. You're in your aunt's house and you'd better stop swearing."

Jake suppressed his desire to laugh, thinking, "That rowdy'll soon find out who's the real boss around here." He could not keep the smile out of his eyes as he watched Valeria scrub face, neck and hands, removing every vestige of rouge and lipstick and mascara as well as dirt and blood.

"Now, Jake, can you lift her a little while I get these clothes off?"

Mother, sitting close by, was slitting an old nightgown down the back.

With sure hands, working slowly as Jake lifted, Valeria removed the mud-stained coat, dress, underwear, shoes and stockings, as well as the bedclothes until the girl, now with closed eyes and moaning again, lay on clean sheets, her head neatly bandaged. Once she opened her eyes and looked at Jake. "You the doctor?"

He smiled, "Sure am."

The girl's hands lay limp and she closed her eyes but suddenly she opened them again as her face expressed fear and panic. "I'm expecting a baby."

It was Mother's hand laid against her cheek and Mother's gentle voice that answered, "We know that. You'll be taken care of. Good care."

Valeria gathered up clothes, towels and soiled rags and handed the bundle to Jake. "Put it in the shed." Presently she held a tablet to the girl's lips. "Swallow this." She gave her a sip of water. "Now try to go to sleep. It's a miracle that you're alive. You're all right. Go to sleep."

As Valeria turned to leave the room, a shriek rose that was nerve-racking. The girl was clutching at the bedclothes, then reaching out beseechingly for Mother's hands. "It's coming. Don't leave me."

In the kitchen, Valeria found Phil putting on his overcoat. "Oh, Phil, you can't do that hill again tonight." She turned to Jake who was returning from the woodshed. "He mustn't, Jake, stop him."

Jake spoke with authority. "Val's right. Hand me your keys, Phil. I'll get Dr. Northrop."

"But you're the one that's needed here." They were arguing

when they turned to see Louise Marcrae standing in the doorway. She spoke without the slightest indication of panic. "It's too late." She smiled reassuringly, "Now just remember that I'm the mother of six children. To Jake on the farm, birth is a commonplace event. Phil, will you take over in the kitchen and give us an adequate supply of boiling water? Val, go upstairs and find old sheets?"

Already Jake had thrown off his coat and was scrubbing at the sink but Phil was unconvinced. "Let me try for Northrop, Mother. How do you know?"

Mother's smile expressed patience. "A woman *knows*. There is no time, Phil."

It was two o'clock that night when Jake stood grinning at the girl baby lying on a pillow in the clothes basket as the new mother slept deeply in the darkened bedroom. "She looks all right to me, perfectly normal, kind of pretty too." He had returned from helping Mother up the stairs to sleep in Valeria's room.

Valeria was stirring oatmeal and making coffee. "Mother likes to quote something Mr. Waters said about you, Jake. He said, 'Some men are good for nothing but Jake's a fellow who's good for everything.'"

She did not see the expression in Jake's eyes as he thought, "Good for everything but what I most want to be, your husband. Not good enough for that." Aloud he said, "What about your school this morning, Val?"

"I've been thinking. The term's nearly over and I would have been through anyway. I couldn't leave Mother with this. She was wonderful tonight but I must keep her upstairs, carry her meals and see that she rests now. Jake, if you'd telephone around, I'll give you the names, stop the children coming. I think they'll have to close the school."

She wrote the list as he drank his coffee. As he pulled on his coat, he smiled. "Some night. I hope Phil's getting a little sleep. I'll be down later in the morning. I'll get Northrop up as soon as he'll come, might have to go for him. It's turned cold and the road's still treacherous."

He had fixed the furnace and now he was gone. She drank two cups of coffee before she set the table and began arranging trays. Then she slept for a while in her mother's chair.

Phil came down so quietly she did not hear him until he stood beside her. His skin looked gray-white and drawn, his eyes brilliant. His hand shook when he lifted his coffee cup.

"Did you sleep at all, Phil?"

"When do *you* get any sleep?"

"I'm all right." She tried to speak casually even as she wondered why Phil should be taking this so hard. Why was he so nervous? Why did he look and act as though he were ill? "Jake said that if you would drive up the hill, take the long route to the other highway, while it would be some twenty minutes longer, it would be easier and safer driving."

"I'd planned to do that." His eyes rested on a heap of articles piled on a chair. "What's all that?"

"Jake went down and got everything in the car, her bag, satchel, rugs and papers." She sighed, "I suppose the workmen will find the car and it will be countryside talk in a few hours."

His lip curled in the bitterest smile she had ever seen on his face. "What a mess on your hands, Val. What a pretty mess for your Thanksgiving celebration; the boys coming home, our gay, fashionable sister from Cleveland honoring us with her presence, Mother nearly prostrated, useless Miri and your even more useless oldest brother."

"Don't, Phil. Don't talk like that. I can manage. I'm well and awfully strong. I'm used to all this, it's just a little extra." She tried to speak humorously, "We looked in her purse and found only three dollars. Poor thing. No wonder she was frightened. After those first pains, she was really quite heroic."

"Wonderful! Am I supposed to admire her?"

"Don't, Phil."

It was she who needed to control herself for she wanted to

cry as she watched him pull on the old coat. His hand was on the doorknob when he suddenly turned and came to her chair. He laid his arm across her shoulder and kissed her. "Val, I swear that some day I'll make some of this up for you. Some day you won't be a drudge and slavey. I'm going to get more money for you right now. Don't worry about the expense. I can attend to that."

He was gone. She saw the car pass down the drive. She thought, "Why is it that no matter how I try, no matter what I do or say, no matter how hard I work, no matter how much I laugh and 'keep smiling' I can't bring one bit of happiness to Phil and I love him so. He hates that bank job. He loathes it. He has an intimate friend in the city and he has never brought him home. He won't even talk about him. He doesn't tell me what he is doing. Writing music? Trying to get songs published? He won't let me get close to him any more. Oh, Phil!" And they were going to need more of Phil's money, not less, and he was somehow financing the boys at college. What were they going to do without her little salary? The girl, she might as well get used to calling her Jessie, the girl evidently had nothing and there would be doctor's bills and the extra food for her and the baby.

Uncle William. Sometimes she thought she would write to him and ask to borrow a goodly sum. How could she ever be sure of paying it back?

Mother? Mother would say, "Pray, Val. Pray and leave it all in God's hands." As the dawn stole into the kitchen windows, she rested her forehead in her hands and prayed.

CHAPTER XI

VALERIA LEARNED that there was one thing a person could be sure of in life. No matter how one planned, or managed or visualized or confidently expected an event, later, as one looked back on it, some utterly different picture remained in the memory, perhaps more joyous, or more heartbreaking, but always different from the one dreamed of. So she found the memory of this Thanksgiving.

During the days of grace before the boys and Bobbie were to arrive, the school superintendent called upon her to express his regrets and present her with a bonus indicating their appreciation of her work. While she clutched the envelope tightly in her hand, she thanked him for all his good wishes. Was she entering normal college? She smiled. "I have no plans at present."

The man in charge of the road work had the car removed to a garage in the village and later Jessie received a small sum of money for the parts that could be salvaged. Dr. Northrop came, made examinations, visited Mrs. Macrae and gave directions concerning the care and feeding of the baby. Valeria paid him with money counted out from her little envelope. She said soberly that she hoped he would not have to come again.

Jake helped her carry in the cot which had been stored in the barn and they made a new room for Miriam at the end of the hall. Curtained and with a small chest of drawers, the little girl found it delightful. "I can lie in bed and see everyone coming in or out of the front door. I like it, Val." Valeria hugged her. "You're a darling, Miri." That at least was a success.

The village paper carried a sensational account of the accident and the city papers mentioned it. A few days after the birth of the baby, men appeared with telephone equipment and Valeria tried to send them away. "It must be for one of the farmers on the upper road." They showed her the order signed by Philip A. Macrae.

That noon Phil called. "Yes, I ordered it, Val. I want to be able to speak to you and I want you to be able to call a doctor or me at any time. Now you can get Jake without sending Miri up the hill." Then he asked, "How's our distinguished guest?"

"Everything's fine, Phil. The baby's healthy and sleeps a lot. Jessie's sitting up. She says she must be like some pioneer women she's read about who had a baby by the roadside and a few hours later got back into the covered wagon and jogged on."

He answered dryly, "I believe they've found skeletons of babies and mothers who stayed by the roadside."

"Well, she's hungry and eating and feeling better. Oh, Phil, isn't this wonderful to talk to you?"

"It's overdue. Good bye."

She had told the men to install the telephone in the front hall and now she stood thinking that when she talked to Phil the entire household would stop to listen. That was not really talking to Phil. She sighed and went into the bedroom to collect Jessie's tray.

Resting against the pillows, the clothesbasket and infant beside her, the girl's face looked pinched and pale, utterly woebegone. There were dark, deep hollows under her eyes; the arms were thin, the fingers picking at the sheets. With the removal of that which had made the body appear barrel-like, she seemed emaciated. Valeria had combed and brushed the platinum blond hair. Now she thought, "She seems starved but she's clean."

They both looked at the empty dishes. There was a belligerent note in Jessie's voice as she shrugged her thin shoulders. "I licked it clean. You've got a starved rat on your hands."

Unsmilingly, Valeria answered, "I wouldn't call the mother of that sweet baby a rat."

"Do you want it?"

Valeria stopped short, the tray in her hands. "No. Don't you?"

Jessie laughed. "No. Not on your life."

There was an angry light in Valeria's eyes, then her expression softened as she remembered what Jessie had gone through. "When you get stronger you'll feel differently about that."

"So says you."

A week had passed when, one day, she said, "By the way, what became of my clothes? Doc said I could dress as soon as I felt like it. I'd like to dress and get out and sit at a table and learn to fix these bottles for *it*."

"I've washed and cleaned everything but I haven't finished ironing. I'm going to do that this afternoon."

"What do you know! I think I'm looking at what they call a good woman."

With color mounting in her face and anger in her eyes, Valeria walked out without answering, but thinking, "And I'm looking at a tough. Just wait until my mother gets hold of you."

Presently she went upstairs for the other tray. Mother said gently, "You're running a hospital, dear. You must get some sleep. See that Miri helps you with the dishes and errands. Does Jessie speak of the father? Does she discuss the question of support or a name for the baby?"

Valeria could laugh now. "No, Mother, I think we're waiting for you."

She left with the tray, Mother's eyes following her. After her nap that afternoon, Mrs. Macrae reached for her clothes and dressed.

The sun on that short November day was already lost behind the hills when Valeria carried into the bedroom all the clean clothes. Both black coat and dress were neatly pressed, the underclothes spotless; even the muddy shoes were polished. "There you are," she remarked. "You can get up as soon as you feel able. If you want help, call me." Then she glanced at Jessie. The girl's eyes were red-rimmed, her face wet with tears and she was reaching out her hand imploringly, "Val, I have dog-ears. I heard you and your mother talking."

Valeria took the hand and sat on the edge of the bed. "I don't know what you're crying about but I know it's bad for you. You and the baby are going to be cared for until you are strong enough to leave."

"And won't you be glad when that moment comes! How you all despise me—you and that giant who's in love with you, the one I thought was a doctor, and your hunchback brother. What's become of him? You all look at me as though I was a piece of dirt that got into your clean house. You don't let that little girl come near this room for fear she'll be contaminated."

Valeria had no chance to speak for like water that had burst its dam, the words came in a flood. "You may as well know now that there is no father; there is no money; there's nothing but me."

Neither turned as Mrs. Macrae, leaning heavily on her cane, stood in the doorway. The hysterical voice went on, "I wouldn't have come near you if I had known how poor you were. My father always understood that his young brother John had become a prosperous lawyer. He said there were six children and somehow I wanted a look at my relatives. Of course I don't want that baby. I thought I could find a hospital, have it and leave it. What could I ever do with it? I ran away. I stole what little money my father had and bought that car and drove all over California, then over the Rockies, hoping for an accident that would end it all. I'll tell you who's the father of that baby —a no-good friend of *my* father's who left me without a cent. I knew I'd rather die than marry him. Why wasn't I killed on that road? Why didn't I go down into the bottom of that ravine? Why did they have to find me? Why did that baby have to be born alive?"

She was sobbing hysterically. "Don't get me wrong. I wasn't any innocent. I knew what I was doing. I've always been a tramp. You don't want me here. I don't blame you. I'm just a piece of dirt to you."

Mrs. Macrae pushed Valeria aside and sank heavily into the chair by the bed. Her modulated, cultured voice, was stern. "Now that you've unburdened your soul, you'll stop crying and listen to what I have to say." Turning to Valeria, "Get me a basin of water, soap and towels and a clean pillow slip. Then make some tea."

How well Valeria knew the firmness and gentleness of the touch in the hands that washed and dried the pinched face. After the pillow-slip had been changed and she was returning with the tea, she found her mother leaning over the girl, a hand pressed on either side of the forehead, heard her voice stern and authoritative. She was finishing, "You see your ideas and mine seem to be quite different but we are both women, frail human beings with virtues and faults. I know why you came here. God sent you. I know why you were not killed on mountains or on that road. God has use for your life and for that child's life. Now it's up to you. You are neither a weakling nor a fool. You are a bright, smart girl. The doctor says you have a strong healthy body and I know God has use for your strength and youth. Now sit up and drink your tea."

Jessie's eyes were fastened on Mother's face. "I don't think you're kidding me. You mean what you say."

"From the bottom of my heart I mean every word I say. I don't want to hear coarse talking. I don't want to hear you swear. I don't want you to refer again to my son as a hunchback. He has had long illnesses and we forget them. We may be poor from some viewpoints but we're self-reliant, and have no fault to find with our lot. We are a united, happy family and want to remain one. For His own purpose I am sure God sent you here to be one of us until you can find a new order for your life. You will call me Aunt Louise and I shall look at you as my niece with some of the same blood that flows through my children's veins."

Several times Jessie started to speak, then stopped short and Valeria wanted to laugh thinking that Mother by forbidding the oaths had so cramped her vocabulary that she could not express herself. She drank the tea and reached for more cookies. "Seems as though I can't get filled up."

"Nothing could be better."

With the tea cups set aside, "Now, suppose we discuss a name for the baby. Later, after Thanksgiving, we might have a christening party, even a baptism by our minister."

"I don't think we'd better advertise this baby. We'd better keep quiet about her."

Mother shook her head. "A baby is one thing in life that can't be hidden. This child is innocent. She is not responsible for her origins so we're going to give her a name and a chance."

Jessie stared at the speaker. "I'd like to have you name her. If I had my choice it'd be Louise. I always loved that name."

"How nice. Still, it is sometimes awkward to have two in the family of the same name."

Mother thought. Finally she smiled. "Why not compromise on a simple but beautiful name—Mary. How is this? Mary Louise Macrae?"

As though unbelieving Jessie said, "You'll allow her to be called Mary *Louise Macrae?*"

"If you like it. I do."

Valeria helped her mother rise, handed her the cane and assisted her until she sank into her cushioned chair in the bay. Her legs were swollen and stiff, her back was concentrated pain. Gently Valeria massaged her spine and her mother laughed. "I wonder which of us is better able to climb those stairs."

"She is. I'm going to change the beds directly after supper."

"What have you planned? Where are you putting her?"

"I am giving her Miri's room—all fixed up for Bobbie, we thought."

Mother mused, "The best laid plans of mice and men—"

"This whole house has certainly 'gone agley.' I don't see anything else to do. It's nearest the bathroom and large enough for both her and the baby. Bobbie will have to sleep with me."

As Valeria turned away, Mother said, "Suppose you open a jar of those special peaches and cream some chicken. Let's make supper tonight a little celebration."

A hot color rose in Valeria's cheeks, an angry flash showed momentarily in her dark eyes. Mother spoke in a low tone. "Come here, Val." She took firm hold of her daughter's hand. "What is bothering you so, dear? I don't understand you. Now that we know the worst, the entire sordid, sad tale, we must be kind. It will all work out if we use good judgement."

The door was closed but Valeria spoke scarcely above a whisper. "I don't mind the work or her. If it were only you and I it would be all right."

"I don't understand."

Valeria's face was red. "It's having her here on Thanksgiving with Bobbie and—and—it's having her here with Phil and the boys coming."

But, seeing her Mother's expression, Val knew she really didn't understand. "She's too good," Val thought. "She isn't capable of feeling resentment—as I am."

CHAPTER XII

ON TUESDAY came one of those early snowfalls that suggest Nature is in a playful mood, is saying, "So you want snow for Thanksgiving? Well, here it is!"

It was the kind that produces soft, squashy flakes the size of quarters, forms tall white caps on fence posts, clings to every branch and twig, causes every bit of stubble in the fields and every withered weed along the highway to be transformed into a thing of beauty wrapping around itself an ermine coat.

When Miriam went to the barn for the pumpkin, she took down from the wall where it had been hooked, the small sled with the iron runners. She set the pumpkin on it but before it had reached the kitchen it was wearing a white hat.

Jake was talking over plans with Valeria and her mother. "Grandfather Waters says the climate is changing." Jake was imitating the old man's drawl. "When he was a boy the ground was frozen a foot deep by Thanksgiving and all the relatives from far and near drove in sleds with spans of prancing horses to his place for Thanksgiving dinner. Drove over hard-packed roads too." They all laughed. "I never talked to any old party who didn't tell me the climate's changing, either hotter in summer or colder, or hotter or colder in winter. I suppose when Miri's an old lady she'll tell her grandchildren how she had to bring the pumpkin and the corn for popping from the barn on a sled over three to five feet of deep snow."

Mother smiled. "If I could do the ordering, I'd keep the fields and trees and shrubs white and beautiful and melt it on the road so you can keep your cars running safely."

"That's about what is happening." He turned to Valeria.

"Shall I give you a ring tomorrow morning? In case of more snow we'll have to start by five-thirty."

Mrs. Macrae answered. "Don't you dare ring. We're not used to that telephone yet and the entire family, including the baby, responds to it as though it were a fire alarm. I'm sure Val won't need anyone to call her, but I'll be the alarm clock."

Hearing footsteps above and the whimpering of an infant, he looked toward the ceiling. "How's it going?"

Mrs. Macrae said, "Very well, she's getting adjusted."

Jake didn't like that word, "adjusted." Getting adjusted to what? He looked at Valeria but her face told him nothing.

He had tended the furnace, left a great pile of kindling, the largest tom-turkey they had ever seen, two chickens and a bushel basket filled with vegetables and fruit enough to last a week, their value to her reflected in the glow of pleasure on Valeria's face. Now he went out, his whistling heard, then the sound of the motor as he passed the windows.

The accident had brought great concern to the men working on the road. Those in charge of operations brought extra gangs and shovels were pushed, pick axes and hammers were swung, as the finished lane was cleaned, the edges were reinforced and post after post was set in place with connecting chains. Should there come deep freezing, work on the second lane might be impeded but travel up and down now seemed relatively safe.

Before the day was over long pantry shelves and commodious tins were filled with such an array of pumpkin pies, mince pies, rich fruit cakes, frosted cakes, jars overflowing with cookies as might make eyes to widen and mouths to water.

Jessie, when called for supper, came down carrying the inevitable bundle of baby washing. Louise Macrae noticed her red-rimmed eyes and the pinched and peevish expression in her face as she called out in a high-pitched whining tone, "What the devil can I do about washing or using the bathroom when this mob you're expecting gets here? One bathroom and how many people?"

Valeria was pouring boiling water into the tea pot. She was tired after the day's work but excited and happy, her eyes shining with eagerness and anticipation. She replied, "Guess you'll wait your turn. In emergencies, Mother allows vagrants into her domain." Without glancing at Jessie, "We haven't been brought up on hotel bedrooms with private baths. Put the diapers down in the shed, I'll do them tonight. With six children we've even been used to diapers." She added lightly, "Walk into the pantry and see what else we've been used to."

Jessie disposed of the bundle then went into the pantry and looked around. She started to exclaim "My G—" but swallowed the second word.

Louise, waiting at the table, was again disturbed by the latent antagonism between the two young women. Looking at Jessie, who was wearing a faded wash dress of Valeria's, she spoke with gentleness, "Jessie, I've also been thinking about the one bathroom. Suppose while my three sons and Bobbie are here we bring the basket and the baby things down into my room. If Mary cries at night it won't disturb the whole family. It's been years since we've been used to that." Louise was smiling. "Between us we can look after everything. Then about your own clothes. I know you'd be unhappy in that dress."

"I won't be seen in it. That Jake always gives me the once over from head to feet, can't stand seeing Val's clothes on me."

"You imagine that." Louise went on serenely, "No, I don't blame you. Wear your black and next week after they're all gone, we'll plan what to do. Can you sew?"

Jessie snorted. "Sew? Sew what? Me sew! I've always bought my dresses off the line, usually at bargain sales, except when someone else was paying for them. No, I can't sew and you don't want me to wear the red dress around here. That's all I've got. When I cleared out that was all I could carry. I suppose my father sold what I left. He'd sell my last pair of shoes for a glass of beer."

There was a painful silence as Mother poured the tea. There

had also been the painful subject of the red dress. When Jessie first got up she had wrapped around her thin figure a robe of Mother's, then one morning she came down in a flimsy, flaming red, imitation silk, too short, too tight, too cheap, too vulgar. Quick to note the disapproval in Mother's eyes she had tossed her head. "You don't like it, huh?"

Mother had spoken with authority. "I can't enjoy looking at a potentially pretty young mother in that dress. You need some wash dresses for the house and later a warm wool. Please take that off. I'm sorry that neither Val nor I have much extra in our wardrobes but anything would seem better to me than that."

Now Valeria spoke hesitantly, "I think, Mother, my blue wool would look nice on Jessie. I have the brown."

Jessie spoke belligerently, "Thanks, I don't want your clothes. I'll wear my black. You can lend me aprons."

Louise Macrae sipped her tea and looked from one face to the other. "No, Jessie's right. She must have her own clothes. After Thanksgiving we'll buy material and I'll teach her to sew. We're going to need slips and dresses for the baby. We'll make them." Her smile was a little forced as she turned to Jessie. "I remember what pleasure it was to make pretty clothes for a baby and how fascinating it was to see pretty dresses on a little girl."

Valeria was looking at the swollen knuckles on her mother's hands, knowing how painful it was for her to do even the mending. Her lips set in the unyielding line and she rose to gather up the dishes.

When Jessie offered to help with the drying, Valeria spoke too sharply, "Don't you hear the baby crying? You'd better go up to her."

Jessie threw down the dish towel. "You don't want me around. You do the washing because you don't think I get diapers clean. You don't think I can do anything right. I suppose you can sew. I'll show you some day what I can do that you can't. I'll show you." She flung herself out of the room.

Mother was in her chair, knitting needles flying fast as she finished a sweater for Andy; there was the click of china as Miriam wiped, the sound of her light step as she went back and forth placing the dishes on the pantry shelves.

When all was completed, Valeria dropped down in a chair near her mother, all the glow gone from her face.

There was a silence, then Louise spoke. "It's up to you, Val. It's not going to be easy."

"Why does she hate me? I have tried to be friends. I have. She sort of fascinates me but I can't understand her. Just as we are doing something together and I think how well we're getting along, she flares up and I see how she hates me. How is it up to me? I'd give her anything I own because I do feel so sorry for her."

"Perhaps you'd better stop letting her see that you do feel sorry for her. Perhaps you'd better try to see her as she is—a wild bird whose wings have been clipped and her feet tied. She's in a cage. Perhaps she's breathing air that stifles her. The baby to her is like a lock on the cage. She has led a wild, free, adventurous life—always with men. She has never lived in a family, never known a home or women relatives. I can see her driving that car through California, then through the Rockies, through deserts, in and out of cities, beating her way, wangling meals out of men as her dollars got fewer and fewer. I can see her enjoying the wild adventure of that icy hill."

Mother's brow was knitted in a frown. "We've got to remember and keep on remembering that she's a wild thing in a cage. I don't know how it will all come out. I can't see her future. All we must do is try to keep our own integrity. We are not going to be the weak ones, allowing her to spoil our Thanksgiving party. It *is* up to you. Loosen up those lips. Smile. Be yourself. I'll manage her and the baby when Bobbie and the boys get here. Get her off your mind. Be yourself, Val. Now go to bed. What time do you want to get up?"

"I'll set the breakfast table tonight."

"Very well. You need your sleep because it will be a busy

time, a happy time if you and I make it that. Help me up, dear. I'm going to pray and I'm going to sleep. You go do the same."

When Valeria leaned over to help her mother, the crippled hands drew her down; her mother kissed her and smiled. "Val, there is an inner strength. You must find it. No matter what your physical strength may be, that never fails."

It was dark and penetratingly cold that November morning as Valeria stood by the gate watching up the hill for the lights of the car. She wore her winter coat, a knitted red scarf about her neck and on her head a small sealskin cap that Mother had fashioned out of an old cape. Never had she looked more beautiful, never had her lips curved in a sweeter smile or her eyes glowed more radiantly. The car lights drew nearer and nearer, then the door was opened and she slipped into the front seat beside Jake.

How comfortable and how good it was to feel the old friendship with Jake. It was so easy. "Easy as an old shoe." That was her mother's expression. Now that they had even brought a baby into the world, working together, the old solid friendship, with no embarrassing talk about love, had been reestablished.

"You're good, Jake." She laughed with appreciation and excitement as he let the car gather speed on the hill.

There were still some flakes of snow gathering on the windshield but not the big, splashy ones; these were small hard balls, the kind they expected in real winter. The single lane was white and slippery.

She remarked that Jake was not driving his own car. This was one of Mr. Waters' big ones.

Jake with eyes on the road, strong hands on the steering wheel, foot ready for the brake, laughed. "The best is not too good when a real princess is going to ride."

Valeria laughed. "I hope she won't act like a real princess."

He didn't say he was not referring to Bobbie. He knew Valeria received flattery and compliments about as awkwardly as he did. He let it go. His happiness this morning was too great to spoil by getting personal. "The boys get in at seven tonight?"

"Phil will be at the station to meet them."

"Get your pies and cake made?"

"You'd better stop in and look at my pantry."

He was wishing it were not her pantry. Now, down on the two-lane highway, although the driving still was not easy, he stole glances at her radiant face. A girl as beautiful as that should be having her own pantry. He'd better watch his tongue.

When they reached the city they had some trouble getting past the huge machine with the rotating brushes that was clearing the main street. After it let them by, they reached the station with ease and Jake found a place to park not too far from the tracks. They watched the long train pull into the station, backing and jogging as the one Pullman was dropped off onto a side track. After taking on passengers it pulled out.

Soon the porters opened a door of the Pullman and set the portable steps in place. One by one passengers got off. Jake's eyes were on his companion. "We may have a long wait; better sit back and take it easy." She had been leaning forward peering at the car. He got out and cleaned the snow off the windshield.

Of course they had seen Bobbie off and on through the years but those had been hurried visits, mere calls, as Uncle William came through on business. She had never come alone to stay.

Val settled for a long wait knowing Bobbie never did like to get up in the morning. There was the insistent honking of a horn as a car drew in beside them and soon they were all laughing excitedly as Phil stepped out. "Couldn't miss this show."

"Come in." Jake opened the rear door. Hardly had Phil sat down when Valeria called, "There she is." She was tugging at the door, then racing toward the train calling, "Bobbie, Bobbie, here we are."

Surely this was a real princess. A mere glance was enough to recognize wealth and social ease. She wore a gray fur coat, soft as a kitten's fur, a hat to match, a smart, many-colored quill at the side resting on her blond curls. A wide smile displayed her pretty teeth while her blue eyes were turned from face to face. "Val, Phil and—oh, I remember, Jake. You fed us."

Valeria felt as though she could crush her in her arms. It was so wonderful to see her. Her sister.

Jake was putting expensive looking bags into the back of the car as Bobbie said, "I'm so hungry—just starved. Wasn't there a good restaurant near the station? Can't we have coffee before we go?"

Phil answered, "One of the best." When Jake had arranged the last of the three bags he locked the car as Phil led the way and soon they were seated around a bare table in the station restaurant.

A waitress came and cleaned away crumbs and coffee drippings then stood waiting for the order. Bobbie looked up still laughing. "I'm on a spree so I'm going to have orange juice, coffee, toast and ham and eggs. Do you remember, Phil, once we ate mince pie for breakfast? I don't remember what happened to us after."

Phil smiled. "Probably felt stronger and better for it all day."

Jake looked up at the waitress. "Make that four orders."

Oh, what happiness. They were all on a spree, young, carefree, hungry and each conscious of that best of sauces—a healthy appetite.

Bobbie did most of the talking as they ate, telling amusing incidents of the trip. "Uncle William tipped the porter and gave him instructions about me and he treated me as though I were either an infant or a decrepit old lady."

Once, after Valeria had been speaking, Bobbie exclaimed, "Val you talk just like Mother. I'm afraid I've acquired a Western accent. Uncle William talked about your beautiful voice when he came home last time. He always talks a lot about you, Val. I think you are his favorite."

Valeria looked shyly pleased as she replied, "I always liked Uncle William. We got quite well acquainted."

Phil had been glancing at his watch. "I'm sorry but I'll have to leave this charming party." He was reaching into his pocket and now extracted a piece of paper. He looked at Valeria. "Mother telephoned. There was a telegram for you, came just after you left. She called me because she thought I might do something about it. Not that you want my advice, but I'll give it to you before you read this. Let me send a return message—about two words—either 'other engagement' or 'deep regrets,' both of which could be true."

He was handing the folded piece of paper to Valeria. "I took it down as Mother dictated."

Smilingly, a wondering expression in her eyes, she opened it and as she read a pink flush crept into her face suffusing even her forehead.

GOT THANKSGIVING DAY OFF COMING TO SEE YOU ON SLEEPER WEDNESDAY NIGHT DINNER AND DANCE AT COUNTRY CLUB THURSDAY NIGHT WITH YOU STAY AT INN WILL BORROW CAR.

JIM

She heard Phil saying, "We're one of those families that go along with absolutely nothing out of the ordinary happening for weeks and months on end; then every darned thing happens at once. Just as we settled down to steady work this winter, Val teaching in our little school, Mother better and all serene, we have a sensation, a car hurtling into the ravine and a cousin whom we had scarcely known existed, catapulted into our midst. Then when we are trying to get over feeling bad about her being there when our beloved Bobbie was coming, what did we get? A baby. On top of all that, an old friend of mine, and of Val's of course, elects to come for the exact day when we have planned all our Thanksgiving festivities. Although we'd enjoy seeing him I think it wise to suggest another time, politely of course

—two words." He glanced casually at Jake. "You remember Jim Ferris? We'd like to see him, but not now."

Bobbie thought for a moment. "I remember him. He was awfully nice."

Jake did not speak. His eyes were fastened on Valeria.

Phil was standing back of her chair, his fingers pressing her shoulder. "Will you take my advice, Val? Let me send the telegram? It was Mother's suggestion."

She looked up into his eyes. "No, Phil, I'll answer it."

"Sure you'll answer it?"

She dropped her eyes. "I want to think, Phil."

"Can't you think now?"

Firmly, "No."

"It's up to you." He bade them all a pleasant farewell. "Until tonight, folks." To Bobbie, "I'm meeting the boys tonight. You're going to be proud of two six-foot athletes, both handsome and smart."

"You're plenty handsome yourself, Phil."

"Thanks. I'll live on that all day," and he hurried away.

Jake jumped up and followed him. There was a little skirmish at the cashier's desk, both the men with bills in their hands, but Valeria did not know who paid for the breakfast.

Soon they were in Jake's car, Bobbie excitedly asking about the accident and the unknown cousin.

On the way home, Valeria told the tragic tale. When Bobbie asked, "What is she like?" Valeria looked hopelessly at Jake. "You describe her, Jake."

"That's no job for me. Might call her an adventuress."

Bobbie gasped. "An adventuress? How wonderful to have an adventuress in our old-fashioned staid family. We're all so conventional in Cleveland. I can't wait to see Cousin Jessie."

Valeria had put the piece of paper in her pocket. There was enough to talk about until they drove up the single lane and saw Mother standing in the doorway, waiting.

CHAPTER XIII

TRY AS SHE WOULD, Valeria could not get to sleep. There on the pillow so close to hers was Bobbie's blond head. How lovely she had looked in her crêpe de Chine nightgown; how fascinating it had been to watch her unpack the bags and lay blue and gold enameled toilet articles on Valeria's dressing table, shake out pretty dresses and a sweater of an enchanting pastel shade, and hang them in the closet. There was plenty of room in that closet.

Bobbie had chatted and laughed in her inconsequential way. "I have a school friend in New York and I took a chance on Aunt Sophie's letting me go on there for a visit, just for a week as long as I'm in the East. Never know what I'll need."

She was holding up a dancing frock. "Isn't this just ravishing?" Valeria had noticed how often Bobbie used that word, she had even exclaimed that the baby was "ravishing." Now she turned the gown around slowly as Valeria studied the exquisite details, lifting the hem to note the ruffled net underskirt, admiring the narrow gold edging, the simplicity of the whole. She spoke warmly, "It's a dream of a dress."

Bobbie went on, "Aunt Sophie always says no first, then when I tease I usually get her to come around." As she hung it up, "I wear my gold slippers with it."

As she watched, Val thought, "Mother might as well allow Uncle William to adopt her legally for she'll never give up all this luxury. I wouldn't want her to and she's been educated for this, brought up to it and it all seems right for her."

It had been an exciting, happy evening with all six of them

together. Mark and Andy following Bobbie about the kitchen, at first shy then having fun with her, talking football scores and players with Phil, answering Mother's smiling inquiry, "What about your work?" with shrugs, "It's tough. Cornell's noted for that. You work or get out. So far we've been able to slide by." They had been polite to Jessie but they were still too young and awkward not to show their embarrassment. They glanced at the baby then turned away abruptly, not having acquired the art of dissimulation.

And Jessie. She had brushed her hair until it shone like smooth pale gold. She had appeared chic and stylish in the black dress that Mother had transformed, taking out the elastic and fullness that had marked it as a maternity dress. How had she made up her face to get that creamy look? She had large blue eyes that she could use flirtatiously when she talked to Phil or Mark. She had sat back on the sofa and kept very quiet.

Such a happy evening. When Bobbie teased Phil to play "just a little," he played just a little, a few gay tunes, not Phil at all. Mother had been obliged to order them to bed.

Only two weeks ago, Valeria had been quietly planning for their usual family, five of them and Mother. She had been busy thinking of all the boys' favorite dishes, wishing there were such a thing as an inexhaustible supply of applesauce, and now look at this big party!

If she could only get to sleep. She could not toss or turn or shake up her pillow or roam about for fear of waking Bobbie. She must lie still and think; try to get the whirling sensation out of her head.

She had not sent the telegram. She couldn't. From the moment when she had read the name, Jim, it was as though something sweet, something painful, something like hunger yet something frightening had caused a hard lump to form in her chest. She felt confused and unsteady. She was afraid to see him, yet her longing to see him made her heart turn into an ache. He hadn't forgotten her. Would he find her old? Wouldn't it be wonderful if he could be a real friend like—Jake? Of course that about being lovers was a childish affair of school days. He had been through a war, graduated from Harvard and was studying medicine in New York—yet there must have been something that caused him to want to come back and see her.

Some tears wet her cheeks as she wondered what it would have been like had she possessed any money at all or pretty dresses, dainty dancing slippers, all the lovely personal things like the ones Bobbie owned. She would have been able to accept his invitations to college dances. She thought of those cards he had sent her from Europe and she with no way to answer them. Hidden in her treasure box was the snapshot of him in his uniform.

Now was he remembering those days in the ravine? When they were engaged "forever and ever"? When she had promised never in her life to love anyone else? Of course it was silly and childish but when she drew her hands away from her eyes, they were wet with tears as she remembered the sweetness.

She had better stop thinking about all that and plan for tomorrow. Should she wait in the morning until he telephoned or should she call the Inn? Suppose he drove up and found her in her work dress? When could she get time to see him? About the Club dinner and dance—her best dress was a good brown wool. She had dinner to take care of and she wished, until her heart ached, that there never had been such a thing as Thanksgiving dinner. Given all the hours in the day she would not have too much time to prepare and serve and clean up after this big one for all the people sleeping under this roof.

Jessie had borrowed clothes. If she could only borrow one of Bobbie's dresses. How silly! Bobbie's dresses, like her shoes, were at least a size too small for Val. Mother disliked people who felt sorry for themselves. She would dislike her daughter tonight for she felt sorry for herself—so sorry she cried into the pillow. If Jessie only had been any good! She was not the only one who had her wings clipped and her feet tied. If only Bobbie had not been—well, Bobbie! If only Mother were well and strong and there had not been that baby!

There was her one wonderful friend, Jake. He couldn't help her now. Had she asked him, he would have moved heaven and earth and at any other time Mrs. Simms, their housekeeper, would have come down to help; but Mrs. Simms had her own big Thanksgiving dinner to attend to for the Waters. All her life Val thought she would hate Thanksgiving day.

Mother talked about "inner strength." No one must guess her inner weakness.

She had had two offers of marriage. But the memory of Jim overshadowed all the love they could promise.

She could not get to sleep. She should pray? Pray for what? Send her pretty clothes? Give her inner strength? Help her to live through tomorrow? Yes, that last was all she could pray for.

She needed to switch on the electric lights for it was still dark when she came down in the morning to set the breakfast table. Mother's sharp ears heard her moving about. She went into the bedroom saying, "Good Morning" cheerfully enough. The basket and sleeping baby were close to the bed and Mother was smiling. "She's been so good. I could pick her up in time and I'm sure she never waked anyone and Jessie must have had a good night's sleep."

"In Bobbie's bed." The words slipped out before she could stop them.

She saw Mother look up sharply. If her countenance had what Mother called "the belligerent look" she could not help it. This morning she felt belligerent. Her head was clear and her mind was functioning. If her lips were set in the "unyielding line" she could not help that either. She would speak to the point.

"Mother, I want to be free from three o'clock to supper time today. I'm going to serve a light breakfast for. I shall have dinner on the table at one o'clock sharp. The boys want to go to a football game. That helps. I want time to put away the food. If I don't get the dishes finished I'll do them with the supper dishes." Her heart was pounding. "As you know, Jim Ferris is here. I want to see him and that would be my only chance."

Before Mother could speak, she walked away then stopped at the door. "Do you want me to help you or do anything now for the baby?"

"No, Val. I can attend to everything."

In the brightly lighted kitchen she moved about swiftly and with no lost motions. The huge turkey was dressed and waiting in the oven, the vegetables cleaned and ready, dishes filled with cranberry sauce, celery and pickles were in a row on the pantry shelf.

It was eight o'clock, the cereal cooked, the table set, when she did an unprecedented thing. She went into the shed and took down an old farmer's dinner bell and, standing at the foot of the stairs, she swung it back and forth until the walls echoed the blatant noise. Like a porter going through a train she called lustily, "Breakfast is being served. Dining room will be closed in one half hour."

There were whistles and merry calls and Andy's tousled head and laughing face peering at her over the banister; but there was also the sound of feet rushing for the bathroom.

She went back to the kitchen and set the bell down. She stood a moment listening, a smile curving her own lips and her eyes gleaming.

Now was her chance. Should she call the Inn or wait? The decision was taken out of her hands. The telephone was ringing.

With no fumbling, she picked up the receiver. "Hello."

"Hello, Val, did I wake you up?"

"Oh, no, I was just about to call you."

"Gosh, it's nice to hear your voice. You do remember me?"

"Yes, I have a good memory."

"Say, Val, I guess I must be excited about seeing you. I couldn't sleep much. If I come to pick you up can you come and have breakfast with me at the Inn? Then we can go for a drive and find some place in the country for lunch."

For a moment she felt as though something were in her throat choking her. Oh, if she were only free for that. It was as though a door had been flung open revealing a glimpse of Paradise and she had been invited to enter. She took a long breath and the door slammed shut. "I can't do that because I have an extra big family and they have to have breakfast and a Thanksgiving dinner; but, Jim, I've planned the day so I'll be free from three o'clock to supper time. Could we go some place then?"

A silence that made her feel faint; then, "That's a long time to wait."

"I know. I don't like it either but it's the best I can manage."

There was such a quiet in the house. Were they all listening? She was beginning to feel a little sick and dizzy.

"Guess I'll take a sleeping pill and go back to bed in that case."

"I'm sorry but it's the best I can do."

"It's going to be all right about the dinner and dance tonight?"

"Could we talk about that later?"

"Don't you say no, this time. Don't let me down again, Val. I've come a long way to see you. You know you used to let me down regularly when I was in college."

"Did I?"

"Where's your good memory now?"

She managed to laugh although she felt weak with happiness. "I'll be ready at three o'clock."

"At three? All right. May I skip the family until later? Just pick you up?"

"Yes, of course. I'll be waiting."

As she hung up the receiver she could only hope that nothing in her outward appearance suggested her inner tumult. Andy ran down the stairs, grabbed her affectionately and whirled her about. "One of your beaus, Val? Dating?"

"Just an old friend. Perhaps you remember Jim Ferris?"

"Sure. He was your steady at one time. Never forget how he lent us Nell."

She knew her laughter sounded a little jittery. "That was a long time ago. I'll soon be an old maid. I understand it's a great convenience to have one around in a large family."

"Not for you. I'll bring down some bachelor before I'll let that happen." They were in the kitchen. "Phil told us the story about our cousin. Who ever heard of her? Kind of raw, isn't it? You want to get her off *your* neck."

"You're right I want to."

"Well, why doesn't she move on?"

"The old story." She was ladling out oatmeal as Andy carried the dishes to the table. "Plus a baby, minus a bank-book."

"And no father, Phil says."

"Another important minus."

Mark came in and swung the bell, then Phil, Jessie following in her black dress, the make-up not so glamorous in the morning light. They were all at the table, Mother ready to say grace when Bobbie, wrapping about her an exquisite rose-colored house gown, ran to her place, laughing.

Valeria gave the dinner time schedule. "Right on the minute, one o'clock. Light supper at seven and you're to keep out of the kitchen while I'm cooking. Don't be underfoot."

Everything went according to schedule, she watching the clock and timing her cooking. Each of them, Andy, Mark and Phil came to offer help but she sent them away. But how sweet those boys could be! She saw Jake but they all kept in or around the barn. Only for a moment Jake looked into the kitchen to hand her beautiful bunches of grapes and long stems of raisins.

She was setting the table when she heard the doorbell, then Jessie, who had answered, brought in a gorgeous bunch of chrysanthemums, yellow and white and from a city florist.

"For you, Val."

"Set it down, I'll attend to it." She was aware of Jessie's sharp, sidelong glance as she tossed her head and left the room.

She undid the wrapping and found the card, "From Jim." She buried her face in the fragrant blossoms and knew the sort of happiness that one can remember all through life.

With shining eyes she found a vase, arranged the flowers and placed them in the center of the table. She rearranged the fruit, placing two dishes one on either side of the flowers—apples, oranges, pears, plums, grapes and over them all the trailing stems of raisins.

Phil came to carve the turkey and soon they were all seated with bowed heads as Mother fervently thanked God for all their blessings, all her children together, Jessie's life spared for His purposes, their health, their intelligence, their great opportunities and for His greatest gift—the gift of life and its dedication to love and serve Him.

It was beautifully delivered; it was sincere and for a moment as they raised their heads there was a reverent silence.

When the food was all put away and the dishes stacked ready for washing, the three boys marched in, singing a college song at the top of their voices. Phil, with shirt sleeves rolled up, donned a large apron and pushed Valeria aside.

All through dinner she had felt his eyes watching her, probably noting the small amount of food she had consumed, noting her constant activity as she served or replenished dishes. "I don't approve of you today. I can't countenance your plans and purposes, so clear out. Go doll up if you must, look your prettiest and take the consequences."

The boys had seized the towels and waited as Phil filled the dishpan. For a moment she stood with flushed face, then she fled up the stairs.

Doll up? How unsophisticated she was. Her hair was curly and she wished it were bobbed like Jessie's or Bobbie's. She brushed and braided and fluffed up the soft waves over her forehead and put on her good brown dress and sealskin cap.

Should she go out and wait at the gate as she would if it were Jake coming? Should she wait in the hall? When she knew it was near three o'clock she decided on the latter. She put on the winter coat, carefully knotted the red scarf about her neck and answered Miriam's question, "Jessie says you are going riding with a beau. Are you?"

"With an old friend."

When she saw the car coming up the hill she walked down the path. As she reached the gate the car stopped and Jim jumped out. The same Jim; tall, good-looking, easy perfect manners but, she felt it instantly, not a boy but a man; filled out, older, with a self assurance that she lacked as he smilingly shook hands. Then he walked around the car, opened the door and helped her in.

Before he started, he turned and looked into her eyes. "Am I dreaming, Val?"

Surprising herself, she laughed. "I'm sure I am but I don't want to wake up."

When they were past the Waters' place with no houses in sight, he stopped and took her into his arms, kissing her lips.

She felt faint and could find nothing to answer when he said, "My memory was good too. I hadn't forgotten what a beautiful girl you are. It is years, isn't it? I could always see your feet dangling in the pool—the prettiest feet and ankles I have ever seen—and your eyes." He chuckled, "When I got part way up the hill, I got out of the car, crept under the chain and looked down at our old pool. With the ice and snow on it, I guess our toes would freeze today but I had to have a look. Have you ever gone there with anyone else, Val?"

She shook her head.

"I wouldn't either."

Minutes that were hours and hours that were minutes and an eternity of happiness crowded into that afternoon. Once when they were on a road which she had never seen before, he stopped near a woodland off the main highway. He turned to her. "I wish I had a Bible handy, I'd make you swear to tell the truth, the whole truth and nothing but the truth."

Her eyes were lustrous as she laughed. "Does anyone ever tell the *whole* truth? Do you think anyone can tell the whole truth if one tried?"

"Never thought about that but here goes. First, that summer when I was dragged around Europe for the noble purpose of teaching me to forget you, why did you never answer my letters or acknowledge my postal cards? I was trying to take you with me with those cards. Not one letter, not one word from you."

"Why? Because I never received one letter from you, only the cards, which I loved, Jim. I couldn't answer because I had no address. And I never received a letter, not one."

For a moment his eyes narrowed and he looked off into the woods. "What a Mama I inherited! I wrote the cards out anywhere I happened to be and mailed them in the nearest box. What a fool. You should have seen me sweating over the letters I wrote you and then trusted them to go with Mama's mail. Mama wrote Papa nearly every day."

Suddenly he grabbed her hands as he laughed. "It's the whole truth?"

"The whole truth and nothing but the truth."

"Now for the other. Why did you always—always let me down when I wanted you to come out to Cambridge?"

Here eyes were downcast, her face flushed.

He dropped her hands. "That's where someone else came in. The fellow up on the hill? I've heard he's become very important in the community."

"Jake? Jake is a neighbor and good friend. He is like one of the family." She hardly raised her eyes as she stumbled on, "You see, Jim, after my father died, things haven't been easy for us because Mother is crippled with arthritis and has had several other troubles. I am the oldest girl and naturally I have to take her place."

She wanted desperately to tell him that a girl couldn't travel with him, or in his set, or go to college dances or football games without the proper clothes, without money. She couldn't. Never had she felt more sensitive, proud and dumb.

There was something almost flippant in his manner now. "You see I was in love, Val, and jealous as the dickens. I heard you were running around with that lawyer, Conrad Whiting. I heard that you and Jake Young were always together."

She tried to laugh. "I was in love too and I imagined all the pretty girls you were running around with and you stopped writing to me and you went away summers and your people moved to the city and you were in the war and then in New York and never came here or wrote."

"Sounds as though we were even." Again his arms were about her, his lips pressing hers. He drew back to look into her eyes. "Val, is that the reason? Is that the whole truth?"

She wanted to cry but she managed to smile. "No, Jim, it's the truth but not the whole truth."

"You don't want to tell me the whole truth?"

She looked half frightened. "Yes, I do. I'm going to tell you. It was never like what you think. I *couldn't* go. I had no money or proper clothes. There was always Mother sick and the housework and the boys and Miri to look after—and—and—"

He held her close. "You inherited more than a Mama. You got a whole family. Look, Val, I finish my hospital work in August, next August, then I suppose I'll start practicing and sit in an office somewhere pretending to earn my living until one by one some trusting soul or Mama's friends have confidence enough in me to start taking my pills." He laughed easily. "I did get a little windfall from my grandfather but it evaporated like dew on the grass when the sun comes out. I'm still dependent on Mama and Papa for spare change. I'm not over-ambitious but someday I hope to be independent."

She spoke now as though she were talking to Andy. "Of course you'll get on. I'm sure you'll be a wonderful doctor."

He laughed. "You're the sweetest thing God ever made."

Then he added lightly, "Let's not lose track of each other again, Val. You've got to come down to New York. It will be fun showing you the big city."

"Yes, that would be fun." Her voice trailed off weakly.

"Now, about tonight. You're coming with me to the club?"

She felt that there was nothing but a pain where her heart should be. "I can't do that, Jim. I can't."

"There you go again."

"I can't help it. I have—I can't come." Should she say, "I can't go through that experience again"?

For the first time in their lives she saw anger in his eyes, anger and hurt. He started the car and their conversation was casual and nothing more until they reached the house. He turned into the drive. "I suppose if I have any manners I should go in and see your mother. I'd like to see Phil. Is it all right?"

"I hoped you'd come in. I haven't even told you that Bobbie is here and a cousin with her baby."

They were walking up the drive. "Who's Bobbie?"

"Don't you remember my sister Barbara? We called her Barb. She went to Cleveland to live with our uncle and aunt."

"Sure, I remember Barb."

He left his handsome coat in the hall and was soon shaking hands with Mother, being introduced to Jessie and being charming to Miriam. Soon the twins entered, then Phil with Bobbie. Jim made them laugh when he said to Bobbie. "*You* aren't little Barb? The kid with bare feet and curls?"

The conversation became merry and general; about the boys and their college plans, Phil in the bank, Bobbie's life in Cleveland. It was impossible to follow it all and remember how they turned to the question of the dance that evening. In his easy way, Jim joked about Val refusing his invitation. They should pity him as one of those stags standing by the wall, seizing a girl once in a while when he got a chance. Why didn't they allow singles to dance around the room alone? If you wanted to dance, why stand still?

Bobbie exclaimed that she loved to dance. Jessie was standing near Jim, holding the baby in her arms and appearing quite maternal and sweet. She turned to him and spoke urgently, "Why don't you ask Bobbie? She happens to have a ball gown and even her dancing slippers with her. I'm sure Bobbie would love to go."

Bobbie's eyes were smiling into Jim's. She told how she planned to go on to see a friend in New York. They laughed as Jim with mock formality invited her and she accepted.

"Only I couldn't eat another dinner. I've felt stuffed all afternoon."

Could she endure watching him and the others eat? She could. Would she be ready at seven thirty? She would.

After he had shaken hands and bade them all good bye, both Valeria and Bobbie followed him into the hall. At the door, he looked into Valeria's eyes for only a moment. "I'll be writing you, Val."

He was gone. Bobbie, with a little squeal of delight, ran up the stairs. Valeria went through the hall to the kitchen. She had no room to go to and be alone. She walked over to the table and stood staring blindly at nothing. A hand hard on her arm and she looked up into Phil's eyes. She could not conceal the jealousy, the pain and misery that seemed to consume her.

Phil's voice was low. "He isn't worth it, Val."

She turned away. She must not cry. She started preparing the late supper.

CHAPTER XIV

THE CLOCK HAD STRUCK THREE when Valeria heard the front door open and close, heard the light footsteps coming up the stairs. She turned over, her back to the light, and feigned sleep.

Bobbie closed the door and now made no effort to be quiet. Valeria lay motionless with closed eyes but soon she felt Bobbie's hand on her shoulder. "Are you asleep, Val?" That pretense had been unsuccessful and now Valeria sat up, watching Bobbie remove the dream of a frock, kick off her slippers and strip off her underclothes.

"Oh, Val, it was such fun. So many of the girls remembered me and Jim was so sweet. I think I've fallen in love with him. He is such a perfect gentleman. I think really you have more wonderful men friends than I have. Jim is devoted to you and I noticed right away that Jake adores you and Miri says some lawyer wants to marry you.

"We stayed to the end and then because some friend of Jim's was driving back to New York he decided to go with him and we had to go to the Inn and the garage, then they brought me home. Imagine, they'll be driving all night after taking all those drinks."

She was slipping the blue nightgown over her head, then cleaning her face with cream. "I'm going to telephone Aunt Sophie the first thing in the morning. Now I've simply got to go and visit Clare. Wasn't it luck I had a party dress with me when you didn't want to go to the dance? I'll always bless Jessie for making the suggestion. I wanted to but of course I couldn't."

She got into bed. "I never drank so much champagne before

in my life. Aunt Sophie is old-fashioned and strict about that. I'd better get to sleep so I won't sound groggy when I talk to her in the morning. I'm sure she'll let me go. I'm crazy to see Jim again."

On Saturday, Phil drove her to the city where she boarded the train for New York.

The snow fell steadily through those December days, laying a white blanket over the fields. Sometimes when the sky cleared and the sun shone it was almost blinding to look across the white stretches. Though the snowplows finally came through, it was dangerous driving and Phil remained in the city.

In spite of Mother's protestations that if Valeria would have patience, Jake would come or send a boy, Val would pull on a pair of heavy boots, a hood and old jacket and shovel a path first to the gate, then one to the barn.

"Why to the barn, dear?"

She could not explain that she must get out. She needed some hours away from the kitchen where Jessie was learning to sew. In the barn she was among Phil's things—his books, his music. It was strange how just sitting at his work table gave her happiness. Sometimes she kindled a wood fire in the Franklin stove and sat idly watching the burning logs, sighing with regret when she felt obliged to return to the house where, garment after garment, Mother was producing Jessie's wardrobe. It was simple enough—another black dress, two wash ginghams, changes of underclothes.

In her spare moments Valeria made slips and dresses for the baby and more and more the care of the infant was left to her.

It was to be a quiet Christmas. The boys came home happy in their freedom but were busy shoveling snow, piling up small logs for the fireplace, filling baskets with kindling and studying.

When Valeria remarked on the amount of reading they did during their vacation Andy spoke seriously, "I tell you, Val, it's tough going, but Mark and I talked it over. We can't let Phil down. We've got to make the grade. Of course Mother cares and we're taking her money but it's really Phil that's bent on seeing us through. I offered to quit and get a job but Phil raised the devil. I don't know why he's so set on my keeping with Mark but he is. I guess I've got to plug and get through."

Valeria sat on the small chair close to the desk where he was working.

"Is it really so hard, Andy?"

"Sure is, but so far I'm getting by."

"It will be all the more credit to you if you graduate. The jobs you do cut into your study time."

"I suppose so." Then, "Val, don't tell Phil this. I wouldn't want him disappointed if it doesn't come off but I think Mark is going to make the crew."

"How wonderful! Oh, I'd be so proud."

"Say, Val,"—he was grinning—"does it take you long to write those letters you send us about every two weeks?"

"No. I just dash them off. I wondered if you found time to read them."

"Read them! We keep them till night and we nearly split our sides laughing. We read that last one over twice—the way you described that hen chase—the hen caught in the wire net, Rover ahold of the hen's wing, you holding Rover's tail, all stuck solid like the Statue of Liberty and you wondering which would come off first, the hen's wing or Rover's tail or your arm and Jake finally coming to the rescue. We read it to some of the fellows and they shouted.

"Then the way you described Jessie in that flaming red dress and Mother's reactions! Gosh, we laughed. You don't know how funny you can write. You make it seem just as though we were there. Of course we like Mother's letters but we wish you would write once a week."

"I was afraid they were silly." She smiled with pleasure. "I wish I could get hold of an old typewriter, then I could write as fast as I want to put it down."

There was mischief in his smile. "I bet Dr. Loring or Jake could find you one."

She pulled his hair and went out. She remembered sitting at Phil's table in the barn writing that letter about the hen. She remembered how depressed and heartbroken she had felt that day. To keep from crying she had made herself write. Now, as she went about her work she wondered if Phil was like that also. Do you laugh to keep from crying?

Again and again she thought, "Do you laugh to keep from crying? Is Phil like that?" How could she earn a little money and buy an old typewriter?

The days grew longer and colder through January and February and although March brought fearful storms and gales that ripped off branches of the trees, one began to feel the heat of a noonday sun. By the middle of April the ditches at the sides of the road were little rivers. Even as the water in the stream at the bottom of the ravine seemed to leap and tumble and laugh and shout in the joy of escaping from snow and ice, so the inmates of the house unlocked doors and windows and sought release on the open highway.

Now Phil resumed his weekends at home. One Sunday morning he joined Valeria as she made her way through the woods to a spot she knew well. Here she carefully brushed aside wet leaves and some snow and found that choicest of spring's treasures—trailing arbutus.

While Valeria was finding arbutus, Jessie found her way to the village. Daily, rain or shine, she pulled on her black coat and with a careless, "Guess I'll take a walk," went out.

When Valeria expressed her amazement that Jessie could spend so many hours in so small a place, Mother expressed satisfaction. "How well and strong she is now. She is actually beginning to diet, says her clothes are getting too tight for her. Who could believe she is the bedraggled creature who was carried into this house last Thanksgiving! And she has changed in other ways—her speech, her manners, her smile. I am glad she is taking these long walks. I have admired the way she has lived through the pent-up days of this winter. She has become quite expert with the sewing machine and has helped me day after day in the sewing. She deserves some freedom now."

"Do you give her money to go to the movies at night? I asked her if she minded walking up the hill near midnight and she said she loved it. What was there to be afraid of?" Valeria laughed, "I don't believe she ever heard of simple timidity."

"No, there isn't a timid hair on her head. She seems to have made a friend or two and goes when she is invited."

"Invited? Who would invite her all the time?"

Mother spoke as though reluctantly. "I have reason to think that Phil sometimes gives her some spending money."

"Phil gives Jessie *money!*" She stopped before her mother, both astonishment and anger expressed in face and voice.

Mother frowned. "I don't like to hear you speak like that, Val. I would be glad to give her an allowance if I could afford it. Just a little in her otherwise empty pocketbook to give her some sense of dignity."

"Don't you think it odd that she never speaks of her future, never discusses some way she could earn money? Get a job? Is she going to settle down and let us support her as though she were—like Miriam?"

"I mean to bring the subject up tactfully, some day. You will let me handle it?"

Valeria laughed. "I certainly will." She saw the rural free delivery man's car coming down the hill and went out to the post box to meet him, thinking, "What a mean, jealous, suspicious person I am. Mother can't see how Jessie makes up to Phil. How she brushes her hair and fixes her eyes when he is coming home. How gentle she appears and how she smiles at him and jokes with him and follows him to the barn. And Phil? I noticed one night he hardly took his eyes off her throughout the entire meal and she really was fascinating, describing those western deserts and canyons. He gives me money, gives Miri money and now Jessie is one of us."

She took the letters and papers as she chatted a moment with the postman. There was a letter from Mark. She turned another over seeing the Cleveland postmark, one of those brief notes from Bobbie.

She opened Bobbie's. It was addressed to "Dear Mother." She hoped they were all well and sent bushels of love. Uncle William had had something the doctor called a heart attack and Aunt Sophie was worried but he got right over it and was fine now.

There was a p.s.

> Tell Val that Jim is coming out for a week end and we are all going up to the lake house. I'd forgotten to tell Val that Jim was out for a week of dancing and fun at Easter time.

Valeria handed the letter to Mother who was busy with the baby and did not look up. She passed through the shed and went out to the barn, climbed the ladder and sat down at Phil's table where she hid her face on outstretched arms.

She was surrounded by Phil's manuscripts. As clearly as though he were speaking she could hear Phil's voice as he once told her, "Great music has been wrung out of the suffering of musicians. Verdi saw his beloved little three-year-old girl die, then his baby boy die; then his beautiful young wife go with tuberculosis when he was too poor to buy food, when the public was laughing at and booing his operas. At that moment, perhaps the saddest of his life, he was handed an order by a producer. For what? For a comic opera! How's that for irony? The brokenhearted genius must write music to make the clownish public laugh!"

She sat a long time thinking of Verdi. Then she reached for her writing paper. She must tell the boys how Phil and Jake were going to dam up the brook in the woods and stock it with trout. She would write about that funny affair with the cat fish. She wished she could get hold of a typewriter.

She could think of dozens of funny things that had happened as they all grew up. That affair of the fondant and the dough, the parrot when father was living, the frog's legs. Why, she could fill a book with them. Of course no one would want to read it but Andy and Mark and Phil. They liked the pen and ink sketches she drew around the edges of the paper. It was fun to draw those pictures; not clever, just fun.

She wrote a long letter and drew some ridiculous pictures. She thought, "This is my version of Verdi's comic opera. When you want to cry, laugh."

She was drawing a scraggly cackling hen as the signature of her letter when she heard Mother's voice. She seemed to be chatting in her amiable way. A voice answered. Robert Loring?

She listened as the voices came nearer.

Twice he had called in the evening but on neither occasion had she, Valeria, spoken to him really alone. When those visits had ended she had told herself, "He finds Mother interesting. He finds Jessie's talk of the West and of Mexico interesting. I can find nothing to say to him. I sit like a dummy. I almost wish he would never come again."

Now Mother was calling, "Val, I am showing Robert our studio barn. May I send him up to Phil's music room?"

Robert! He and Mother were getting to be real friends. Imagine calling him Robert...

He ascended the ladder while the older woman went back to the house.

She was on her own, unaware of her beauty as with flushed cheeks and shining eyes she explained the manuscripts and books that had represented so much of her grandfather's life.

When she turned to the table she began putting in order the sheets of letter paper numbered one to seven in large numerals.

He stood beside her. "Curiosity is eating me. May I know what you were doing?"

Her laughter rang out spontaneously. "I was signing a letter. See? That's the way I sign my letters to the boys—a flustered hen."

He joined in her laughter. "Lucky boys to get a letter like that."

"Oh, it's just silly—mere nonsense."

His amusement and interest were flattering. His smiling eyes looked into hers as he asked, "Have I ever told you that I think you have real talent, Val? It is not a matter of fluency—perhaps an originality, a turn of words—"

"I love to tell stories but they're commonplace."

He smiled, "I wish you would let me read some of the commonplace stories."

Her cheeks were crimson. "Oh, I never could do that."

"Perhaps you will when we know each other better."

She placed the sheets of paper in the envelope and when he offered to mail it in the village, she stamped it and handed it to him.

As they walked across the lawn she was surprised by the feeling of peace and contentment his presence gave her. She had been alone with him for over an hour and they had found something to talk about. It was almost as though he had come to see her alone.

She walked with him to the gate and stood watching until he disappeared down the road.

In June the family had a serious decision to make. Mark wrote that Jake had offered them good jobs on his place; then their professor had got them an opening in a firm in Schenectady, work along the lines of their studies with wages enough to cover their living expenses and still save for winter. Which should they accept?

They waited for Phil and sat late talking it over. Louise Macrae's heart yearned for her boys. "They will be going out into the world so soon. Can't we have this summer while they are still boys?"

Phil walked restlessly up and down the kitchen floor. He and Valeria wanted those boys home also. He finally said, "Mother, in that big electrical company they will come in contact with big men and big enterprises and see the world they want to enter. They may make contacts that will change their future. We must let them go. Shall you write the letter or will I?"

"I will write it, Phil. It's another break but I must accept it."

"It's not so far from home. They can get some Sundays here."

"Yes, Phil, I'll write in the morning."

"They'll have a week's vacation, over the Fourth, before they go away."

Valeria would remember that week's vacation. They came in the evening with Phil and there was the usual lively talk until bedtime. Early the next morning Phil asked her to come out to the barn. She wondered what he could want as she climbed after him up the ladder. She was surprised to find Mark and Andy already there. They were grinning widely. "Something on the table for you, Val."

She looked. A black box. "Open it." A typewriter. She could hardly read the scrawl on a piece of paper. "For Val from the hoodlums she writes about—Mark and Andy."

Phil was smiling. "I had nothing to do with it, Val."

She was so inadequate. She wanted to cry as she laughed, "Where did you get it?"

"You have no manners. You don't ask Santa Claus where he got the doll?" She hugged them and wiped her eyes.

As the summer days lengthened there were other things one did not ask out loud. One did not ask—why, when Phil is home Saturday afternoons, does Jessie give up her walks to the village and slip out the back door and disappear into the barn? Where she, Valeria, would not intrude? What could Phil and Jessie find to talk about? Were they getting to be friends? Should she speak to Mother about it? Ask Phil? She would do neither. After all, wasn't Jessie now a member of their family? If Phil found amusement or interest in her company, wasn't that all right? Where could she, Valeria, ever get any of that "inner strength" that Mother talked about? Was there nothing but jealousy, envy and hate in her heart?

There was something worse. Must she give up her lovely walks in the woods? In the late afternoons Jessie took Valeria's own private path across the field, up the hill, and disappeared into the shadows of the dark pines. Could she follow and appear to be trailing her? Sometimes Jessie was late for supper, coming back flushed and with a curious brightness in her eyes. What was she up to?

The explanations and the blow fell on a hot August afternoon. The postman was late. Val wandered out to the road, ducked under the chain and, holding to the trunks of small trees, made her way to the top of the declivity. Never again would she visit the pool or do any remembering. She stood looking down at the water tumbling over rocks, then retraced her steps as the postman's car came down the hill. There were no letters from the boys. A letter from Cleveland. . . Then she noticed it was addressed to her, not to Mother.

She stood with the hot August sun beating down on her head, opened it and read,

"Dearest Val: I am writing to you because you will be so interested. Jim and I are announcing our engagement at a big party Aunt Sophie is arranging.

Jim finished his hospital work this month and Uncle William has persuaded him that Cleveland is a far better place to start medical practice than New York. You know how generous Uncle is. He is going to set Jim up, introduce him at clubs and give him a fine start. We are planning to be married at Christmas time although we don't like such a long wait. I am so happy, Val, I want to dance all day but I have to get my mind on a trousseau and plans. I am so happy and I know you will be just as happy for me.

Hugs and kisses, Bobbie."

Valeria crushed the paper in her hand and walked quickly around the house direct to her own path, up the hill, hurrying into the dark coolness of the pine forest. She walked on and on, climbing, sometimes half running until she reached a point where she could look into the next valley. She threw herself down on the soft, fragrant pine needles, her entire body shaken with sobs. Once she called aloud, "Oh, Jim, Jim."

The sun had moved a long way across the hot August sky when she sat up and wiped her face on the skirt of her gingham dress. She sat with arms tight about her knees, her dark eyes looking far into the distance. As though those eyes were looking up into his face, she spoke to him, "You loved me, Jim. I think you really love *me*. Everything has gone wrong. Bobbie is not the person you need. You are making a mistake and I can't save you or save myself. We were always so happy together. Phil is wrong. I could have made you worth all my love."

Sometimes the landscape was but a blur; sometimes the beauty of the rolling hills, the wide valley, the fertile fields seemed to bring some healing to her tortured spirit.

From her childhood her mother had said she took everything "too hard." Whether it was happiness or sorrow, success or failure, she took it too hard. Now she dreaded going back to the house. She must smooth out that piece of paper and show it to her mother. Could she ask her not to tell Miri or Jessie? What did it matter? They would have to know sooner or later. If she could only stay here, far in the woods, shielded from human eyes.

At last she rose, smoothed her skirt and slowly, very slowly began to retrace her steps. She passed over the brow of the hill, walked through the deep forest, her footsteps soundless on the soft pine needles.

She was within a hundred feet of the clearing but still in the shadow of the woods when she heard voices. Seldom before had she encountered anyone on this her beloved, private walk. Was Mother right? Was the new road bringing past their door cars and more cars never seen there before and now people who would prowl about their woods? She stood still. On each side were huge rocks. No, she would not be turned from her path by strangers. Then she heard a laugh and knew the intruders were not strangers. That was Jessie's voice.

She walked quickly now, stepping on twigs, hoping the sound would be heard. In a moment she stopped, pulled back into the shadow and stood breathless, rigid as though all the energy latent in her body were concentrated in listening. Two voices mingled in laughter. The man's voice? Phil! Oh no, dear God, she couldn't believe her ears. Phil? Oh, no.

"I'd better get going." Phil's voice clear and resonant. The sound of someone moving toward her. She scarcely breathed as he passed within ten feet of her, his back visible as he found the trail that circled through the woods down to the rear entrance of the barn.

He had disappeared and again only the deep silence of the woods. Slowly as though her feet had become leaden weights, Valeria moved forward into the clearing. In a moment she came upon Jessie in her blue dress lying in a spot she, Valeria, had always loved, an enclosure something like a room surrounded by brush and trees. The sound of her coming was heard. Jessie turned her head, sat up, then, as the full import of this intrusion was understood, she sprang to her feet, her eyes blazing.

Speechless with shock and fear, Valeria merely stared at her.

Jessie laughed aloud. "So you're spying."

The pallor of Valeria's face gave way to a crimson flood of shame and anger, her lips pressed hard together but she did not speak.

Now there was a different quality in Jessie's laugh. "Your neurotic brother. You think you have him, like Jake, eating out of your hand, don't you?"

"Don't you even speak of my brother."

"Oh, you poor fool. Why don't you get wise to yourself? You know, Val, often this winter I've really wanted to help you, sort of open your eyes to see what life is all about. I feel so sorry for you, in love with that Jim. Why didn't you go out and get him? Not let him slip through your fingers. That Bobbie knows a thing or two. You think you have Jake tied up like a puppy. You don't want him but you smile at him enough with those eyes of yours to keep him from seeing anyone else. But you don't know anything about men. You don't know what they want. There's only one thing in life besides money they want. Get wise to yourself."

Valeria stood with her back pressed hard against the trunk of a tree. Her eyes never left Jessie's face.

After a moment Jessie's eyes wavered. She shrugged. "All right, let's go home."

"*You* go home. This is *my* woods, not yours."

"Cut it out. Don't act like a tragedy queen just because you found me giving your unhappy brother a pleasant afternoon. You should be grateful to me. He gets so little fun or even pleasure out of life." Her eyes narrowed. "At that you'd better not make me hate you any more than I do now or I'll pay you off in more ways than I have already. You and your aristocracy and your brains and your morals and your culture, plus your putrid poverty. You make me sick. I hate you and your kind. I would have helped you. I withdraw the offer. You're not worth the trouble."

Long after Jessie was lost to view, Valeria stood as still as though she were part of the tree. Only, once or twice, her hand tightened on the crumpled letter.

CHAPTER XV

FOR THE NEXT THREE DAYS, Jessie went about as usual. She fed the baby, put it to bed and disappeared down the road to the village in the evening.

Valeria had been carrying the crumpled letter in her pocket but tonight she felt so self-controlled and calm that she determined to bring it out and read it. Yes, that would be good discipline—read it aloud.

Miriam listened with Mother and after Valeria heard their exclamations she went into the parlor and practiced some difficult passages in a Beethoven sonata.

She went to her room early, loving the privacy behind the closed door. Sometime, out of a deep sleep she felt herself wide awake. Jessie returning? She thought she heard the clicking of a door latch. She listened for steps on the stairs but there seemed to be only the deep silence of the night. She lay wondering about the time and whether Jessie were in or out when the clock in the lower hall struck two. Now she heard her mother cough. Apparently she too had been awakened.

Valeria was getting drowsy when the baby began to cry, first a small whining sound but soon rising to a crescendo that could awaken Miriam. Again she listened, expecting to hear Jessie soothing the child. The baby's cries were fast becoming ear-piercing when Valeria slipped out of bed, crossed the hall and spoke at Jessie's door.

"Are you awake, Jessie?"

There was no sound but the crying child. Valeria pushed open the door and switched on the light. The bed was empty.

She picked up the baby and took her into her own room where she finally managed to get her back to sleep.

At breakfast Valeria could see that her mother was worried. Had Jessie met with trouble? "With the new road so many people pass this way. I don't think a young woman should come up alone in the middle of the night."

It was when Valeria was making the beds that she stepped again into Jessie's room. Aware that something was different she stood in the middle of the floor looking about. That was it. The bureau. Her brush and comb and toilet articles were not in their place. Then she saw in the corner Jessie's small black satchel. Something impelled her to open it. It was empty. She went quickly to the closet. Her clothes were gone. Not until later did they find that Jessie had helped herself to Phil's suitcase. Now, Valeria was bewildered. She left her work and ran downstairs to tell her mother who exclaimed, "This is incredible. The baby—why, the baby!" Mother and daughter looked into each other's eyes.

Throughout the morning Louise Macrae hoped for a telephone message. Later she thought that when Jessie reached her destination, wherever that might be, she would telephone or write. Perhaps they should be patient and wait for an explanation. "I am hoping it is merely one of those—what she would term a spree. Perhaps some friend has invited her."

At that idea Valeria was forced to laugh. "Mother, you seem to be conjuring up quite a circle of friends for Jessie. Who are these friends? What social circle has she been moving in? I hadn't heard. Don't forget she has taken all her clothes."

"Phil will be here by three o'clock. He will be shocked. I can't think what to do. Suppose she has met with foul play? We should notify the police."

"Oh, no, Mother. Don't start anything." There was the sound of a motor in the drive and Valeria looked out. "It's the man with the extracts. We're nearly out of vanilla."

The man stepped into the kitchen, opened his case and,

chatting pleasantly, Mother chose her bottle of flavoring. "Will you get change from my room, Val?"

Valeria opened the drawer in her mother's little table. There was change in a small purse but not quite enough to pay for the extract. Mother kept her bills in a leather folder beneath the purse but the folder was not in its usual place. Valeria searched through the drawer then went into the kitchen. "Mother, do you mind looking? There wasn't enough change and I couldn't see a bill." The minutes dragged as Mother searched.

The man said, "It's all right, Miss Macrae. I'll pick it up some day when I'm passing. Don't have your mother bother now."

"Thank you. I'll remember the amount."

She saw Phil's car on the road, waiting for the peddler to back out. She went into her mother's room. "You must have put your bill case somewhere else, Mother."

Her mother was standing in the middle of the floor looking utterly distracted. "No, Val, I haven't put it anywhere but in that drawer. My bill case has been removed by someone else."

"Oh, Mother. How much was in it?"

"Seventy-two dollars, the largest amount I have had there in some time. It was my quarterly insurance payment and all Phil gave me for the boys' and Miri's dentist bills. Jessie knew I had that money."

Phil stood in the doorway looking from face to face. "What's up?"

Valeria answered, "Jessie's gone and taken all her clothes and we're afraid all Mother's money also."

"Why, I saw the baby."

"She left the baby."

He turned quickly and walked into the kitchen where he dropped down in a chair by the table. Mother was saying, "It seems incredible after all this winter and summer. I can't believe it. Surely she will send back my money. I don't mind about the clothes which were my gift. She seemed happy with me, almost affectionate."

Phil jumped up and there was that wretched color and anger burning in his eyes. As he crossed the room toward the sink he muttered something Val couldn't hear. He drank a glass of water, then he turned to look at the baby in Valeria's arms. "There's an orphans' home outside the city. We'll soon get her child out of here. I only wish we could rid the place of even our memories of her." He was wrought up and he spoke rapidly, "One of the reasons I wanted the boys away this summer was because of her."

Mother's hands hung limp at the sides of her armchair. "Oh Phil, let's not condemn her. She may explain herself and send back my money. Let's be lenient in our judgement and wait and see."

On Sunday morning Valeria was alone in the kitchen. She filled the small tin tub with warm water and gave the baby its bath then laid her on a towel, drying and powdering her tender skin. Nine months old. "You little naked baby girl. You're growing so big you'll soon be running in the garden before I know it." She held one tiny foot in her hand, then kissed it. "Your feet and hands are like little flowers. Your mouth is a rose bud and your eyes are a piece of the sky. Are you laughing at my silly baby talk?" She clasped her hands about the baby's head and looked into her eyes. "Oh, Mary Louise, why did you allow yourself to get born? Why didn't you roll on down the ravine? This world is no place for you because you have no mother, no father, no home, not even a name. They'll put you in an orphan asylum and you'll grow up wearing uniforms and you'll long to know your mother and some day you will and I pity you, I pity you. . ."

She wrapped the towel about the baby and snuggled her against her shoulder as the arms clung to her neck. Again and again she kissed the soft cheek. She whispered, "Would you like to be my baby?"

Phil had been standing in the doorway watching her. He spoke sharply, "Don't get fond of her, Val."

Her face flushed. "I've been fond of her for nine months. No one could bathe and dress and feed a beautiful baby for nine months and not get fond of her."

"No one?" He laughed. "Sometimes I think you're about the wisest old party I know; then again I think you're an imbecile, an innocent. The trouble is, Val, you've never got out into the world, never come in contact with the masses of human vermin that inhabit it."

"They're not all evil. Even Jessie is not all evil."

"Let's not try to figure percentages. A lot of people spend their lives in that useless occupation. The point is Jessie came, Jessie went and now her baby must go."

Val raised her lovely eyes, her lips unsteady as she smiled, "I'd hate to figure out my own percentage. I'm mostly hate, jealousy, envy, depression, loneliness, restlessness and filled up to the brim with all the sins of omission the Bible talks about. Even my mind is going to seed." She tried to laugh. "I've even dreamed of doing what Jessie did—run away from everything and everybody, only I wouldn't take all *my* clothes. Sometimes I hate the mended, patched, darned rags." Before he could interrupt she went on, "And don't think I'm such an innocent. I know more than you think I do. I know more than I want to know."

With penetrating eyes he watched her during this unheard of outburst and, without speaking, he walked out to the lawn where Mother was resting in her chair under the apple tree. "What's happened this week? Anything unusual?"

"Except this about Jessie there was only the surprising letter from Bobbie."

"What was that?"

She told him about the engagement. His response was a low whistle.

Later, he came into the kitchen. Sitting at the table, his

nervous hands twisted and turned the dishes Valeria was setting on the table as she prepared dinner. He looked up at her. "And when you're up to the brim, you go and write a funny story for the boys. What you don't know is that you're a wonderful person, Val, really wonderful and you're not going to vegetate in this place, a cook, nursemaid, washwoman and general slavey. Soon you'll be a genteel old maid at everyone's beck and call. Now listen, I've had this on my mind for a long time—night and day I've been thinking and planning. We've got the boys on the road and we're certain after this tough year they can make the grade. I'm going to see them through. Miri has four years ahead in high school before we have to worry about her future. Are you listening?"

She was basting a chicken in the oven. "Of course I'm listening. Don't you know I care as much as you do?"

"All right. We've got Jessie out of the way. She's welcome to the money and I'd say it's cheap to get rid of her. I don't think we'll ever see or hear from her again. We'll get the baby off our hands as quickly as I can make arrangements at the home. Now I want to know this. Which would you rather do, go to college and then teach or come to the business school in the city and prepare to be a secretary? They make fine salaries, come in contact with interesting people and are independent. After you get settled in a job you could write nights and I tell you you have talent. That would require one year, college four. Now wait, don't answer yet. Mother? Miri? We will get a good woman from the village to come here and take care of them. Jake would find her. He knows everyone. We would come home weekends."

She came over to him, laid her hand on his shoulder. "I never should complain about anything in the world as long as I have you." She seemed immensely amused. "I wonder which of us is really the imbecile. The innocent? You talk like a millionnaire, a rich Uncle William. Have you been writing to him? Have you drawn his attention to the fact that there are other children in his brother John's family besides Bobbie? Has Aunt Sophie fallen in love with *you?*"

He sat punishing the napkin at his place, folding and refolding it. "It happens to be you who likes Uncle William, not I. I have a good position, Val, and I'm making money. I could be dead sure of swinging the one year in the business school and the woman helper here. If your heart is set on college it's all right with me."

"Dinner is ready, Phil. Can we talk later? I'm dizzy. There is so much to think out."

"Come out in the barn tonight. I want to see Jake. What's become of him? Hasn't been down all day. I'll go up on the hill later but when you see the light, come out."

She was setting the highchair for the baby next to her place at the table. Throughout the meal she knew that Phil was watching her as she fed the child. Once he asked, "She eats everything?"

"Not everything, but soft food, vegetables, scraped meat, cereal and lots of milk."

"Nine months? I think she's still under the age limit for the infant's home."

Miriam stopped eating, her eyes filling up with tears as she looked at him reproachfully, "You can't take her away. She's *our* baby."

He looked annoyed. "She's definitely not our baby. She's Jessie Macrae's baby and we're not going to forget that."

Their mother did not speak. She appeared tired and sad and ate little.

That afternoon in her room, Valeria walked up and down with the baby until the eyelids drooped when she gently laid her on her own bed for the afternoon nap.

Now she sat on the edge of the bed looking down at the little creature. Yes, she must think it out. She might be wrong about the value or importance of one human soul but to her no flower in her garden, no jewel, no painting conceived or executed by the greatest artist, no music, nothing in all the world could be more beautiful, more exquisite, more perfect than a little baby girl. She touched the silk-like down on the child's head, looked at her perfect features, the lovely symmetry of the body, the flower-like hands and feet, thinking of the intricate machinery functioning in them all.

Softly she whispered, "Where did you come from? Who planned your creation? Is Emerson right? Are you a little human soul part of that All Being, that Spirit we call God? How can one keep that God part alive? How can anyone take a little child and train her so that the percentage will be at least mostly good? Mother would say God put evil in the world to test our strength, to develop our strength. Why are some babies given devoted mothers and fathers who pray and teach and train them to know good and help them to be strong? Why are some babies brought into the world as Jessie was without a good mother, with a father who was the black sheep of his family? I had everything. Is Jessie to blame because she had nothing?"

She bent over and pressed her lips against the tiny foot. It was strange, very strange that she had helped bring this baby into the world. She thought of that awful night and the baby's first cry and their relief when they knew she was going to live. Live for what? To grow up in orphan asylums, then be claimed by Jessie? Who planned that for her? God? Was is merely accident? Then was everything accident? With the mother living, no one could legally adopt her without that mother's consent. Why was all this planned for this lovely little creature?

She walked to the window looking out across the fields. "Why do I feel from my very soul that she belongs to me? Why do I feel that I am responsible for her life? Why, dear God, must it be Phil and his dreams *or* the baby?"

That night when the long day ended, when darkness and cool breezes brought relief from the heat of the day, she saw the light in the barn and went out. Presently she must climb the little ladder. Could she make a choice between Phil's dreams or the baby?

CHAPTER XVI

INSTEAD OF GOING DIRECTLY to the barn, she sought a moment of respite, conscious of the coolness of the earth beneath her feet, of the freshness of the night breeze and of that wonder—an August night sky. Almost of their own volition her feet turned toward the road. She ducked under the chain and stood looking into the dark depths of the ravine where the trickling stream could be heard like a soft murmur.

Returning to the road, she was aware of a man's figure approaching and knew instantly from the easy stride that it was Robert Loring. Once she would have fled in embarrassment but now they were friends and instinctively she knew he would not think her "queer" when he found her standing alone, gazing up at the night sky.

After a surprised but pleased greeting, he explained that he was going over the hill to spend an evening with friends. She spoke of the beauty of the sky. "The trouble is I really know so little about Astronomy."

"Valeria, you have a reaching mind."

She spoke impulsively. "One of the clearest memories of my father is of one night when he lifted me to his shoulder so I could get nearer to the stars. I remember wanting to pick one as I would a daisy in the field." She went on pouring out the thoughts. "Since then I have read books and studied charts and know just a little about those great masses of matter that make up the universe." She remembered what they were called. "Incandescent bodies made visible by their own light and dark bodies revolving around them." She laughed a little, then went on, "Stars and nebulae, and I think I remember the difference; our own sun which was a star and then the little earth, considered as part of the universe utterly insignificant." She laughed again. "That makes *me* feel insignificant."

He was smiling as he watched her. He agreed with her that one human being appeared small enough among the uncountable existences of people who had lived on this planet. Yet was it not astonishing that there could be a human brain capable of looking into those skies and delving into its secrets, formulating the rules by which the stars and nebulae were governed? "Isn't it the amazing thing that man knows he doesn't know?"

There was eagerness in his voice as he offered to lend her some recently published books which he was sure she would find interesting. She thanked him, suddenly shy. He lingered a few moments then went on up the road walking with his quick, easy stride and she stood watching him until he vanished into the darkness.

She walked slowly across the lawn circling the house, thinking of his words, "Man knows he doesn't know." He always went to the heart of the matter. He stimulated her, made her think. It was wonderful to feel that she had such a friend. No matter how drab and sordid life seemed at times, whenever she was with him she regained a feeling of dignity—and hope.

Hope for what? As she slowly went toward the barn, she thought, what is it all about? How does my obscure life fit into the great whole? Am I only like one of the millions and trillions of ants that one steps on? The ant was born and lived and died. Can our finite minds grasp the meaning of words like infinite and eternal? What brought these galaxies of stars into being?

Science had had no answers to her questions but Mother and Emerson had answers. Emerson was sure that in every man was part of that All Being, that God who created the universe. Mother never doubted. Could she, Valeria, ever find that "inner strength" that Mother had? She thought of the teachings of Jesus, that Soul and Spirit that had moved the world. Thomas

Jefferson had made a little Bible for his own use out of the words of that Son of God.

Suddenly, as she stood looking up into the starry sky, she felt a hungry longing to talk about all this with Robert. She wished she had the courage to call him Robert as Mother did. She wouldn't mind his knowing all the mean little problems of her life. Wasn't that the test of friendship? To know the worst about you yet be always *for* you?

As she stood on the path she felt sure he would always be *for* her. The thought astonished her yet it brought some deep happiness to her troubled heart—something she had never felt before. She envied the friends with whom he was going to spend an evening.

She looked toward the light in the barn. She did not want to go in. It was wonderful to walk up and down the path, free, released from all the problems and decisions, from Jessie, from the whole question of right and wrong. Tonight, the sky was to her like music. Music carried one away from daily living into some realm of beauty. What was music? Not the mathematical system of sound and the mechanics of an order or a material instrument. It was part of what she was gazing at—the stars, the infinite universe. When Phil played she could forget everything of earth and sometimes it was hard to come back to thinking when his hands were lifted from the keys.

Not in haste but slowly she walked toward the barn. She was standing at the foot of the ladder when she heard Phil talking. To whom? Should she go up or make it an excuse for going back to the house?

He stopped speaking. He had heard her. "Val? Is that you, Val? Come right up."

She ascended the ladder and there, sitting at Phil's table with his back toward her, was Jake.

"Come in. Jake and I are talking things over. We have no secrets from Jake."

She took the empty chair by the table feeling Jake's eyes on her but not once did she glance at him. Instead she began to look over the circulars and booklets neatly arranged before Phil.

"You see, Val, I've been working on this for some time, inquiring from those who ought to know—and sometimes don't—how you can make up deficiencies or brush up. I talked to Loring who has always had a personal interest in you. He said he would be anxious to help you.

"Jake doesn't like the Business Institute, neither does Loring. I knew Jake would know the right woman to live with Mother and Miri. There's a Mrs. Corning, a widow who goes about the village nursing and caring for children. Jake will talk to her as soon as we get the other things decided. How does that sound?"

Her eyes were on the pamphlet she held in her hand. Her lips softened in a smile. "Why do you bother to ask me? I seem to be the pawn you are moving about."

Phil laughed. "Does sound rather high-handed. You don't mind having a brother and a friend who are anxious about you and your future and are going to do something about it?"

She smiled. "I am lost in admiration."

"Don't steal my sarcasm. It isn't becoming to you."

Her face flushed a little but she didn't look up. "I can't believe you're really talking about me. I've probably forgotten how to study. I'm sure I'd look like an old woman and feel like one. I'm sure you don't realize what it would cost besides the tuition. Even if I waited on tables or worked in dormitories to earn my way, there's the question of clothes.

"I guess pride is one of my sins. Girls are changed, even the girls who go to high school now. They cut their hair short, make up their faces and know how to look smart. I'm an old fogy. Then suppose I failed? No, we can't think of college for me. I think the Business Institute is more suitable. I'd get to earning money much sooner. I'd be near home and until the roads are impassable I could get here in time to prepare supper and help Mother nights."

Phil smiled. "Quite a speech."

"I think it makes sense. I might get a position in the factory office."

"I'm dead sure you could; however, it seems a trifle grubby—down to earth. I like to soar. I'd like to see you get out in a different world, meet people with brains and get a degree that serves as a key to open the type of door you ought to enter. Speech number two."

He was merry and now turned to Jake. "Your turn, Jake."

"Guess I agree with Phil."

Phil laughed. "Not much of a speech. We've proved already that it's Val who is college timber. She can make the longest speech."

Val had not looked at Jake but she laughed too, and felt relieved and happy in the pleasant atmosphere which Phil had somehow created. His eyes were bright and he reached eagerly for the booklets. "You can't read these now, but study them tomorrow." His good humor and enthusiasm were contagious. "Look what college has done for the boys in only one year. Already they are in summer jobs where they're getting in touch with the world I want to see them enter. They'll make good. At first I was a little nervous about Andy. He has to plug more than Mark but he's keeping up. Mark is perhaps more brilliant but Andy has staying qualities. Now we'll get Val launched."

Valeria laughed. "Phil is like a general who loves to plan campaigns. He has always been the one to soar." Then she added thoughtfully, "I think you must be like Father. He was so ambitious and he made the grade." Then her face grew serious as she asked, "What are you planning about the baby?"

"Jake and I agree that she goes to a home."

"Then you can forget the whole idea. I have made up my mind. I am going to keep Mary Louise. I am going to bring her up. I am going to give her a chance. I brought her into the world and I feel that she belongs to me."

There was a silence and while she waited the thought almost overwhelmed her. How silly that must sound. After all, it was

Jake and Mother who had had most to do with bringing her into the world. They had accomplished that task together.

Phil was tipping back in his chair, running his hands through his hair and whistling a melodic phrase.

She made it worse. "I feel that I am her mother."

Phil laughed. He stopped and then began laughing again. She felt her face burning, knowing they were both watching her and probably thinking what an idiot she was.

She raised her eyes and looked steadily into Phil's face. "I do appreciate everything, Phil. I want you to know this. I used to dream night and day of going to college and studying and knowing wonderful teachers and I would picture to myself all the girls I would be friends with and how I would graduate and get a position in a fine school or college. But that was nothing to the way I dreamed of *your* life, Phil. It didn't happen to us but it is coming true with Mark and Andy and now I see my place until they get through. You've got all this wrong about the baby. You are laughing because you think I'm a little girl with a doll, ready to cry because you want to take my doll away. I can't explain it to you, but nobody—no one on earth but Jessie can take Mary Louise away from me. She could but I think she is glad to get rid of her. You can't change me. I know what I'm going to do."

She took a long breath and hurried on before he could interrupt. "*If* I could get my rusty brains working, *if* Mrs. Corning were the right person to look after Mother, Miri and the baby, *if* Mother keeps well enough for me to leave her, I'd work so hard—harder than I've ever worked in my life."

No one spoke. There was a pleading note in her voice, "Promise me, Phil, promise me that no matter what happens you won't take the baby away from me."

Phil wasn't laughing now. "Why do you want to tie a millstone around your neck? You haven't thought it through, Val. It's fun to play with a pretty baby or wash and dress her just as you used to wash and dress Miri. I remember that. Father didn't like your little mother business any too well. I was old enough to know. Because Mother was ill so much of the time she threw the entire burden of the family on you. It's nothing but a bad habit now. I'm trying to break it. The point is, Miri was your sister, one of us. This baby is not one of us and never will be. You get that? Never will be. Keeping her might even bring Jessie back if it suited her purpose."

"I know that."

It was Phil's voice that held the pleading note now. "Val, I can't sit by and see you messing up your life like this. Jake knows as well as I do that you allowed Jim Ferris to mess it up enough. I could strangle him. You're holding on to some romantic ideas or ideals of him that keep you from marrying anyone else. Now you want to take on this brat that'll tie you hand and foot and God only knows what trouble waits in the future. Snap out of it, Val. This is your chance."

Her eyes were downcast, staring at the boards in the plank table without seeing them. She was frightened. Never before in all her life had fear gripped her so unmercifully. She felt sick and there was a pain tightening in her chest. Jessie had "paid her off" by sending Bobbie to the party; now could she pay her off with Phil? Phil or the baby?

Clearly she saw his vision and his plans all made at a great sacrifice to himself. He was the one who would grub and grind and worry and sweat to see them all educated and steered into paths where they could earn good livings, where their various abilities could be used to advantage. How dared she thwart his plans! For what? For Jessie Macrae's baby? He hardly seemed to think of it as a human being. To Phil the baby was a tramp like her mother.

Phil still sat tilted back in his chair, his fingers reaching nervously for a cigarette. He lighted it, breaking the match then throwing it down. A glance told her there was an angry light in his eyes. He repeated, "Snap out of it, Val."

"I can't. If I saw the baby sent away, I'd feel guilty all the rest of my life."

"And I'd feel guilty all the rest of my life if I allowed you, an unmarried woman without a cent in the world or any way of earning a cent except by hard labor, to take on the support and care of Jessie Macrae's child. What's happened to your mind, Val?"

Her eyes flashed angrily back into his. "I only wish she were mine instead of Jessie's."

A sudden laugh and Phil brought his chair down with a bang. He turned to Jake. "You old farmer. What are you sitting there for without a word? You're not earning your passage. What do you think we ought to do about this?"

Jake squirmed in his seat. "Have you talked this over with your mother?"

Valeria echoed, "Have you talked with Mother?"

"I have not. Of course when it comes to the question of engaging Mrs. Corning, Mother must be consulted, but this is a matter between Val and me. Val is asking me to support that baby and I think I'd be a fool to do such a thing. We were six, then we were five; now Val wants to make it six again with perhaps eighteen years ahead to feed and clothe and to pay doctors' bills and educate her. Here's Miri grown up and a help to Mother and a mighty nice companion. Now Val wants me to start over and bring up this infant."

Valeria's voice broke as she cried, "Oh, Phil, I don't want you to support her. If you will let her stay until I can earn money, I'll never ask for anything and I'll pay you back every cent she costs. Only let me have her, Phil."

"My God!" He rose and began pacing up and down the floor.

She went on, "I've never asked for anything before—not even for party shoes."

"That's part of the bad habit I'm talking about. You'd better learn to ask for pretty shoes, not for babies that grow up to be women. As life goes on you and Jessie are going to be partners in that treasure. Can't you see that?"

"I'm sorry but I can't change myself."

Jake cleared his throat then spoke slowly. "I see how Val feels. The only thing I can offer is to bring down all the food she can use. I guess it's you that has to give in, Phil."

Phil painstakingly destroyed his cigarette. "Let's get to bed. It must be near midnight. Get down the ladder before I put the light out. Don't wait for me. Take this stuff with you, Val. Tomorrow Robert Loring will telephone you and you can arrange an appointment."

Valeria gathered up the papers and went down first. Out in the coolness and beauty of the night they waited but Phil did not join them. She spoke weakly, "Good night, Jake."

"Good night, Val." He strode off down the drive toward the road and she went in the kitchen door.

Mother's room was dark. She took off her shoes and quietly ascended the stairs, thinking, "Tomorrow I'll get Miri to help me and we'll get the crib out from behind the crates. She must have her own bed."

The baby was asleep in Valeria's wide bed. She undressed and crept in beside her. Tenderly she kissed the soft cheek. "I couldn't do it to you, Mary Louise. I couldn't."

She could not sleep. Why didn't Phil come? At last she heard him. As he passed her door she spoke softly, "Oh, Phil, forgive me."

"Get to sleep, Val."

CHAPTER XVII

THE DEW WAS HEAVY on the grass, the sun laying patterns of gold on kitchen table and floor when Valeria set the baby, clothed only in diapers and diminutive shirt, in her highchair. The fragrant odor of coffee filled the kitchen as she shook dry cereal into little bowls.

She was startled to see Phil, fully half an hour early. Usually he hurried down, ate his breakfast and in minutes was gone to the barn for his car. Though she thought he looked almost ill, she was astonished and pleased when he went directly to the highchair, placed his finger under the baby's chin and, raising the pretty face, smiled. Could it be possible that there was neither sarcasm nor irony in the voice as he spoke?

"The top of the morning to you, Mary Louise. So you are my latest gift from that heaven which has bestowed so many unearned gifts." He turned to Miriam who entered, as always a trifle tardy, offering to help with the breakfast. "Go put your socks and shoes on, Miri. Don't you know you are our young lady now? About yesterday you were our baby but this morning you're almost as tall as Val, much taller than Bobbie whose development was stunted by high life in Cleveland. No more tree-climbing or broken legs. You are to spend more time at home and less up at the Waters' place playing tennis with Ned, going fishing with Ned or running through the woods like a pack of wild turkeys. Next month you will enter high school. You are going to have smart plaid skirts to suit your bobbed hair and what's more you're going to be held to strict account for your grades."

Miriam stood still, sleepily staring at him as he went on, "You are a little slow and lazy. Go put on your socks, honey. This baby has taken your place."

As he ate his cereal his eyes rested on the child in the highchair. Valeria, pouring the coffee, wondered if he ever slept. Did the lids ever close over those brilliant eyes? Did the nervous fingers ever find complete relaxation and rest?

He watched the baby being fed. "Can you make any guesses concerning the potentialities in *our* child, Val? Music is out. That gift came through the Ainsworth side. Our baby manages to get Mother's name, Louise, but not a drop of Ainsworth blood flows through her veins.

"Line up the four Macraes we know anything about—Father, Uncle William, Uncle Sam and Jessie! What in heaven's name have you? Then there is that unknown quality—from the baby's father."

"My guess is that if she is loved and cared for there will be nothing to worry about."

"The old controversy—heredity versus environment." He rose.

Valeria followed him to the shed and they stood at the open door looking out into the fresh beauty of the August morning. He lingered, his eyes following the contour of distant field and hill. There was a gentleness in his manner. "Jake, that old farmer on the hill, usually sees things pretty straight. That is why I like to talk to him. I like his animal reactions, even the mud on his boots—a substance that is unknown in my city environment. I like his mind. He knows how to blow off the froth and look down into the cup and see what's there.

"About the stuff I gave you, look it over, Val. It's *your* life. I ought not to have tried to meddle in it. Make any choice or *no* choice. It's your life. Live it the way you want to."

Valeria looked into his face and never had she seen a sadder expression there or a more downcast curve to the lips as he spoke.

"Val, have you ever thought much about hermits, men who

go off into the mountains or wilds somewhere and live out their existences completely removed from human contacts? No 'getting on' in the world, no ambition, no cut-throat competition, no strangers jostling you, no hypocritical smiles, no *money*! Oh, Lord, *to live where there is no money*! Never mind about streets paved with gold or angel wings or marrying or not marrying, just give me a place where there is no money and that would be heaven. Up in the Catskills or Adirondacks there are still little hamlets in out-of-the-way places where one could build a shed for shelter." He turned to her with his characteristic smile and a glint of humor in his eyes. "Perhaps when I get my family all launched into paths of success, I'll manage that—an old hunchback with matted white hair and beard, with a serene mind and peace in his heart."

She was speechless and he laughed. "Today, give me my piano and plenty of manuscript and I'd jump at a chance at that existence. You see, Val, Jake was right. I was the one who had to give in. Now you do what you want with your life. I'll stick with you."

He was gone and she returned to her work, performing tasks absently as she thought. What was so wrong with Phil? She was conscious of an insight into his mind and into thoughts that he usually kept hidden. He appeared to take such pride in the success of Mark and Andy. He had been determined to keep Andy working side by side with Mark when he wanted to drop out.

He seemed so cheerful when he went over accounts with Mother and paid the doctor, the dentist and grocer or the bills for cotton or woolen goods to be made into dresses. He always expressed his admiration for Mother's knitting, the sweaters and caps and socks and shawls. With his charm and cheerfulness he could make a simple birthday dinner a celebration to be remembered always.

Did any of them realize how completely they depended on

him? "We will tell Phil, we will ask Phil, Phil will attend to it, Phil will decide."

Did he loathe the life he was forced to live, not the bank but the confinement in the bank? Did the soul of the musician, the artist, cry out for the chance to create? Even long for the loneliness that is part and parcel of the creative instinct?

Never before in all their lives had she heard him use that hated word "hunchback." No one in the family would think of using it. She remembered long ago when she had snapped at Uncle William for saying it.

Even as she ate with Miriam, helped her mother dress, followed the pattern of daily work automatically, she tried to think it out. Hadn't she and Phil always been partners in finding means and ways of bringing up the family? Why was he treating her as only another sister to be launched into independence? Weren't they partners any more? He out earning the money and she holding the family together? She was more than puzzled, she was deeply hurt.

Perhaps some day, some time, Phil could find independence from them all and she could work for and dream of that day. Then it came to her with something of a physical pain, stabbing at her heart—it was she who had hung the millstone, not on her neck but on his. He would earn the money for the baby and for all the years ahead. He had said "*our* baby."

She was preparing lunch when the telephone rang and she answered Robert Loring's pleasant voice, "Phil suggested I come up and talk over your work."

"I haven't made any decisions yet."

"Perhaps I can help you. Would you be free about four o'clock?"

She would be.

As she hung up the receiver she felt jittery and nervous, thinking, I don't want to go to any business institute and I don't want to go to any college. I have no ambition—none whatever. I want to stay home and take care of Mother and bring up my baby and write stories every week for Andy and Mark and send them cake and cookies and always be ready for their days at home. I want to climb hills and roam through the woods and make my garden. I hate to sew and I don't care if I never have a party dress or dancing slippers. I know now I never want to see Jim again or even Bobbie Macrae. I love to sit up there in the barn and waste my time writing stories. Andy and Mark get fun out of them. No, I haven't one bit of ambition.

She was smiling as she braided and pinned up her hair, put on a fresh gingham dress, socks and sneakers. What's more I don't want to live in a cave or be a hermit. I want to live right in this house, on this farm. So, I'm a rustic and I ought to have married Jake but I won't. I'll end up being an eccentric old maid, physically as strong as a horse and mentally as weak as a feather.

She was still smiling as she ran down the stairs and entered the parlor where Mother was sitting in her easy chair.

It was unusual to see those hands lying idle in her lap. Even tighter the skin seemed to be drawn over the fine bones of the face, more cavernous the large dark eyes. "I find it cooler in the house than out of doors. That pink gingham is very becoming to you, Val."

"Mother, I want to cut my hair short like yours. Would you do it? Not for style but for comfort and saving time. If I could get behind myself, I'd have done it this afternoon."

Mother smiled. "I'll cut it tomorrow morning."

Valeria sat down noting how ill her mother looked, seeing the idle hands and wondering. "Can I do anything for you before I go out?"

"Nothing, dear. I talked to Phil yesterday about a wheel chair. My knees and back! I'm afraid I soon will be unable to walk at all and I could get about in a chair." Without waiting for comment she went on, "I'm glad Robert Loring decided to stay on here. The community is very fortunate in having so brilliant a young man here even for a few years. One day when you were out, he called and we had such a fine talk. Somehow one has to know the beginnings and background of a person in order to appreciate him."

"What about him?" She tried to keep the eagerness out of her voice.

"He told me that his father was a minister and they lived where his father preached in a suburb of New York City. His father died leaving the mother almost penniless, with four boys. She moved into a shabby apartment in the city, a poor neighborhood but close to free schools and a city college. The church helped her while the boys carried papers, worked in grocery stores, did janitor work, everything and anything until each one graduated from college.

"Now Ben, the oldest son, is a prosperous lawyer, accepted in a distinguished firm; another is an interne in a city hospital, getting ready to launch out into a practice of his own; the youngest is following his father into the ministry and our friend, Robert, after getting his degree, snapped up the first position offered him which was in our own high school. He intends to be a writer. This last June he was offered a college position but he says he likes our country, has leisure for writing, so he has cut his vacation short, rented a small house in the village and is bringing his mother to live with him. I'm looking forward to meeting her."

Valeria was drinking in every word, her face sobering as she listened. "I hadn't thought of him like that. Why, they were just a little like us."

"Except that the mother was well and strong and had the nerve and courage to live where there was free—even college—education."

There were steps on the walk. "And here he is."

Valeria went to the door, her cheeks slightly flushed as she brought Robert Loring into the parlor.

With her charming manner, Louise Macrae welcomed him

briefly, asked about his mother and sped them on their way as he asked if they might walk.

"Can we try the ravine? We need rain. The stream is down to a mere brook."

The ravine? Jim's ravine? She hesitated a moment, then slid under the chain.

He followed her as she lightly and sure-footedly let herself down the steep bank. When he joined her, standing on dry stones, she laughed. "It's hard to believe that the water reaches up that bank nearly to the top in the spring."

They made their way over flat stones or along the edges where he stopped to examine moss, shrub, flower or overhanging bush until she showed him her fringed gentians and pink lady-slippers. Near the woods they found a mossy bank and sat down to rest.

As with bent head he examined some seeds through a small glass, she watched him. It was as though she had never seen him before or as though he suddenly had become a new person, for she had never even wondered about his family or background. She thought him not handsome like Phil but very distinguished looking. Was it that suggestion of prematurely gray hair at his temples? Did he deliberately choose gray suits that matched his gray eyes?

Or was it herself she was seeing for the first time? No longer was she a shy little schoolgirl, flattered if he walked for a moment beside her but virtually tongue-tied. She knew and felt herself to be a woman, chatting easily and conscious that she was attractive in his eyes; knowing he had formed the habit of stopping a few minutes at the house when on his long walks and also knowing that his eyes followed her even when he was talking to Phil or Mother.

When she started to say, "Doctor Loring," he interrupted, "What about Robert?"

She looked into his eyes and smiled, not knowing she was beautiful, with the little beads of perspiration on her pretty forehead, the flush of exercise bringing high color into her cheeks, the sweet curve of her lips and the glow in her eyes.

"Val, what about this question of college versus business institute? What do you want to do?"

"Nothing."

He waited. She remained silent.

He laughed, then quoted,

> "Cromwell, I charge thee, fling away ambition:
> By that sin fell the angels; how can man then,
> The image of his Maker, hope to win by it?"

She thought a moment then questioned, "Cardinal Woolsey to Cromwell?"

He nodded, "Good. Excellent memory."

"Perhaps a good teacher?" What fun it was to talk to him not as a mere pupil with a "reaching mind" but with the stimulating give and take she enjoyed with Phil. "I don't have to fling away ambition, I simply have none." She added more seriously, "I know what Phil wants. Ever since my father died he has felt the terrible responsibility of educating the whole family. He feels Barbara is safe, and Mark and Andy are on their way to be engineers. No sacrifice is too great to see them through Cornell. I was next on his list."

"I don't think I am divulging a secret when I tell you that Phil gave me a number of those letters you have been writing to the boys. It seems they have saved every one and I have written them asking for the lot. I am sorting them, editing a little in regard to personal family affairs and I would like, with your permission, to submit them to a publisher I know in New York, to get an opinion."

Her face reddened in embarrassment. "Oh, please don't. With all those silly pictures! No one would think them funny except ourselves. You know us and you would be prejudiced."

"Deeply prejudiced." There was something more than humor in his eyes, some undisguised tenderness and ardor in his voice as he went on, "You have a talent that is worth cultivating, Val."

She flung her hands out in a gesture of impatience. "Oh, no. Please don't overestimate me."

"I couldn't overestimate your description of Jessie and the night of the accident ending in the birth of a baby—the tough mother—where did you get that vocabulary? You have made a most remarkable tragic-comic sketch of it with those pen and ink—"

She supplied the word—"Scratches. I'm no artist." She dropped her eyes and the color deepened in her face. "I was ashamed of that after I sent it. At the time I hated her." She sat tearing at the grass, flinging it aside. "I have taken her baby. I'm going to be its mother. Then—I can't, I simply won't leave my mother. No one else realizes how helpless she is. I have taken care of her for years, done for her all the little intimate things that I can't describe. I know it would be wicked and cruel to leave her to strangers. Just because she is cheerful and charming, no one knows how she suffers and how ill she is. Then Miri. She has been *my* baby. She is sometimes thoughtless and lazy but she's a darling and she needs me. I can't and won't walk out on them and the new baby. I want to do what I am doing. I mean it. I have no ambition."

"What is to prevent your doing what you want to do?"

"Phil, I suppose."

"You are mistaken. Phil understands you better than you understand yourself. Perhaps I do too."

Her eyes opened wide and she gazed at him in astonishment. He stood up, looking at his watch. "I have a carpenter coming at five-thirty—about time to get back." He held out his hands took both of hers tight in his and lifted her lightly to her feet. She did not resist or pull away as he held her hands against his chest. There was both tenderness and a glint of humor in his eyes as he looked into hers. "Ambition is out the window. Let's leave it at that for this afternoon. All right?"

She was close to him, standing with eyes sometimes downcast, sometimes looking shyly into his. She was tremulous and strangely comforted and even more strangely happy.

He spoke gently. "You feel things deeply. You are a passionate soul, loyal to a fault. Let's develop that latent talent of yours and forget other decisions for the present."

They walked back down the road in the lengthening shadows beneath the maples as he talked of his house, his work and his mother's coming. At the gate he held out his hand.

She managed to smile. "I can't see why you bother with me. You are overestimating me."

"Let me be the judge of that."

CHAPTER XVIII

SHE WALKED SLOWLY down the path seeing the shadows as the late afternoon sun slanted across the tree-lawn, hearing the voices of Miri and her friends, the gurgling laughter of the baby back in the orchard but thinking of her two friends, Jake and Robert Loring.

Jake, her old friend. She knew what Phil meant by "animal reactions" and "mud on his boots." Yes, she knew all about that. There were advantages in being brought up on a farm and in a farm community. One imbibed all knowledge of animal life, both of man and beast, without recourse to the stilted, embarrassing devices of talks about "birds and bees." One knew the natural gravitation of farmhands toward haystacks, and the girl who went along traveled that course of her own accord with full knowledge of the hazards. A country girl knew what she was doing or not doing and Valeria knew what the daughters of most farmers were *not* doing.

One took all that knowledge in one's stride and looked at the picture of life with neither shock nor prudery. There were the sensational moments—the "shotgun marriages" that gave the gossips a holiday, some accepted illegitimate children—but mostly wholesome, happy marriages. One simply knew all about it— the various ways of life that seemed the natural ways of life.

Jessie? Why was that so different? The woman who smiled tolerantly when Mattie Jones' bouncing baby boy arrived a few months early, hated the inhabitant of a certain hovel up at Perkin's Hollow where men's cars were parked back of a paintless house. Here was no young love, no youthful spontaneous animal reactions, no careless fun, no happy laughter but something commercial and to their minds dirty, poisonous, and mothers watched and warned their young sons.

Valeria sat down on the lower step for it was good to be alone and have time to savor the experience of this afternoon.

Robert Loring. She would like to call him Robert but she would have to get used to that. As she thought about him there was a feeling of comfort, excitement and a surge of happiness in knowing she could talk to him as an equal and laugh with him.

How wonderful that he should think her worthy of his friendship. Was he merely overestimating her? At least it was a challenge. How good it would be for Mother if Mrs. Loring turned out to be a friend, an educated, cultured woman, not any better but different from the farm women who came in often.

About Jim, would anyone know what she meant if she told them that she was sorry *for* Jim? More sorry for Jim than she was for herself? It was puzzling but it was the truth.

She rose, opened the door and entered the hall. The house was quiet. No voice answered her call, "Mother?"

She looked into the parlor and saw the empty armchair. Again calling, "Mother" she entered the bedroom. There on the floor Louise lay with ashen face and closed eyes, one leg doubled under her. For only an instant Valeria stood immobilized with shock and fear. Then quickly she called Miri, ran to the closest for restoratives, forcing the lips apart, bathing the face with cold water.

"Miri, call Dr. Northrop and ask him to come right away. It's supper time so he'll probably be home; then try to get Jake. Send Ned and tell him to run."

Working quietly and coolly she saw the eyes open. "You must have fainted, Mother. Everything is all right. Lie still. A pillow?"

She placed the pillow under the head. "Your leg? Don't try to move it, dear. I've sent for Dr. Northrop."

Weakly, Mother explained, "I felt faint and tried to get to my bed."

"Don't talk, dear."

Jake, who also was at the supper table, arrived first but soon they heard the car in the drive and the doctor entered. He examined and straightened the leg then he and Jake lifted her to the bed.

"Get her clothes off, Val." Then, cheerfully to Mother, "It's nothing but a faint—heat probably, but you'll have to stop prancing around with that cane. No, nothing's broken."

"Phil is getting the wheelchair, Doctor."

"Good. I want you to lie in bed a few days before you try anything."

The dark eyes looked up at him anxiously. "Doctor, my hands. I couldn't sew. I couldn't manage the needle. I couldn't knit. It seemed to come all at once—this morning—like a paralysis."

The doctor looked first at her, then at the anxious faces above him as he drew a chair to the side of the bed. "Mrs. Macrae, here are two strong young girls with twenty fingers to do the sewing and knitting. I sometimes wonder if anyone on earth but a family doctor knows what a mother is. The clothes, the sweaters and mittens and socks those fingers of yours have produced, the nursing, the cooking, the cleaning and once the music they have accomplished. Let's give those hands a little rest now."

It was unprecedented; they saw Mother's eyes fill with tears. "But I loved doing it. I had six little children and now a baby is with us."

"Yes, I heard about your keeping that baby. I'll know where to come in case I find myself homeless."

Miriam ran out to the crying child and now Jake withdrew as the doctor continued his examination.

At the door he turned to Valeria. "Complete rest. I'll get a prescription filled. Jake can bring it up. There is nerve exhaustion. We'll hope for improvement."

"She won't use her hands again?" Valeria spoke as she felt as though she were choking.

"I'm afraid not, Val. I can deprive people of liquor or tobacco or various activities but to deprive a mother of work is tough. I have to thank God you're here." Then he added thoughtfully, "It was a mistake to keep that baby. I could place her in a good home."

Valeria's eyes did not waver. "She's *in* a good home. She's my responsibility. I'll take care of her."

The doctor smiled. "Well—well," and went off to his car.

Back in the bedroom she bathed her mother's face, brushed back her hair and accomplished all she could to make her comfortable even as she noted how long Jake and the doctor stood talking in the drive.

In the kitchen she watched Miriam quiet the baby, settle her in her highchair and give her a toy to play with. She came to the young girl's side. "Honey, do you realize that when I was your age, you were my baby? That was the winter when Mother was in bed with some acute rheumatic trouble."

Miriam followed her about the kitchen, trying to be of real help. "You got into High a year before my age, Val."

"What about it? Mother pushed us. Now I'm here to help you. One thing you already do better than I. You sew better and like it. I'll have to buckle down to that."

"Mother says I can knit my own sweaters."

Valeria laughed. "And mine and Andy's and Mark's?"

"I know I could."

"Go ahead. I'll buy the yarn."

Jake came in, his face first grave then smiling as he watched the two girls. "I'll go down and get the prescription. One thing, Val, you must not lift your mother." He lowered his voice. "She must not lie in bed because there's danger of pneumonia. She must be lifted into the chair and I'm going to do it. She doesn't mind me."

"Mind you?" Valeria laughed, "You think your last name's

Young but I think it's Macrae. When I'm in trouble you're the first person I call for."

His eyes followed her as she prepared the supper. "What about your plans, Val?"

"My plans?"

"I saw you walking with Loring. Did you decide between college and business? Shall I speak to Mrs. Corning?"

"Oh."

He might well wonder at the expression of quiet happiness in her face, the serenity, the brightness of her eyes.

A mischievous smile curved her lips. "He quoted Shakespeare and examined bugs and seeds and advised me to fling away ambition." She laughed outright at the expression in Jake's face. "That's the truth." Then she added, "You see what happens when I turn my back on my family for a few hours."

He watched her narrowly as she finished, "I'm staying right here, Jake."

"You *are* the family." As Miriam passed him he ruffled her hair. "That's the truth, too, isn't it Miri? I'm glad I'm part of the family." He turned abruptly and walked out.

They celebrated the baby's first birthday with a tiny pink candle on a frosted cupcake. On Thanksgiving day, no one could have guessed at any hidden heartache, any anxiety, any worry as Valeria set the huge turkey on the side table for Phil's sharp knife to carve.

Perhaps it was only Valeria who was acutely conscious that no city florist's display of chrysanthemums flanked the fruit dish in the center of the table. If they remembered that a year ago Jessie in her black dress and bleached hair sat there and Bobbie in her pretty sweater chattered incessantly, they did not speak of any loss.

Mark and Andy vied with each other in finding opportunities to assist Mother or do chores. When Mark came in from the woodshed, he laughed, "Gosh, it's good to swing that axe again."

Andy, his eyes expressing the affection he felt, watched Mother manipulate the wheelchair with her nearly useless hands. "I seem to be indestructible, Andy. It's my heart. The doctor says that good, strong heart has seen me through."

That evening, with Mother in the wheelchair where the low armchair had once stood, they acted like children as they gathered about the fireplace, cracking nuts and popping corn. However, there was one question they might discuss while they were alone together with no visitors. To Val, Louise said, "You might get Aunt Sophie's letter and let me read it."

She managed to adjust her spectacles and read a long letter, beginning, "Dear Louise."

It was all about the coming wedding. Bobbie was going to be heartbroken if none of her family could come. She would like to have Mark and Andy as two of the six ushers.

There was an interruption as both snorted and rolled over on the carpet with bursts of laughter. "Tell her nix, Mother, nothing doing." She read on. About Val. Bobbie had wanted Val to be her maid of honor but realizing that Mother was now helpless—here Mother stopped to shake her head indignantly, saying, "I am not helpless"—her next choice would be Miri.

Aunt Sophie scarcely remembered Miri but she understood she resembled Bobbie in looks. If Miri would come, she, Aunt Sophie, would like her measurements and would have her dress, shoes, wraps and underthings all made to order; also she would gladly pay for any other needed clothes.

Mother laid the letter down in her lap and all eyes turned to Miriam. Mark asked, "What about it, Miri?"

"Oh, no. I'd be scared to death."

Had no one noticed that Phil was the only one who had not been mentioned in the letter? Mother had noticed. She turned to him. "What do you think, Phil?"

His most sarcastic smile twisted his lips. "When it concerns our great Uncle William or his spouse, I don't think, I merely feel. As Val gets most of the jobs around here requiring brains, I think she'd better make the decision."

They turned to her. She had read and reread the letter, and now she spoke quietly, surprising them. "We allowed Bobbie to go away from us. I think someone should go to her when the occasion is something as important as her wedding. I want Miri to go. It will be in her vacation time. I think we might allow Aunt Sophie to buy her clothes. She would come back with one or two pretty party dresses and things to go with them. She needn't be afraid. There will be rehearsals and she knows how to dance. I want her to go."

No one missed the sharpness in Phil's laugh as he rose and went to the piano. "That's final, Miri. Let's give the sacrificial lamb its first lesson. Andy, you are Uncle William walking up the aisle with her. Don't push or shove but act reluctant like a gentleman sorry to part with a treasure. Mark, you're the groom waiting at the altar with the ring, another sacrificial lamb and I bet he knows it. Sorry we have no best man. Now Miri, come up the aisle about one step to every two measures in the music."

Hilariously they took their places as his fingers on the keys brought forth the strains of the Lohengrin march.

Hardly had they started when Phil stopped the music. "Lamb, don't look at your feet. Look toward the altar but have your *mind* on your feet. Back to your places." They began again while Mother laughed.

They were back in their chairs still laughing when Phil struck those first compelling, deeply somber chords from Händel's "Saul"— the funeral march. With a little cry, Mother raised her hand, "No, Phil, please."

He rose laughing. "You don't think that an appropriate ending for this marriage? I do."

There was an interruption, the banging of a car door, steps, hellos, and Jake, followed by young Ned and Celia Waters, entered. Jake set a gallon bottle of sweet cider on the kitchen table.

Ned and Celia had been Miriam's playmates from the days when they all rode in the Ford to the one-room schoolhouse over the hill. Now, Ned, two years older than Miriam, was a tall gangling youth in high school. Once Jake had said he looked like a puppet held together by strings, skinny, legs too long, arms dangling and ending in hands that never seemed to know what to do with themselves, glasses sitting on a freckled nose and, above all, unruly reddish hair. "Only," Jake would add, "don't fool yourself. Those bony fists can pack a wallop and he can outrun a deer."

After they had piled their outdoor coats on a kitchen chair, Phil played dance music while they pushed back tables and chairs clearing the kitchen floor. They pushed Mother's chair to the door where she could watch as Mark and Andy taught the girls new dance steps, the dancers matching the music in frenzied whirling.

Sometimes Jake watched, sometimes he took part for like many heavy men he was light on his feet. They did a square, Phil playing the tunes and calling the numbers.

> "Duck for the oyster
> Duck for the clam,
> Duck for your home
> And the happy land."

Andy called, "Now a sentimental Good Night Ladies. Miri's got to learn the latest cheek by jowl goo or she won't be popular in Cleveland society." Mark added, "The lights ought to be dimmed. Who could hug a girl with this electric light blazing overhead?"

They were quite ready to drop down into their chairs, ready for the cider, the apples and doughnuts.

When the guests left, Louise's chair was wheeled into her bedroom. No more could she be left in her armchair by the fire to watch the coals burn out. When Valeria had prepared her for the night there were strong arms waiting to lift her into the bed.

While Phil was putting the lights out, he stopped a moment at her door. "Mother, you'll be answering that letter. I know the wedding dresses have to match so let them pay for that but please don't allow them to send any money here for Miri's clothes. I want to buy her a new coat and all she'll need. Don't accept a cent of money."

"You have just bought this expensive chair, dear."

"I can manage it. You won't accept money?"

"No, Phil. I feel exactly as you do. You think it wise to let her go?"

"That was up to Val. Good night."

"Good night. What a happy evening! I did so enjoy it."

"Good night."

The few days of the vacation passed like a moment. Mark and Andy were packing their suitcases ready to go with Phil to take the night train.

Phil was blowing the horn and the others were outside but Andy lingered. He kissed his mother again and there was something of anxiety in his eyes.

She smiled at him. "I am doing wonderfully well, dear, as I told you, practically indestructible, and I'm going to see you both graduated."

"It's a promise?"

"With God's help, I promise."

CHAPTER XIX

IN THE MORNING, Mother repeated. "What a happy time we have all had. Now it will be plans for Christmas and getting Miri ready for the wedding. We must remember that Phil is paying for everything and not one dollar must be wasted."

Before the week was over Valeria had accompanied her sister to the city where they lunched with Phil and went from store to store looking, comparing, discussing and finally at Phil's suggestion sending garments home on approval.

On Saturday while the trying on was still in progress, Phil laughed at them. Should they buy the green coat which was a little too loose but would last until she should grow large enough to fill it, perhaps two years, or should they decided on the sweet French blue with the little beaver collar, the one that fitted so perfectly?

"Great guns! Only a life time of training in *not* spending could produce this result." He walked around Miriam, critically examining the coat. "Put the green one back in the box. We keep the blue."

So it was with each garment until the wardrobe was complete.

There were other things worrying Miriam. She followed Valeria about talking it all over. "Phil says it's a fast set. They drink and pet and everything."

Valeria was patient. "Listen, honey, a girl either learns to take care of herself or she's nothing but a softy, what the boys call a 'pushover.' Ask for lemonade and if they can't produce it ask for water. I'd be ashamed of you if you can't go to your sister's wedding and enjoy yourself."

Phil laughed at her. "If the boys bother you, go sit by Uncle William. That ought to be dull enough to suit you."

However, neither Valeria nor Phil knew whether to laugh or cry when they at last drove to the city and put her on the train. Phil arranged her bags and left her with a pat, then a kiss on her trembling lips. Outside they stood on the platform waving at the woebegone face as the train pulled out.

"I never would have believed it. Our reckless Miri who climbs to the top of a pine, dives into the deepest pool, wanders through any dark woods at night and now is frightened to death at leaving home."

Valeria sighed. "Phil, I've been more frightened at what she's facing than I would be at meeting a wildcat at night. Only this time I know Miri will have the proper clothes and be with Aunt Sophie and Bobbie. She will be protected."

"You're the architect of her fate."

Valeria did not answer for some time. Then she said thoughtfully, "I'm right. I'm going to see that Miri has what I couldn't have, pretty dresses and experience at something besides our village dances. Ned is going to Cornell and if he asks her for dances or football games, she's going and she's going to feel at home when she gets there. I'd let her miss a whole term in school for this experience."

Phil was driving carefully over an icy road. "I got that and more without your telling me, Val. It was not *all* you wanted."

No, it was not all she wanted. That would come later.

A telegram from Uncle William assured them of Miri's safe arrival. Two days later a picture postal said, "It is wonderful. I've been all over the city. The rehearsal was fun. Tell Phil I kept my mind on my feet."

More postals. "Aunt Sophie says if it weren't for school she'd keep me here while they're on their wedding trip."

Phil said, "First danger signal," and they were relieved when Uncle William telephoned when he was putting her on the train.

Weeks passed after her return before Valeria got that "all" she wanted. At first there was astonishment at Miri's radiance. She tossed her head and laughed when they twitted her about her fears. Everything had been "wonderful," the church, the flowers, the six bridesmaids, the crowds, the reception, the dances, the wealth, the beautiful home with a bathroom for nearly every bedroom, and a butler, cook and extra maids.

The boxes containing her clothes came by express and Celia, Ned and Jake came in to see the froth of pale pink tulle over silk and the flower head-dress and gold slippers and ermine trimmed wrap. At every item Ned ejaculated, "Gee," Celia gasped, "Gosh." Jake grinned. "What use are they now?" Valeria answered, "We'll simplify them. I expect she'll use everything."

There was a package containing newspapers with many pictures of the bride and groom and wedding party. Valeria studied them again and again.

Then one by one through the weeks came disclosures. "Uncle William had to leave the reception because he couldn't stand so long and had a heart attack." "Aunt Sophie has some serious stomach trouble and may have to have an operation."

And, whispered to Valeria, "I am sure Jim was almost drunk even at the wedding. One of the boys told me he drinks like a fish. He and Bobbie are going to live with Aunt Sophie in the big house and Jim told me he wanted to live in an apartment. I don't believe he really likes Aunt Sophie. She does boss everyone, even Uncle William.

"I danced with Jim more than with anyone else and he talked about you all the time. I asked Jim if he liked being a doctor and he said he wasn't a doctor, he was a sycophant. I had to look it up in the dictionary."

One day, Valeria took firm hold of Miriam's shoulders. "Listen, honey, I want you to promise me something on your word of honor. Promise you will never tell any of these things—like Jim's being drunk—to anyone else. Never breathe a word. Promise?"

"I promise. If I tell you something will you keep it secret?"

"I promise."

"Ned and I are secretly engaged. When he goes to Cornell he's going to ask me to everything. Do you think I'll be able to go?"

"You bet your life you're going. That's wonderful, honey. I'll keep the secret."

"Val, I feel sorry for Bobbie, not having a sister living with her. We don't do her much good."

"What's the matter with Bobbie?"

"I think she's fast. I wouldn't want Mother to know the way she talks."

"About what?"

"Oh, about drinking and affairs with men and divorces. I know now what Phil meant when he said they were a fast set. I think Bobbie is fast."

"Remember this, Miri. Bobbie didn't have what we have had. We've had so much fun, always together. We've had Mother. We allowed Bobbie to go away from home."

It was on a cold day in January. From early morning snow had fallen on snow until the banks were so high that fence posts hardly appeared above the hard crust. By afternoon, gusts of wind were hurling clouds of white that almost obliterated the view from the northeast windows.

Miriam came in from school looking like a snow man. She stamped and shook her coat, leaving wet spots on the kitchen floor, before going into the parlor where Mother was reading near the fireplace. "Where's Val?"

"Out in the barn. I see smoke from the chimney so I know she's made a fire. I almost wish Jake wouldn't tell the man to shovel that path."

"She writes out there, Mother."

"I know."

"Val never minds being cold. She's sort of an Eskimo. She

keeps her window wide open at night and when there's snow on the carpet she walks right into it. She says she likes to feel the snow on her bare toes."

"I know."

The January days were lengthening but soon the sun was sending slanting rays across the fields. Mother guided her chair to the window where she could watch the beauty of the sunset.

She exclaimed, "Miri, I believe that is Robert Loring coming up the hill. Yes, he's coming in. Go to the door."

There was laughter as he started to remove his coat and overshoes. No, he loved the cold and please don't feel sorry for him. He was wiping his eyes. "These are not tears of sorrow—just the confounded wind. You remember the Walrus,

> 'Holding his pocket-handkerchief
> Before his streaming eyes'?"

Mother told him Val was out in the barn. Miriam should call her. Oh, could he go out?

Valeria was sitting at Phil's plank table when she heard the barn door creaking on its hinges, then a step on the ladder and his voice, "Val, am I intruding? May I come up?"

"Of course."

For a moment she felt flustered. Why did she have to be wearing her oldest, darned, faded sweater? Who would have expected him on such a day?

Her cheeks were flushed as she stood at the top of the ladder. Immediately she felt some excitement, something different in his face and manner.

At the top of the ladder he stopped. "You haven't heard from Phil this afternoon?"

"No. I've been out here quite a while."

He turned to the table. "I think Phil will call you later, probably tied up at the bank now."

"No bad news?"

"Good news, but he must tell you." He smiled into her eyes.

"I've brought good news also and I claim the happiness of telling it. That his news and mine happened on the same day was sheer coincidence—the sort of coincidence you must never put in a story."

He took the chair opposite her and drew out of his pocket a long envelope. "I hope we can celebrate the return of this day many times, Val. I know Phil will."

He unfolded the papers but she looked only puzzled.

"You don't guess what it is?"

She shook her head.

"It's a contract for you to sign. It's the contract from the publisher who is taking your book. About a dozen times I've had almost to bite my tongue from telling you that it looked favorable, they were interested and all that but I knew how many slips there can be between interest and a contract. Now you're an author with a publisher."

Her face was crimson, her lips slightly open and only all the details convinced her of the truth.

"I can't believe it. I'm awfully stupid but couldn't they change their minds?"

She hardly knew that his hands were holding hers in a tight grasp. "They want an option on your next book."

"Next book! Why, I didn't write a book! I never could write another. That's all there was, all I could think of."

"What are all these papers?"

Again her face flushed red. "I was trying a story. It's nothing."

"Nothing?" His fingers flipped over two or three of the popular magazines, then he pushed them aside.

She said lamely, "Phil says some of these magazines pay hundreds of dollars for five thousand word stories. I tried to study them."

"Well?"

"I knew all the time I couldn't do it. I don't know enough about life."

"About life?"

"Yes, I was discouraged. Of course I didn't read the ones about sports or deep-sea fishing or bull fights or traveling around Europe going from one hotel to another because I know nothing about all that. I read the love stories but I knew I couldn't write the kind they like. I got discouraged."

"Then what were you doing?"

"I was writing a funny story for Andy and Mark about a silly guy who couldn't write at all, much less about matadors or murders or stunning beauties with red hair and green eyes."

Suddenly she seemed transformed as her merriest laugh rang out to echo from the old rafters of the barn. "Don't you remember Andy's all time low was that E you gave him in English? I could see Andy trying to write one of these stories. Andy is the silly guy."

"I remember that." His fine gray eyes were filled with amusement as they looked steadily into hers. "Keep on writing to Andy." Again he held her hands in a close grasp and she did not try to withdraw them as he went on, "You are a reader. You have read and reread the great books and great stories written by the great writers. You have found in them strong meat, interpretation of the eternal conflict in the human soul. *What is life?*"

Her eyes opened wide as she looked into his with deep seriousness. "I don't know. I only know these stories didn't mean anything to me."

"Does birth, the strange coming into this world of a new human being mean anything to you? Does death and the going out into that great unknown mean anything to you? Does the struggle for bread, the struggle to find a place among other human beings mean anything to you? Do you know good and evil, weakness and strength? Does that unending conflict in the human soul, mean anything to you? Do you know loneliness? Do you know the joys and hazards of companionship? Do you know family life? Do you know why a bad woman isn't all bad?

Why a good woman isn't all good? Do you know that the word love means something so complicated that a long novel can't explain it? Do you know anything about greed, selfishness, selflessness, charity, devotion, work? Do you know when work is the best of medicines and when it is brutal, enslaving?"

She turned her eyes away and stared long into space. She spoke slowly, "Yes, Robert, I know a little about those things, I think." She seemed a little breathless as she continued, "I'll tell you what I wanted to write. I wanted to write a love story but I couldn't get it into so few words and then I knew it was the wrong kind."

"Why wrong?"

"The kind I wanted to write about doesn't grow like a weed. I was going to tell about that kind. The kind I meant grows like an oak. That would take a lot more words."

"Take your time. Finish this story for Andy. Let the long love story live back in your mind and someday you will write it. Don't hurry. Don't try to do what you are not fitted to do. You are right in thinking of a book as a mighty oak. The growth of the tree is slow, taking its nourishment from the soil, bending in the storm before devastating gales, basking in the sunshine and adding year by year to its full development, just as a man, though he disclaims putting into the book any single person he has known, in reality has written of all the people he has known, all the suffering, especially what he has experienced in his own heart, all the joys, all the struggles. Wait and work. Most of a good writer's hardest work is done before he sits down at his desk."

They were startled when Miriam called, "Do you know that it's pitch dark and I've had supper ready for nearly half an hour?"

They jumped up, gathering together the papers. "No, you go first. I'll put the light out. I'm used to coming down in the dark."

They followed Miriam down the path between the banks of

snow which had ceased falling as the cold increased. The moon was breaking through clouds, sending a pale silver over the fields, over the stark skeletons of trees in the old orchard, the dark masses of pine. The world seemed mysterious, bathed in the soft light.

He lingered a moment on the path. "You remember Thoreau said, 'I love Nature partly because she is not man, but a retreat from man. None of his institutions pervade or control her.' Isn't that something else you understand?"

At Louise Macrae's warm invitation, he stayed for supper. It was at the table he brought out the contract and Valeria found a new truth. Her happiness was enhanced a hundred fold by sharing it with Mother and Miriam. She turned to Robert. "You're sure Phil doesn't know?"

"I wouldn't rob you of that pleasure."

"I think I could get him now." She went to the phone, closing the door.

Miriam was looking ruefully at her plate. "Her supper's cold. Are they going to talk all night?"

Valeria came in walking slowly to her place but she did not sit down. She grasped the edge of the table looking from face to face, then with wonder shining in her eyes, she turned to Robert Loring. "You kept both secrets. No, you couldn't put it in a story because it wouldn't seem true. It *is* true." Her shining eyes turned to her mother. "It's happened. Phil is publishing three songs and his quartette. I almost forgot to tell him about my little book which is really Robert's book because he edited it and found a publisher. My little funny book is nothing. If it weren't for this storm Phil would drive out. He'll call you at nine o'clock, Mother."

"Sit down, dear, your supper is cold." She turned to Robert. "This is tremendous news to us. I can't quite explain."

Not to anyone could she quite explain. For a moment she closed her eyes and her emaciated fingers pressed hard on them, then passed slowly back and forth on her forehead. No, she could not explain that she had spent her girlhood living through her father's successes and failures and agonized waiting and deferred hopes and so often his despair. She spoke gently, "There will be moments of great happiness and moments of doubt and sometimes black days of indecision." Again she turned to Robert. "I am somewhat overcome. All their lives Val and Phil have done things together, even working together to keep this home prosperous and intact. They are both talented—surely God's great gift to them—and now, now—they will go on—my two talented children."

Val was wondering why her mother had been so happy about her own little book and why an agonized expression came into her eyes when told that Phil would publish some songs and a quartette. Couldn't any of them realize what she, Val, knew? She might possess a small talent but Phil was a genius. Couldn't they realize that Phil must be released from all that grind at the bank? Limited in physical strength, he had so little time. They, his family, were consuming his life. How could he be liberated?

It was April, weeks after she had finished the story, again edited by Robert, about the silly guy who couldn't write that she received a letter from a magazine accepting it with a check and a request for more of the same kind.

That night after all the excitement of the news had passed, after most of the lights were out, she went once again into her mother's room. She knelt by the bed, feeling the nearly useless hands fumblingly trying to caress her hair.

"Mother, it wasn't the money. It wasn't much and Phil said to remember we don't need it. It's something else. I feel so happy. I feel so rich inside me. I feel like a cup all filled to the brim so that it runs over. I feel so rich, Mother."

"We are rich, Val. Sometimes I feel we are about the richest people in the world. As I look back I know that living with my father was a rich life. Even little Mary Louise. You were so right about her. She has added more than her weight in gold to the richness of our lives. We must thank God for it."

Val went up to her room where she opened wide the window, drinking in the fragrance of the spring night. Spring. The buds opening, the roots coming to life drinking up sustenance from the bounty of the soil, millions of growing things coming up to breathe and live, the birds seeking mates and building homes.

Spring. She stood a long time at the window.

Book III: The Accounting

CHAPTER XX

ON THE ROAD before the white farmhouse the soft maples were strewing a wealth of gold on the earth which had turned russet brown. The sumacs were aflame with a crimson that subdued the red of the old barn, and along the edges of the fields over the old stone walls there was a running fire. There was pink and purple dogwood, copper and gold changing day by day in the great oaks, the continuous chirping of crickets, the last calls of birds as they flew far overhead starting their journey south; while in the parlor, kitchen and bedrooms of the house there was a light as though the sun shining through the small panes of glass had transformed them into cathedral windows.

The peculiar glory of the American fall? And no headlines in the newspapers calling attention to the miracle? No. The papers told the millions of city dwellers that President Coolidge had accepted the resignation of a secretary, that a British prince was making his first visit to America, that a Russian had died, the Dawes plan for reparations had been accepted, the stock market was climbing up and up, a boy of nineteen had murdered a boy of thirteen, a movie star was divorcing her third husband.

There were no headlines celebrating the return of this American glory but up on the Waters' farm the corn had been gathered into shocks and along the straight rows lay golden pumpkins; the crimson-cheeked apples had been gathered into barrels, the windfalls were in the cider barrels, cabbages were buried and one heard the rat-a-tat-tat of the woodpecker and knew the woodchucks, half asleep, were digging into the ground.

The season of fruition, and Louise Macrae, sometimes in her chair but often lying almost helpless in her bed, had lived to glory in its wonder and beauty once again.

She had kept her promise; she had lived to see her two sons graduate from Cornell in the previous June. For the first time in their twenty-one years of life they faced a permanent separation. In their hearts there was some grieving over this but they allowed no outward sign to appear. After only a day or two at home following graduation, Mark had left for a position in Schenectady. Andy, however, had been stricken with the first serious illness of his life, pneumonia. It had been bad enough to persuade him to rest and then spend the remainder of the summer working for Jake on the farm.

Now as he entered his mother's room for his last farewell, he was so tanned that his blue eyes looked almost out of place in the brown skin. He was going to New York, having been offered a position in a firm whose name was nationally known; a young fellow just out of college was not only lucky, he seemed favored by the gods when presented with such a chance.

He stood by the window in his mother's room. Outside, there was an unusual sound—shovels sinking into the earth, throwing up mounds of soil; then the noise of a truck and the racket of stones being dumped. "They're getting on like a house afire. When we come home for Thanksgiving I bet the frame will be up and before the heavy snow comes, they'll have it enclosed."

For Phil was building the wing which they had planned and dreamed of for many years. They would remove the kitchen bay with its charming windows where she had sat and sewed and mended and knit for so many years and place it at the end of the new room outside of which they planned a stone terrace looking into the garden. The clapboards, the shingles must be exactly matched, the roof slanted, all to conserve the unity and beauty of the old house.

"Do you mind the noise, Mother?"

"Not at all. I don't know how I'll manage when they cut the door through but you know I like workmen and I'm dreaming of the day when it will be finished and I see the old mahogany diningroom furniture uncrated and installed." She did not say that she would never see the new bedroom and bath above.

Andy came to her side and sat down.

"You will remember to get in communication with Robert's brother, the lawyer, Ben Loring. It will be a great comfort to me knowing you are in touch with someone whose family I know and admire."

"I'm not so good at barging in, Mother. I hear Phil getting out the car. I guess I must go. You know, Mother, when Mark and I get on our feet we're going to pay Phil back all the money he has spent on us. Of course it will take time."

"Phil would never look for payment any more than your father would have. I'm sure he would be hurt if you considered it a debt."

"I know that. Just the same he's going to get it back."

"Andy," she smiled into his eyes. "There is just one thing I want to say to you. I might say I trust you but you know that. It is this. I want to say that through the many vicissitudes of my life—and you will know many also for no one escapes them—it has been the power of prayer that has seen me through. In happiness, in sorrow, in days of doubt, in days of mistakes, in days of prosperity or need, always pray. Don't doubt your prayer. Don't wait for definitions or analyzing, brush all that aside and simply pray. Prayer will see you through."

"I'll remember, Mother." He kissed her and went out quickly.

Yes, he would remember. The same words had been said to Mark. They might not act on them but they would remember.

Fruition. The highchair had been returned to the barn and a little girl with pale blond hair (perhaps Jessie's had not been wholly synthetic), dressed in gingham, played under the apple trees or watched with fascinated eyes as the workmen laid stone on stone and the foundation grew.

It was Mother who had suggested they drop the Mary and call her Louise. Her origins seemed to have been completely forgotten. That she resembled none of them was immaterial for she was loved and enjoyed by every member of the family. One day Valeria watched Phil as he held her imprisoned between his knees. She saw his narrowed eyes as he seemed to be studying the face with the wide-set gray eyes, the turned-up nose. Suddenly he released her and walked away saying, "Apparently not a drop of Macrae blood showing. You're making quite a gal of her."

Valeria's eyes followed him. "She came into the world crying but she's been laughing ever since. Sometimes she sort of bubbles, sounds like water gurgling out of a bottle. I'll be sorry when she has to go to school and learn to sit still and be solemn. I can't imagine her serious."

He seemed to have grown strangely fond of the child, often bringing her toys, dolls and once a beautiful little muff and tippet made of some shaggy white fur.

He fastened it about her neck. "It looks like a ruff on a bird." Then as she ran out to show it to Miriam, he turned to Valeria. "She's not pretty, not at all pretty, but she's the darnedest, cutest little bird I ever saw. I wonder at what point in her life she'll stop that gurgling laughter. Or have it stopped."

"Perhaps never? If we're careful?"

"Who said, 'man proposes, God disposes'? I get mixed up between Mother, the Bible and some old wives' sage remarks."

They were happy days. There was a young woman a half inch

taller than Valeria sitting at the sewing machine expertly hemming sheets and pillow cases; at odd moments embroidering doilies and guest towels as was the fashion, filling something called by expectant brides a "hope chest." Ned Waters would graduate from the Agricultural College and there would be a wedding next June. Mr. Waters had given his son a few acres on the hill and a house would be built for the bride and groom.

Jake stood by Phil one Sunday morning looking at the excavation at the side of the house. Phil asked, "When do you start the house on the hill?"

"We'll get the foundations done this fall, then when the winter breaks we'll start building. Gosh, I need Ned. You can get helpers but you can't hire responsibility."

Phil laughed. "Do I know that! After I get Miri married —I want to give her a nice wedding, first one in the family—I don't count Bobbie—you know, bridesmaids and trousseau and wedding cake and all the extras—after that, I'm thinking of applying for a job right here." There was a lightness, a note of exhilaration in his voice, a smile in his eyes. "Perhaps you can find use for a part-time bookkeeper up on the hill. That would be neat."

Jake watched him, seeing the lift to his head, some freedom in his walk, in the way he stepped across the grass as though his relief and happiness in the success of Mark and Andy had affected him both mentally and physically. They often talked of the twins. Phil said, laughing, "Andy had a tight squeeze getting through while Mark made the crew and got honor marks. Andy plugged like the dickens; then, can you beat it? He gets the better job, almost twice the salary and he, the mother's boy, gets catapulted into New York while Mark stays within a few miles of home."

"You've done a wonderful job, Phil, making those two boys what they are."

Phil scowled. "Lost your mind, Jake? All I've done is supply some needed cash. Who's kept the family together? Who's kept

Mother alive? Who's made this place a home? Who's worked like a galley-slave washing, ironing, nursing, cooking, educating, cheering everyone, never giving up ideals? Whose mind and spirit dominates this family? You've forgotten Val? I can't even picture this place without her. Have another thought, Jake."

They were sitting on a pile of lumber as Jake whittled at a small stick with his penknife. He seemed to find no comment for a moment. Then he asked, "I suppose Val could make her living, that is all the money she would need, owning the home, by writing those stories?"

"She needs more time. Some days she can squeeze in an hour of writing, some days none. Mother's helplessness and all our coming and going keeps her nose to the grindstone. After Miri's married and Louise goes to school it will be different. Then she can be alone with Mother. I hope to clear out for a while."

Before Jake could question that, he went on, "By the way, I don't want to mention this to either Val or Mother at present. I make it a point to see the Cleveland papers. Since Aunt Sophie's death, Mrs. James Ferris has been prominently in the social news. It's sort of wearing a hair shirt but I follow her career. The last item insinuated she was heading for Reno and a divorce from Jim who seems to be drinking himself to death. I wonder how the great Uncle William and his bad heart stands all that."

"Sorry to hear it. Bobbie wasn't a heavyweight but she was a nice kid, one of the best behaved when I toted them to school."

"She's not any worse than most of the crowd, Jake. She's in the swim, in fashion. We're the ones who are out of step, old-fashioned hill-billies."

Jake did not answer lightly. He seemed lost in thought. "If Jim gets the go-by, what do you think he'll do? Come back here?"

"No. I'm sure there's no chance of that, knowing Jim. If he hasn't lost his confounded smoothness, he'll marry another rich girl, perhaps even get a better wife. No, I'm sure none of us are apt to see him again. I'm beginning to have sympathy for Uncle William. After all, Bobbie's all he has now. She'll probably be able to make him think black is white, though the old boy must hate divorce."

Jake waited some time before he ventured, "You don't think this means anything to Val?"

"No, positively no. It went pretty deep while it lasted as everything does with Val. She has talked freely about it, sees it in perspective. It made me sick with worry at the time but I can laugh now at the way she built such a beautiful castle on shifting sands."

Carefully, Jake fashioned the point on the stick he was whittling. "She was never meant for an old maid. I think she grows more beautiful as she grows older." He did not wait for Phil's reply. "It's Loring?"

Phil glanced sharply at the face bent over the whittling. "That's something she doesn't talk about. Sometimes I think I know Val better than I know myself. Then again I can't fathom her. I guess I don't need to tell you what marriage I would have planned for Val. In spite of my disappointment there, I can see what is happening. I never saw two people better suited to each other. I believe some of the hard-headed scientists say that physical attraction is due to some chemistry of the body. That may be but what I do see—and we both will have to admit it—is that they have so much in common." Phil bit his tongue, aware that he must be hurting Jake, but also knowing Jake deserved the truth.

Jake had stopped whittling. He folded his knife, dropped it into his pocket then sat with elbows resting on his knees as he stared into space.

As the silence grew awkward, Phil added in a gentler voice than usual, "I guess we'll have to admit, Jake, with all his learning, or in spite of it, Robert Loring's a regular guy. He can offer about everything but money and that's a commodity Val cares little about. We're beaten, Jake."

Jake said quietly, "I guess we're all fools about something." Then he changed the subject. "You'd get out of the bank? I understand you and the president's son run neck and neck for high position."

Phil lighted a cigarette, took a few puffs before he answered. "Get out? I hate the sight of Hal Martin's bloated, infantile face. Sunny Boy. I'm going to walk out next August. On the first of September I plan to kick the shackles off my feet. I'm going to fix the barn up next summer. Without too much expense I can enlarge that room into a real studio, get a small piano up there and give all my time to composition. I'm going to do some traveling first, perhaps on a tramp steamer."

He laughed. "Probably I belong in a booby-hatch but with one trio, a quartette and four songs published and sung and played in concert, I'm optimistic. If I can eat and have a place to sleep and keep my body covered with some old clothes, I'll be able to forget money. My grandfather was, as Mother admits, a talented failure. I'm going on where he left off, I hope. Just that chance is all I ask of life."

There was a long silence before Jake spoke. "What became of that fellow you roomed with when you first went to work?"

"Marino? I always wanted to bring him out but he was shy, couldn't speak much English. You don't know? Of course you wouldn't. You don't devour the music news in the magazines and papers before you eat your breakfast. He is in the upper class of violinists, playing in New York in the Philharmonic Orchestra. We were working on a concerto but he's given up composition. I hope to go on with that work. He's a success."

They were interrupted. Valeria walked out, her eyes bright and shining as she looked into the excavation. "Imagine having a cement floor and a modern cold room. It looks deep."

"Deep? Jake hopes to stand upright when you send him down there with barrels of apples and bushels of this and that."

"I don't *send* Jake anywhere. Do I, Jake?"

Jake watched her. "Except home once in a while."

She smiled wryly. "I came out to tell you that Mrs. Simms has telephoned for you."

"Just as I said." They all laughed as he strode off toward the road.

"Dinner's ready, Phil." Valeria had already gone through the trying ordeal of raising her mother's head high enough to enable her to take some nourishment. As Miriam and Louise came in from Sunday School they took their places, Phil at one end, Valeria oppoosite at what was now a small round table, the many leaves removed.

That afternoon in the glory of the fall colors, leaving Miriam writing her long letter to Ned while sitting at the desk in Mother's room, Phil and Valeria with the little girl's hand in hers, followed the path around the edge of the field, up through the fragrant woods.

She must loiter to teach the child to see scarlet partridge berries running through the moss, puffballs to pinch into brown smoke, acorn saucers, woolly oak-galls. Carrying a basket swung over one arm she taught Louise to help gather the brilliant trimmings she wanted for decorating the house for the coming holidays. Soon the basket was filled to overflowing with bittersweet, thornapples, rosehips, vermilion winterberries, lichens, burn-bush seeds and tough brown bracken.

Sometimes Phil, who seemed to tire easily, sat on a log watching them. They had reached the little brook that cut its way between rocks as it tumbled down to empty into the streams at the bottom of the ravine. "You know these woods as you know your kitchen, Val."

Her eyes smiled with some special serenity that he noted as she replied, "I've lived with them a long time but you're mistaken about knowing them. I feel out here the way I feel when I look up at the stars at night. In spite of all Robert has taught me, I merely know enough to guess how much I don't know. I'm always finding something new, something I've been too dull or blind to see before."

Not until they were over the top of the hill and gazing at the valley beyond did she sit down beside him. He threw himself on the grass, pillowing his head on his arms as he stared across the wide valley to the distant masses of green on the hills.

The spot held memories. Was it so long ago that she had fled to this place and sobbed as she tried to accept the fact that Jim was marrying Bobbie? Now, as she wound her arms about her knees and looked off to the distant horizon her countenance expressed tranquility together with thoughtfulness. How bitterly she had fought against accepting the loss that life had transformed into so great riches. Without the tears would she ever have written the funny stories? Without knowing the false would she ever have been able to evaluate the true? Robert. Beloved Robert. Again she felt like a vessel filled to overflowing with love that was part of music, of the stars, of the beauty of Nature, something deep and true.

After a long silence she said, "Jake says our holdings, our forest could be converted into quite a lot of money but I hope, Phil, we'll never have to do that. The thought of lumbermen coming in here, stripping these hills, makes me feel sick. I couldn't endure it. I hope as long as we live we can keep our land. I love the house but without the land it wouldn't be much but a shelter."

He did not speak and she went on, "I never want to live anywhere else, I want to stay here."

"I hope you will. You'll allow me a corner in the old barn?"

They laughed and Louise, not knowing what was funny, laughed with them.

There was a gorgeous sunset and they waited to watch the sky being suffused with purple, crimson, blue and gold. The little girl pointed at her. "Your face is pink, Val."

"So is yours and Phil's and all the earth's. Before long it will all turn brown and the trees will be stripped of leaves—all but the evergreens, and the snow will come and we won't be able to get up here so we'd better enjoy it while it's all rose-colored."

An hour later they rose as she took the child's hand. "You'll be stumbling in the dark if we don't start home."

It was late that same night. The child was asleep in her own room, Miriam was bent over her embroidery, when there came the sound of a high wind rattling shades. Valeria quietly closed the windows in her mother's room, then went upstairs to see what was happening there.

She had seen a little spiral of smoke from the chimney in the barn and Phil's light. How chilling the night could be after the warmth of the noonday sun. As she passed the door of his bedroom she noticed that the breeze had scattered papers on the floor. She closed the window, put on the light and stopped to gather up the scattered sheets.

She was absentmindedly putting them into a neat pile when inadvertently the last sheet of a letter rested on top. Without the slighest intention of seeing them, she read the large sprawling letters,

> You may as well know I am yours to eternity,
> Your ever hating,
> Jessie.

Had her eyes beheld a venemous snake coiled on that bureau they could not have expressed greater horror. For seconds she scarcely breathed. She was so shocked and stunned that she hardly knew that she read lines above. "Sure it's blackmail. Do something about that if you dare."

Her heart throbbing, something tightening in her throat as though choking her, she laid the paper down, turned off the light and went downstairs.

Miriam did not look up to see her stricken face as she said, "Listen for Mother. I'm going out to the barn."

There was no hestiation. With the chilly wind buffeting her she ran down the path, pulled hard at the barn door and then, without the usual hello, climbed up the ladder. Almost out of breath she stood panting, her eyes wide with shock as she looked down into Phil's startled face.

"What's the matter?"

In those moments since she had seen the scrawled words her mind had pieced together the picture. "You're sending Jessie money. She's blackmailing you. She's using Louise as a hostage. You've been keeping it from me. You've been trying to save me."

His face turned as white as the piece of paper on which he had been placing measure after measure of black notes.

Before he could speak the words seemed to rush out of her mouth. "The wind blew sheets of paper onto the floor. I was closing your window and picking them up. I didn't spy. I didn't even know I saw the words. They were there staring at me. It was as though they saw me before I saw them."

It was almost a relief to see the old bitter sarcastic smile on his lips. "That's the first time I ever left one in my pocket. Sit down, Val."

She turned toward a chair and held the back a moment as though she had lost control of her body, then she sank down.

His thin nervous fingers were unsteady as he laid the pen down, screwed the top on the ink bottle, then looked up at her. "I know you wouldn't spy, Val. We'll come clean in a minute."

He gathered together his manuscript, carefully put the sheets in order and placed them in the folder. Pushing it back he turned to her. "I'm sorry you had to know."

"How long has it been going on?"

"Several years, off and on."

"Does she want to see Louise?"

"No. But that's one of her threats—coming back to live with us. Mother and Miri had to be saved from that, as well as you and Louise.

"A few weeks after she left here, she wrote me from New York saying that if I would send her one hundred dollars she would never come near us or ask for anything again. I actually took her at her word and sent her the money. When months, many months, passed, I was confident we had heard the last of her. She said she wanted the money to help set up housekeeping because she was marrying. That seemed final."

He stopped for a moment of coughing. "Then came a letter saying she had been deserted, was coming back and if I didn't help her, she would come into the bank. I lost my head then. I began sending money, sometimes a little, sometimes more. Then she did come back to the city. Sometimes she went away for weeks, called it 'tramping.' She's in New York now. This letter came from there."

He spoke wearily, "As far as I can figure it out her death would be the only solution and I'm not up to encompassing that."

It was only a whisper. "Oh, Phil." Then, "Oh, Phil. You've been living in this hell and not letting me share it."

The bitterness in his laugh was horrifying. "I think hell is to be my present and future abode and it's doubtless where I belong."

"How can we end it?"

"I've spent hundreds of sleepless nights trying to plan an end, knowing there is none."

He was starting to rise when she asked the fatal question. "You have never seen her since she left here?"

His fingers were not steady as he lighted a cigarette. For some time he stared at the lighted match then stamped it out. "Val, even if I tell you, you will not quite understand. She attracted me. You must have noticed in those last weeks when she was here how often she came up to this room. She didn't come to talk. Twice she came to my room in the city, telling my good Italian friends, the Marinos, that she was my sister."

He stopped and looked at her. "You want to know all this?"

"I want to know everything."

"She came a third night and the Devil himself couldn't have planned things better. While she was there, while I was handing her money to get rid of her, Hal Martin came in. They left together. Even I still miscalculated her smartness. Hal was going to California on business. He took her with him. He left her there but when he came back I found I too was in the blackmailing business."

Valeria sat with wide, staring eyes trying to fathom the depths of his misery and unable to see clearly.

He was not looking at his sister. With elbows on the table, his head resting on clenched hands he said, "That's not all of it. Hal drinks and when he gets properly sodden he talks. Probably at some drunken moment he talked about something that put *him* in her power. I know what it was but I am not going to tell you that. Now we both get letters. He sends her money."

She sat still staring into space but shivered a little at the harshness of his voice. "Lord, I am such a fool. I still feel sorry for her. She's wretchedly unhappy. I still feel sorry for her."

He suddenly jumped up. "I hoped it all would be terminated without your having to know anything about it. More fool I! Now you know how low a man can fall."

"I see that and much more than that, Phil."

"Don't tell me, Val. I have to be in the bank when the clock strikes nine tomorrow morning. That grand old man, Ezra Martin, cursed with a son he doesn't know, depends on your brother more than on his son. He likes one to be punctual. I am always punctual."

Never had she heard a more bitter, mocking laugh than that which followed her as she descended the ladder and he put out the light. "There are various chambers in hell. I'm at home in several of them."

CHAPTER XXI

INSTEAD OF WHISTLING as he dressed on the following morning, Phil sang, over and over, some few dozen notes of a singularly beautiful melody. When he stopped for his usual good morning at his mother's door, she asked, "What is that haunting refrain, Phil? I can't place it. Those few measures. What follows?"

He smiled with pleasure. "Glad you can't place it. I'll find out what follows probably on my ride to or from the city."

"I understand." Her eyes smiled up at him. "Often my father got up in the middle of the night to jot down notes. You are so much like him in some ways, yet in others so different."

"How different?"

"He was gentle and often depressed, lacked that force, that ability to overcome all obstacles, lacked some fire, some intensity of feeling that turns talent into genius. Teaching music all day, going over and over the familiar things bored him, dulled his enthusiasm."

"That was sad."

"Sometimes I think I see a great truth—that one has to burn one's self as a sacrifice to produce the flame that kindles then consumes one in creation. Art demands a fearful sacrifice."

"Interesting, Mother."

He went into the kitchen. "Some fuel, Val? A fire needs fuel."

"I heard what Mother said."

"And like a wise old owl you knew the difference between the fuel needed for the body and the fuel needed for burning up the so-called soul. I've been hunting for a theme and that melody came to me in the night. Thanks to you."

"I can't see what I had to do with it."

"Caused an eruption. Some millions of people on this earth build homes, cultivate farms, marry, beget children and spend their lives on the sides of volcanic mountains. Back in their minds there must always be the fear of an eruption. I wonder if, when it comes, there could be a feeling of relief?"

She could see that the partial eruption had indeed brought some strange relief to him. He seemed cheerful, happy, humming as he went out to the barn for his car.

After he had left she thought about that. He had been all alone, not sharing his trouble with her as he had throughout most of his life. Now they could discuss it.

For years she had wanted to talk to him about money. How had he managed so much that was needed to see the boys through college, never hesitating when more and more was required, first for this emergency then for that? She was sure that there had been times when he must have borrowed—perhaps from the rich Hal Martin? Did he pay it back month by month? He hardly owned a change of suits. Except for his music manuscripts did he ever spend a cent on himself? And now this horrible drain of Jessie...

Where was right and where was wrong? How smart Jessie had been, leaving the baby, knowing Valeria would never part with her. How smart she was now, using the child like a hostage. Right? Wrong? She, Valeria, had thought it right to give the innocent little girl a chance and now she saw clearly that she had given Jessie a chance to harass Phil.

What did old Merlin say? Evil always hated good. Evil was a powerful force in the world, always hating, always plotting to destroy good. Good and evil were like two personal antagonists, the advantage lying with evil because it was aggressive, always seeing the guard down and pouncing upon its prey.

Wise old Merlin! Now Jessie was "getting that hunchback,"

as she had said she would. How far would she go? How could it be stopped? Why was she so sure that Phil would not dare to—what?

Without understanding, Valeria was conscious of an inward sickening shudder as she felt with the intuition that is indefinable that there was something sinister here; felt that there was more than she understood.

Through the uneventful weeks and months of that winter there were moments when fear clutched at her heart. Would they have any legal hold on the child? At any moment, would Jessie be clever enough to satisfy the court and come and claim her if it suited her purpose? They had confidently accepted the baby as one of their own. When the boys came home for Thanksgiving or Christmas she saw how they held the little girl in their arms, how their eyes showed their affection, how painstakingly they had hunted for presents to bring her.

Mother loved her as she ran in and out of the bedroom, "like a ray of sunshine." And Miriam was expecting her to be her little flower girl at the coming wedding.

More than that. From her infancy, Valeria had fed her, nursed her, dressed her and when the little one was scratched or hurt or frightened she ran past any arms outstretched to help her until she found refuge with Val. When Valeria went to a concert she knew they had trouble persuading her to sleep. "Where is Val?"

At night when she put her to bed the little hands clung to her and as Valeria turned out the light she knew, "I am her mother. She is my child. Nothing and nobody can take her away."

Now she could question Phil about the letters. She asked and he answered frankly. No, there had been none recently but he cautioned this had happened before. It was in February that he showed her a postal from San Francisco on which was mockingly scrawled, "Better pickings out here." Jessie was not allowing Phil to forget her.

Their hopes had been fulfilled and the new wing had been enclosed when the boys came for Thanksgiving, the doors had been opened and all through the winter days there was the sound of hammering, the voices of workmen, the trucks and cars coming and going. Discussions concerning paper and paint were followed by the making of cretonne draperies and dainty ruffled curtains for the windows.

It was at Easter time that Mark, Andy and Jake opened the crates and carried the old mahogany from the barn. When everything was in place they wheeled Mother around and around as she smiled. "It is perfect." She went through the swing door that made an easy entrance from the kitchen and the double doors that could be opened wide from her room.

She had made one of those remarkable recuperations, gaining strength to spend many hours in her chair and even eat at the table. As Mark wheeled her back through the wide doors to her room she spoke cheerfully, "Someday, when I have no more use for this bedroom, I would like to see you use it for a music room. Working all together, how beautiful you have made this old house."

"Guess it sort of lent itself to the improvements."

"But never forget, Mark, that it is the land, the woods, the fields, the ravine, all Nature's beauty that remains the richness, the setting for the home. You must never part with the land."

"It is really Val's home. You can depend on her never to part with the land."

"Mark," she spoke with deep seriousness, "when I go the property will be left to all my children—all except Barbara who is well provided for. Miriam also has a secure future. Perhaps, if you and Andy are doing well, marrying and doubtless making your homes elsewhere, you will all see fit to make this property over to Val. Then I shall know that Phil will always have a home. Sometimes a man in need of money will sacrifice land or forest or mortgage a place. You see what I mean?"

"I certainly do. Don't you worry about that. This place is Val's."

"I hope you and Andy will bring your children and grandchildren here."

"Gosh! One at a time, Mother."

Yes, it was another dream come true. As the cold decreased and the last vestiges of snow melted away, the tree buds swelled, Valeria found arbutus in the woods and day by day the preparations for the wedding progressed.

Almost daily, Mr. or Mrs. Waters or Mrs. Simms or Jake came down or Miriam hurried up the hill for consultations about the house that was being made ready. As Mrs. Waters said, "We will put in only enough for a start. Then they can have the fun of buying and selecting what they want little by little."

The simple but beautiful wedding dress was made with Mother's old rosepoint collar the only trimming. The dimities and ginghams—for Miriam was to be a farmer's wife—were chosen. There were the parties and little showers arranged by Miriam's friends who also trimmed the church, all the small but meaningful events so dear to a girl's heart and a satisfying fulfillment of Phil's wishes.

He discussed the music with the organist, telling Miriam, "I wish I could be at the organ and up front giving you away at one and the same time." Then he laughed. "What a silly idle gesture that is—giving the bride away. Ned has owned you since your hair was braided in pigtails and now I'm asked to stand up there and try to look sad as I give you to him. I'm tickled to death to hand you over."

Every day and often far into the night Valeria worked, baking the wedding cake, preparing for the small home reception to follow the marriage, trying on her maid of honor dress, training Louise for her important function.

They knew that their mother was anxiously awaiting word from Cleveland for she hoped Bobbie would come to her sister's wedding. It was fortunate that Bobbie's regrets came in a letter to Valeria. The postmark was Reno. She was sorry she could not come but she was sending silver and love.

The day came with the sunshine they had hoped for. Up before dawn, Valeria had the house ready, dressed her mother, then Jake and Mark lifted the wheelchair onto the opened back of a station wagon, the others filled the cars and the procession started down the long hill.

More often than on the bride, Phil's eyes rested on his mother sitting in the wheelchair close to the front row of seats. What stamina and serenity! What a beautiful light in the faded sunken eyes. Twice he saw the pallor increase and saw Mrs. Loring who sat close to her, remove the top of the bottle of smelling salts and gently wave it to and fro. Yet he knew she would endure. After he had delivered the bride he watched her, ready if she needed help, understanding as he never had before what it was in her that was "practically indestructible." Once her eyes met his brilliant piercing glance and she smiled. Then he saw her look from face to face—Miriam, Valeria, Mark, Andy and little Louise. She suddenly closed her eyes and he knew she was praying.

There was a smile lurking in many eyes when Andy who was best man fished for the ring. Had he lost it? Breaking the momentary silence came small Louise's high-pitched treble, "It's in the other pocket, Andy." There was a ripple of laughter with even the minister smiling.

They were married. The procession started back down the aisle. There was the hubbub in the vestibule, the rice throwing. At the house the young folks danced until Miriam and Ned were ready to drive away in their new car for their honeymoon in New York, Washington and points south—as long as their money lasted. As Jake put it, "Everyone on the hill is so happy about Miri and Ned, they can't think of enough ways to spend money on them."

It was quiet in the house after they had all departed. The shadows were deepening in the garden when Valeria undressed her mother and prepared her for her bed. Wondering if she could lift her, she heard a step on the walk—a step she seemed to hear with her heart rather than with her ears. She waited in the hall.

"May I come in? I thought you might need help, Phil being a busy chauffeur."

She looked into Robert's eyes. She loved him. Love? What a little word to designate those unfathomable depths in the human heart. The roots had gone deep. She had learned that "Perfect love casteth out fear." There could be no fear of jealousy, unfaithfulness. There could be no fear. Was not love God's greatest gift to man?

Often, she and Robert had talked of that. They had laughed at his unorthodox views. He had said, "Let me believe three words in the Bible and my mind and heart are steeped in religious faith."

"What three words?"

"God is love."

Often in the quiet of the night, alone in her bed, she remembered that. Once, when they talked of money, he had said, "There is only one abjectly poor man—the man with no love in his heart. He is pitiful, low, common, mean."

She loved him. For a moment she stood close in his arms, then she raised her head and smiled. "I thought you would come back."

They went into the bedroom. Gently he raised Louise Macrae's slight figure and laid her between the sheets. The hands lay motionless on the coverlet as she breathed, "I am very tired but I did not want to miss a minute of it."

"You must stay in bed tomorrow, Mother, and have a complete rest."

"Yes." She looked up at Robert. "It was a beautiful wedding. Miri was my last baby. I'm so thankful I lived to see her married to a boy like Ned. It was a beautiful day."

Her eyes closed and she said, "I'm quite all right, only tired."

When they had left her, Robert helped Valeria pack some of the wedding presents. Upon the departure of the guests, she had changed into her simple gingham dress. Now she looked about. "Jake will tote them up in the morning."

They sat on the terrace, finding the dark quiet of the night refreshing. As her eyes became accustomed to the dim light she could discern the outlines of her flower beds, the wide path leading down through the center with the open circular space and the stone bird bath, while beyond stretched the lawns and fields and the dark bulk of high hills and great pines against the lighter sky.

It had been on such a night as this when Robert first had taken her close in his arms and told her of his love, his longing for the day when she would be his wife. Even in the depth of her happiness she had been almost unbelieving. When he had gone, the passionate kisses still warm on her lips, she had knelt by her window and looked up into the night sky with all its myriad stars and wondered at the depth, the beauty, the fathomless happiness of what she now knew. No more when he went down the road would she imagine he might never return; no more some latent fear of the attractive women he met when in New York—for she still could be envious and jealous; no more could she ever feel herself alone. Whether it was down a smooth grassy path in a garden or over rocky difficult roads, she knew— was sure in the very depths of her being that she would never be alone again until death separated them.

Robert had gone into the kitchen to get a match to light his pipe. Now as he returned he took her hand. "Rather nice to know it's all over. Nice to know Miri will be close by up on the hill."

"Yes."

"You ought to be tired, Val."

"Oh, I guess I'm like Mother, practically indestructible."

"Leave out the practically. There is that in you both that is indestructible."

He leaned over, drawing her close to him. "Val, surely you are free now. If you are hesitating because of your mother, Phil and Louise, we can arrange about all that. My mother has three other sons to welcome her. Can't we hear those few words that will pronounce us man and wife? In church or not, that's immaterial. I love you. I want you. Surely there is nothing now to hold you back."

She laughed softly, happily. "Let me get my breath. Let me get the house straightened up. I don't want anything like this but I want something simple and beautiful—only—"

"Only what?"

She laughed again, teasing him. "Only—give me a little time to think it out"

CHAPTER XXII

SHE STOOD ON THE PATH watching until Robert's car backed out of the drive and turned down the road, feeling the silence, the darkness like a velvet cloak wrapped about her. Above, stars twinkled in the deep-night blue of the sky but not a leaf seemed to move.

The shepherd dog rubbed his head against her knees. As she petted him she murmured, "Poor old Rover. You've grown old with us. Do you miss Andy and Mark and now Miri?" Jake had promised to bring down one of the new litter of puppies for Louise.

Yes, she ought to be tired. She smiled as she thought how people thank God for some talent, some windfall—for money— yet they seldom think it worth while to give thanks for a strong, healthy body, feet agile and strong enough to travel the long road of life, eyes to see the beauty of the world, ears to hear, however dimly, the music of the spheres, hearts—marvelous little engines that keep all the machinery functioning. And? She smiled as she went in and turned off the lights, and what? What was a heart anyway? Something besides a machine, something that could feel, exult, suffer, break.

She was still smiling as her head rested on the pillow. Such a deep sense of happiness and peace and fruition filled her own heart that she wanted to stay awake and think about it. They all thought she lacked ambition, as she herself had insisted long ago. How little they knew. Now with her ambition, for Andy and Mark and Miri realized, she was going to work. Phil would start his transformation of the barn, making it a real studio.

The next great objective was to liberate him from the grind of all these years.

And Phil never cried. Had he learned a lesson as a child? She could remember seeing him sitting on a bank watching the children swimming in the pool on one hot summer's day. What is crying? Only moisture coming out of the eyes? She remembered how he smiled at them or laughed with them as the children came near him that afternoon and yet she felt he had been crying all day. No matter how deep her love for Robert, she must never let Phil down.

Now, if he were only given a chance would that cry be heard in more of those beautiful songs? Perhaps in the concerto on which he was working? Yes, she was ambitious. She was ambitious to see Phil freed for his work in composition, with good food and plenty of rest. He must be given his chance.

She would work. How amazing it was that she, staying right here in her beloved home might learn to earn money enough, added to the rent of their land, for all their needs. With hard work and Robert's help, she might become a successful writer. Why, she was fairly eaten up with ambition.

It was Louise's little hands tugging at her quilts that told her how she had overslept. "Val, wake up. I'm all dressed and Jake's downstairs with the puppy."

It was of her mother, not of the puppy she was thinking as she hurried down the stairs.

Had the tired hands moved through the night? They still lay motionless on the quilt. Bending over her, "Are you awake, Mother?"

The eyes opened, then closed again. "I'm all right, dear, but please don't bring breakfast. I just want to rest."

An hour later, two hours later, she worried. Should she call the doctor? No, surely all her mother needed was rest.

Throughout the day she was busy setting the house to rights, Jake removing all the wedding presents, then the last of Miriam's personal possessions from the bedroom. She cleaned and dusted, preparing the room for Louise who looked on with excited eyes.

"It's to be my room?"

"Yes, your very own."

How long ago it was that she had made those draperies and fixed the room for Bobbie's coming. She could see Jessie and the baby there, and the morning when she had discovered the empty closet. Then once again it had been Miriam's. Now would Louise grow up there until on some happy day she too would leave it a bride?

It was late in the afternoon when she called Dr. Northrop. For some time he sat by the bedside, made his examination, then came to the door. "There is nothing you can do, Val. Nothing much to do but let her rest. When she can take it, give her gruel, warm milk or tea. Don't force her. Let her sleep."

Impatient for Phil's coming, she set the table and prepared supper, her ears alert for the sound of the car.

Six o'clock, seven o'clock, eight o'clock, nine o'clock and she put Louise into her new bed. She walked about restlessly, in and out of her mother's room, listening to the soft breathing, feeling for but hardly able to get the pulse. Again and again she called Phil at the Marinos' but a man's voice, with a decided accent, answered, "He hasn't been here tonight. Except in winter, he seldom sleeps here."

Where was Phil? Why hadn't he telephoned, telling her he would not be home for supper? He almost never stayed in the city now.

When she looked out she saw there were no stars, the wind was coming up and black clouds were lowering with promise of a storm.

She was still standing at the shed door when she heard a car and saw the lights flash into the drive. She waited; then, astonished, she saw Jake helping Mrs. Simms to alight.

They followed her into the kitchen and she saw Jake's face

and she knew how a heart can seem to freeze with sudden fear. "What is it, Jake? What has happened to Phil?"

He stood under the light by the kitchen table and she noticed he carried a bundle of newspapers in his hand.

"Get your raincoat, Val. We've got to go into the city. Mrs. Simms will stay with your mother. One of our men just brought these evening papers out." He was spreading them open. "I'm sorry you've got to see this."

With both hands clenched into hard fists, the nails digging into the palms, she rested them on the table as she leaned over and read the headlines. Even in the more conservative paper the black words stretched across the page. "Defalcation of Bank Funds—Junior officer held for questioning."

Jake was saying, "I telephoned and found they had arrested Phil."

Sometimes the words blurred before her eyes but she followed down the column. "For some time the examiners had known of——"

She turned to the sensational paper. Great black letters—"Junior officer suspected of embezzlement."

For a moment she closed her eyes and clenched her teeth, then without a word she ran to the closet thrusting her arms into her raincoat as she returned.

"Is there anything about your mother I should know, Val?"

She gave details of the doctor's visit. She started toward the door then turned. "Mrs. Simms, you won't allow a soul to come near her? No one in the house who would talk so she can hear?"

"I'll take care of that, Val. She'll never hear a word."

"Take the papers with you, Jake. Don't leave them here."

There was a distant rumbling of thunder but the headlights illuminated a clear dry road as the car turned into the main highway. For miles they rode in silence but at last Jake said, "I tried to get Robert Loring but there was no answer."

"He was leaving early this morning, driving up to Vermont

to settle his mother for the summer on his brother's farm. He was to stay a few days."

"Which brother?"

"The lawyer, Ben, who lives in New York but has bought this summer place."

"Do you know the telephone number?"

"No, but I have the address and know the village nearby." She named them and he repeated the instructions.

"Val, let's try to get over the shock. We're going to need our heads, especially your head. He'll be cleared. We know Phil."

She said, "Phil is not a thief. Phil is not a thief. All his life Phil has *given*. He has given his very life to others; his time, his money, his very soul. Phil is not a thief."

"Don't use that word, Val."

As they drove down the city thoroughfare the rain started to come down in what seemed like sheets of water.

"Where are you going, Jake?"

"To the police station first. They must be holding him in jail waiting for the judge in the morning."

He saw the shivering that shook her whole body as she crouched back into the corner.

Coming down into the business center of the city they passed the Greek temple that was the bank, passed a moving picture house which was emptying, the people jammed under the marquee, caught in the storm, some with newspapers over their heads, some running through the rain for cars.

Some few blocks further, Jake pulled in to the curb. There was the old brick City Hall and back of it the city jail with the iron bars at the windows.

"I'm glad Mrs. Simms thought of an umbrella." He opened it and together they made their way to the entrance where bright lights indicated the activity of men on duty day and night.

They passed through a dingy hall and entered a room where two uniformed men sat at a desk. Without hesitation, Valeria took the lead and walked directly to the desk.

"I am Philip Macrae's sister. May I see him?"

The man who appeared to be in authority looked at her, looked at the clock, then again to her.

She leaned toward him, her face pale even to the trembling lips, her beautiful dark eyes filled with agonized entreaty. "You will let me see him?"

Without speaking the man turned to his companion, made a motion with his thumb toward the hall and nodded.

She started to follow, then stopped, looking toward Jake. "This is Mr. Young, our friend and neighbor. May he come with me?"

Again the curt nod and they followed the policeman down the dingy hall, into a narrower passage to a grilled gate where a guard turned a key and allowed them to enter.

The odor of a city jail assailed her nostrils. Here were lodged drunks, vagrants, all the pitiful riff-raff picked up in brawls, from gutters, all the suspects waiting for the court to open in the morning when their various sentences would be pronounced and their immediate destinies made known. There were women's voices and for a moment she felt faint for a woman was sobbing, another vomiting, a man was snoring, another cursing. They went farther where cells were on the street side. The guard opened a door and they looked in.

It was neat and clean, containing a cot, a chair and a table. There was no light except from the corridor.

Phil was sitting in the chair, bent over, his head resting in his hands.

When she said, "Phil," his head jerked up and he jumped to his feet. *"You* here!"

For only a few seconds she looked into his haggard face, then her arms went tight about his neck and it was with relief she allowed some tears to come.

There was something bitterly ironical in the courteous way he offered her the chair. There seemed no room for big Jake so he sat on the end of the cot but Phil began pacing up and down between them.

Quickly, with lips set in the unyielding line, she said, "They may not allow us to stay long. Try to tell us what you need."

He threw his head back and nothing could have been more jarring than his laugh. "I need to start over. From the beginning."

She drew a long breath. "Phil, no matter what this is all about, I know *you* are not a thief."

For the first time he stopped and looked directly down into her eyes. "The answer to that is yes and no. If I said yes, it would be a lie; if I said no, it would be a lie. I shall probably have to answer yes or no. I was trying to work that out when you came in."

Before she could speak he went on, "If my name were not Philip Ainsworth Macrae, if I had no mother, sisters, brothers, father's memory or grandfather's I wouldn't care what happened to me. I'd get this all over as soon as possible. I'd go to prison—I believe ten years is the maximum for embezzlement—I'd go without an explanation. I don't want to go through that explanation. If I didn't have a family, it would be simple." He laughed again, almost lightly. "Wasn't it the great Uncle William himself who said there is one black sheep in every family?"

"Phil, you must have a lawyer. I don't like the way you talk about not defending yourself. Can you suggest anyone?"

"No. I'll be my own lawyer."

Jake spoke for the first time. "I think I can take care of that. What can *we* do?"

He did not look at Jake as he answered, "All right. What about Mother? She was so tired after the wedding—" he broke off and it was pitiful to see the sudden nervous working of the muscles in his face.

Valeria explained how completely she would shield her, adding, "Until your name is cleared."

When at last Valeria walked out of the building there were blinding tears in her eyes. She slipped on the stone step and Jake found it impossible to hold the umbrella over her as she ran through the rain to the shelter of the car. It was Jake who saw a fair-haired woman, standing unprotected from the rain near a tree. Incredulously, he looked again but she had stepped behind the sheltering trunk.

Coming to the side of the automobile he said, "You wait here, Val. I'm going into that drugstore to make a telephone call."

It was near midnight when they turned into the drive. Mrs. Simms came from the bedroom, ready to leave with Jake. "She only wakened once. She didn't recognize me, called me Val. She's very weak."

Valeria stood looking with curiously dilated eyes from face to face as she answered absently, "Yes, she is very weak."

"I'll come down early in the morning, prepared to spend the day. Celia will take care of Louise and look after everything on the hill."

"Thank you, Mrs. Simms." She turned to look into Jake's face. "You can take me in the morning?"

"I would like to stay here tonight. You ought not to be alone. I could watch your mother while you get some sleep."

"I want to be alone tonight. Come in the morning—early, Jake."

She stood listening as the car started and then the sound of the motor died away. She removed her wet coat and threw it over a chair. Slowly, quietly, she ascended the stairs and looked into the child's room. She bent over the little girl, listening to her regular breathing, then she went down and entered her mother's room.

There was only the shaded light from a lamp on the far side of the room. She drew a chair close to her mother's bed.

There were the tired hands still resting on the cover, the closed eyes, the waxen face. She spoke clearly, "Mother?"

The eyes opened then closed as she murmured, "Val, dear?

It was a beautiful wedding." Then again, "Val, dear—" but when she tried to add words the voice trailed off and lips and eyes remained closed.

Long into that night she sat watching, sometimes trying to get the feeble pulse. Sometimes she heard the rain snapping against the little panes of glass; sometimes she could feel the quiet permeate the room like a presence. On the shelf, the little clock ticked away the seconds but there was no sense of time in Valeria's mind. Past, present, future were but part of eternity. Once she turned her head and spoke as though someone were kneeling at her side. "She is dying."

She slipped down on the carpet, laid her head against her mother's arm and taking the almost lifeless hand in hers, she prayed. Never in her life had she felt she knew how to pray as she did now. The breath came hard from her aching throat as she closed her eyes and moved her lips. "Dear God, take her tonight. I pray that You will take her tonight." Over and over and over the words seemed to be lifted up from the very depths of her being. "Dear God, answer my prayer. Take her tonight."

With the dawn the rain stopped. There was a glow in the eastern sky. She looked at the clock. It was four when she called Jake.

"Yes, Val."

"Will you get Dr. Northrop? Mother died in the night."

CHAPTER XXIII

ABOUT HALF AN HOUR after Valeria and Jake had left, one of the city's most distinguished citizens entered the station house. His chauffeur waited near the door as he walked directly to the desk.

As the tall man with thick white hair, carrying himself erect with conscious dignity, approached, the officer at the desk sprang to his feet. "Good evening, Mr. Martin."

"I wish to see Philip Macrae." It was an order, not a request. "I wish to speak to him in private."

The officer turned to his assistant. "Bring Mr. Macrae and take him into that office."

Their eyes did not meet as Phil with head slightly bent passed into the office followed by the elderly man who carefully closed the door after him. Now it was the white head that was bowed as the owner sank into a chair. He lifted a grief-stricken face and looked into the dark piercing eyes watching him. "Sit down, Phil."

Phil took the nearest chair, his eyes unwavering as he contemplated the bowed head. Was there a sorrow here perhaps beyond his experience? Was that agony beyond his comprehension? Often, he had thought deeply about that father and son. There must have been great rejoicing at the birth of the boy. He remained their only child.

Phil visualized the loved infant, then the fair-haired boy. Did both father and mother spoil him? Deny him nothing he asked for? With what pride the father must have directed his education, looking forward through all the years to the manhood when the boy would be trained to take his distinguished place in the world? There was pride of family, pride of name, and love. . .

There was more than that. Here was a man whose entire life had been built on a code of honor; a man of dignity whose word meant more than any legal paper, a man whose integrity was unassailable.

He was speaking in low measured tones. The bank was bonded. "You remember I once talked to you about that, Phil. The officers thought I carried too heavy insurance. Although I would have trusted every man in my employ—and they have been worthy of my trust—still my responsibility was so great that I felt no precaution too expensive."

He talked on and on. The morning papers would carry details and already there was talk that might cause a run on the bank. They could be destroyed. It had occurred so often in bank history. Though he might pledge every cent of his personal fortune, he might not be able to act in time to avoid the catastrophe.

"All this you know, Phil. From the day when you came into the office, I saw in you the brilliance and ambition of your father. I also felt some honor, some integrity on which I could depend. I knew the heavy burden you carried at home, your love of music and your activities in that field. I knew *you*, Phil. I gave you a larger and larger salary and would have thanked God if you had been my son. I think you know me as well as I know you and when I pledge my word that I will be your benefactor for the remainder of your life, you can trust me. I want you to *save my son*."

The older man seemed to have difficulty meeting the eyes that never left his face.

"Save him from what?" The usual flexibility, the suggestion of gaiety in Phil's voice was gone; the tone was hard and sharp.

The older man was not used to dissemble and now he dropped his eyes and spoke hesitantly, "I never held with the theory that a boy must sow what they call his wild oats, yet I have seen a youth go through such a period and then come to his senses and develop into a dependable, honorable man. Hal has gotten into bad company. I am confident that, if he is saved from this catastrophe, he will become such a man; also, we will both be in your debt for life."

"And you wish me to save him. You are actually asking me 'to take the rap' for him. My name, my family, my future is nothing to you." Phil's voice was clear and resonant. "I have accepted gratuities. For that I must be dismissed—and dishonorably—from the bank. When I have been in a tight place, Hal has offered me gifts. I accepted them as loans that someday I would be able to repay. Altogether they amount to something less than three thousand dollars—a hundred now and then, once five hundred dollars. Even now, by humbling my pride and begging help elsewhere I can raise that amount and pay him back every cent he gave me. I was a fool, and dishonest because I knew his gifts were a form of blackmail. I suspected he was stealing, that he was dishonest, although I never watched his books or his transactions. Both your trusted Smythe and Murphy were in the position to do that. Either of those men could have tipped the examiners off. I am neither a spy nor an informer. Accepting his money and keeping my suspicions to myself is my guilt and all my guilt, Mr. Martin."

"You can't prove that."

"I have kept the items and dates. Perhaps I can't *prove* anything for there were no papers signed. I can't *prove* that at lunch about two weeks ago, Hal offered me five thousand dollars in cash if I would resign from the bank and forget him and his gifts; but Murphy and Smythe could swear to my integrity."

The old man's face was haggard. "You knew exactly what Hal was doing?"

"No. I don't know now. I was merely suspicious. I was not clever enough to prove anything. I knew he was gambling. I knew something of his activities but his personal life was not my business. Why didn't the examiners suspect something? Why didn't Smythe and Murphy come to you?"

There was a painful silence. Then Phil said, "You have just admitted Hal's guilt."

Martin's voice broke as he answered, "He can be proved innocent. My lawyers are already at work. Murphy and Smythe will not desert me."

Phil's face seemed to age as he looked at the white drawn face before him. He spoke with difficulty. "Mr. Martin, it is *you* who is being crucified. It is you and only you who will stand at the bar of justice and tell the truth—and you know the truth; or, on the other hand—save your son and *your* name."

"The law will take its course."

"You don't believe there is a higher tribunal?"

"A man might build his entire life on honor and integrity, Phil, and yet meet a test he could not find strength to pass."

There were moments of silence as Phil's lips twisted, the muscles in his face worked nervously, the expression of anguish deepened in his eyes. He rose. "That is what you have to say to me. You came to threaten me. I will take my own punishment for my guilt. I decline taking Hal's punishment."

There were red blotches on the older man's face and his eyes were bloodshot. Now his voice was hard. "I have done a great deal for you, Phil. Think this over. I have influence and you will have no choice. A confession might bring compassion, a shorter sentence."

"If you are able to carry through what you are planning, Mr. Martin, I will still be enduring the lesser punishment. God pity you through the remaining years of your life. As I said before, you are the one who is being crucified."

He looked down at the bent head a moment before asking, "May I go back to my cell now?"

The old man seemed to have difficulty rising but Phil did not offer to help him. It was Phil who opened the door, walked out, passed the desk, entered the corridor without one backward glance.

The morning papers, though less sensational, carried the news of the embezzlement on the front pages. It was known that lines were already forming at the bank door. The clock in the little courtroom struck ten as the judge took his place. Here were no drunks or vagrants or pickpockets to be disposed of for this case eventually would come before a jury.

Surrounded by reporters scribbling into notebooks and a surging crowd of citizens, Valeria and Jake had taken their places on one of the hard benches. Following the hubbub of conversation, there was a silence that seemed painful after the court came into session. Then the accused was led in.

Suddenly, Valeria grasped Jake's arm and the fingers dug in. He laid his hand on hers and breathed a deep sigh of relief, for two men walked beside her brother. Robert Loring quickly left, finding a seat near the front but the other man stood beside the prisoner.

"It must be Ben. He looks like Robert."

The judge was gazing fixedly at Philip Macrae. He looked ill with his hunched shoulders, head held slightly sidewise, his ghastly pale face, his brilliant dark eyes.

There followed all the preliminaries, the questions asked and answered, the hush in the room as the crucial question came and then Phil's clear voice, "Not guilty."

There was some talk back and forth with the lawyer, words spoken that Valeria could not hear, then the question of bail.

"I must fix the bail at five thousand dollars."

The figure was accepted. The Loring brothers had contributed the sum.

It was all over. The officer led Phil away followed by his lawyer. Bedlam seemed to break loose as the reporters hurried away and dozens of tongues babbled at once.

Robert Loring was making his way across the room to

Valeria's side. He looked into her troubled eyes. "I have just heard about your mother. We can take Phil home. You and Jake had better go right on and we will follow."

"He can come home?"

"Until the trial."

He came home. Alone he went into his mother's room. Not even Valeria would follow him there.

When at last he came out, he did not glance toward the parlor where the others were sitting but went through the hall and stood a moment in the kitchen looking around as though it were a room he never before had seen. Ben Loring joined him. Phil lifted his head. "Could we go out to my room in the barn to talk?" He led the way down the old path, up the ladder and no one disturbed them.

It was a small private funeral with only the Waters and Robert and Ben Loring sitting with them in the parlor while the minister read the words from the Bible. Could any but her children know what that Book had meant to her? Could any but her children know what prayer had meant to her?

And flowers. Where had all the flowers come from? They heaped them about the grave and not until long afterwards did Valeria read and reread the unfamiliar names. There must have been many mothers' hearts that ached in sympathy for that little family and expressed their feelings in sending flowers.

Louise was living at the Waters' place. But Miriam? Somewhere she and Ned were motoring through the South. It was agreed that with so small a chance of success, no effort should be made to find them.

Jake drove Mark and Andy back to their train after Valeria again and again had told them of their mother's happiness in those last hours. But even in the silence of the deep night as she tried in vain to find oblivion in sleep, she could hear the loved voice saying those last words, "Val, dear."

CHAPTER XXIV

THERE WERE LONG summer days to be lived through before the trial for which the date had been set in early September. Must the days be filled with hours of anxiety and sickening dread or could they be filled with hope and faith? Val remembered her mother's words concerning "inner strength" and sighed as she thought how far short of that refuge she had always fallen.

She was grateful for that never failing relief a woman can find in the round of petty activities in a home. Insignificant accomplishments—dusting, seeing a room neat and clean, cooking, making sure appetites were satisfied, knowing bodies were being nourished with good food.

Louise was no problem through the vacation days. Knowing her love of animals, Miriam or Celia Waters delighted in keeping her often up on the farm where she found a never ending circus watching the pigs, cows, chickens and the great bull roaring in his pen. There were the dogs and cats and Celia, who was something of an ornithologist, taught her to know the birds by their songs, their colors and also by their separate ways of flight.

Valeria saw how Phil delighted in the child. A little Polish boy living in a shack across the ravine came to play with her and Phil hung stout ropes from a limb in an apple tree, made a solid wooden seat and swung them higher and higher until they screamed with excitement.

When, after the first days of their acquaintance, the children began to quarrel, Valeria was perplexed. The little fellow with the broad flat face, the pale eyes and straight light brown hair was belligerent. When he pulled an arm off Louise's doll she scratched him unmercifully, sending him home bleeding and crying.

Phil only laughed. "All right, send her to bed with bread and milk for her supper but let her fight. How many times did I have to stop Mark and Andy from tearing each other to pieces! I'm glad she held her own. She'll learn a lesson she'll need when school starts. She won't always find refuge in your arms, Val. I'm glad she's got the stuff in her to fight her way."

The Polish boy came back the next morning, as Phil said, "with some respect for a little girl's doll."

All these trivial events filled the days, for which she was grateful. They were alone. With carefully chosen words, weighing each as though to be certain of the exact truth, he had gone over the story of those years in the bank. Here was the old Phil, often hiding tenderness and affection under a screen of sarcasm but with no walls erected to shut her out. Again she felt that the eruption had brought relief to his heart.

Frankly he talked to her about his music. It was in early August that one popular song "caught on." He endorsed the check and handed it to her. "That was sheer accident. I might or might not be able to repeat it."

One day he came in from the barn and she could see the enthusiasm and excitement filling his whole being. He talked excitedly about his concerto. "Val, I need a piano so badly." He was looking into their mother's room. "I had planned to enlarge that place in the barn and get a small piano installed. All that is a forgotten dream. Would you want to make this room a music room? I've measured and the big piano could fit into that wall. Why not move the bureau and all the bedroom furniture up into the new room that is half vacant? Just for the summer I would like to fix a place to work—not in the parlor."

Jake with two men came down and with much careful manipulating they moved the piano after carrying the bed and furniture upstairs. For days they worked arranging this and that until the room was settled. When much else had been forgotten she would remember the evening when all was finished and Phil walked about, back and forth, back and forth from room to room, through the wide doors to the diningroom, back through the kitchen until he finally stood still in the hall. Never had she seen his face suggest more pleasure, his lips smiling, his eyes glowing as he spoke such simple words: "This is a very pleasant house."

"Andy said Mother told him she wanted that room to be a music room."

"I'm sure this would have pleased her."

"Will you move all your things from the barn?"

"No." He hesitated, his head forward in the suddenly tired gesture. "No. Perhaps I'm used to that old barn. I seem to work better out there with the world shut out. Just now I do need the piano and this change has improved the whole house."

As the summer days passed she began to hear the themes, the variations, the slow and wonderful development of the piano part. Once she asked him, "What about the orchestration, Phil? How did you ever learn all that?"

"Val, I never realized until my intimacy with Marino and his friends what a marvelous teacher I had in Mother. She grounded me as her father had done in educating her. There are many things in music, as in any art, one cannot accomplish without technical training and," he smiled, "there are many things no training can give. Mother knew that and now I know it. How I have wished that defeated old fellow—our grandfather—had lived! I wish he were here this summer."

Valeria had noticed that there were always those words, "this summer." He must work "this summer." It was as though the future was a blackness into which he could not penetrate; but still there was "this summer."

Several times Ben Loring drove down from Vermont, stopping on his way to New York, staying a day or two with Robert and spending hours in the barn with Phil. Never did Phil walk in the woods, never did he move except from the house to the barn and back to the house, and yet he seemed cheerful, happy and intent on his work. Many nights Robert walked up the hill and took supper with them and no one looking in on the four sitting about the table would have dreamed how black a shadow hovered over their heads.

Sometimes in the long evenings, Phil put aside his own work and played for them—Beethoven, Mozart, Chopin and his beloved Schubert. Sometimes Valeria, listening to the glorious sounds echoing through the house, bit her lips to keep back tears. How could a human soul reach such heights of beauty and yet find his life enmeshed in such sordid misery? And as to so many questions she asked of life, she found no answer.

As September approached a tenseness grew that could be felt. One could not help but see the nervous start that caused Phil's hands to close spasmodically whenever the telephone rang.

And then, there came a black day when Phil drove away in Ben Loring's car.

Valeria watched alone as the car passed out of sight down the hill. In the empty house she walked about, sometimes with closed eyes and clenched hands, as she cried, "Oh, God, teach me how to pray."

It was a tedious trial. Choosing the jury was long drawn out. There were long columns in the newspapers filled day after day with endless details. Every morning Valeria drove in with Jake and took her place close to the front row. There came a week when it seemed there would never be an end to the conflicting testimony of handwriting experts. Was the name Philip Macrae signed to some checks, forged as Ben Loring contended? It was a nerve-jarring sound in that courtroom when the decision went against him and Phil laughed aloud. The law taking its course?

"What can't money buy?" Valeria asked that question as she and Jake drove home one afternoon.

"Perhaps it isn't as simple as that, Val."

Had it been money or pity, or their love for Ezra Martin or

their future need for their families that had caused those two loyal employees to assert their high regard for Hal Martin and insinuate their suspicion of Phil? They were men whom hundreds of citizens had known through the years and trusted; men whom even Phil would have thought incapable of actual baseness, although he understood why they had not mentioned their suspicions to Ezra Martin.

That had been a far more crucial day than Valeria realized. She saw Phil, as the two men's evidence was recorded, drop his elbows onto his knees, leaning far over, his face almost hidden but his hands closing and opening convulsively, then clenched. She was conscious of Jake's hard breathing and saw Ben Loring's face turn crimson with anger.

Jake's frown and set jaw made her sick with fear.

"I realized it wasn't simple. It went against Phil and I couldn't quite understand why."

"I felt they were saying what either Ezra Martin or the lawyer had trained them to say. Sometimes men do things for reasons so complicated they themselves don't understand why. It may have been for money but I don't think that is the whole answer."

"It was the worst day."

"Yes, it was the worst day, Val."

That evening Ben Loring came out to the house for some papers. His anger was evident although he only said, "I don't know everything that's ahead but I do know that before I'm through this community is going to know some truths about the life of that son of Martin's. I have advertised and used detectives to trail Jessie Macrae but I could not find her. We were sure she was in hiding not far away. Last night Bob and I were ready for bed when the doorbell rang. Bob answered and there she stood asking for me. A pitiful creature... She asked if she could help Phil."

"*Help* Phil?"

"I explained to her that she could help by keeping out of

sight. She must have been attractive once. Tell me everything you know about her."

Thoughtfully, Valeria explained her background and the details of her life with them not omitting the scene in the woods or the blackmailing. "She constantly threatened to come here to live and claim Louise."

"You need never worry about that now, Val. No court would allow such a woman to take Louise from this home."

When Ben Loring had left, after again reassuring her of Louise's safety, Valeria went about her work, trying to banish from her mind all thoughts of Jessie Macrae, but nothing could remove the pathetic picture from her mind. Why did Jessie run away immediately after she, Valeria, discovered her intimacy with Phil? That Jessie loved Mother, Valeria knew; that she was really happy in those quiet days when she learned to sew, that she enjoyed her pretty new wardrobe, that she appreciated her return to perfect health and strength after emaciation and near-starvation, Valeria felt sure. Why then did she steal Mother's money, run away and become a—"tramp" again?

Were Mother living, Valeria felt sure she would be doing everything possible to help. What could she, Valeria, do now?

She talked to Jake about it. He pondered the question and answered in his slow way, "Ben Loring is right. I only hope she keeps in hiding. Her presence would hurt, not help Phil."

Two days later, when she was sitting in her usual seat with Jake in the courtroom, she gasped as the prosecution called the name, "Jessie Macrae."

Nothing Ben Loring had said prepared her for her cousin's appearance. She wore an old black coat. She had pulled down the brim of a black hat as though trying to hide her hollow cheeks, dark circled eyes, blotched skin. She swayed as she took her place in the witness chair.

Relentlessly, the prosecuting lawyer fired questions, fairly yelling, "Answer yes, or no," as she tried again and again to bring in the name, Hal Martin. Yes, she had received money from Phil Macrae, had had improper relations with him. Her sordid life was revealed.

Once she slumped in her chair and when the matron handed her a glass of water, her hand shook so that it spilled on her coat. When Ben Loring began the questioning that would have brought Hal Martin into the picture, Jessie fainted. She was removed from the courtroom. Beyond question, she had done Phil almost irretrievable harm.

On their drive home, Jake's only comment was, "I wish her name were not Macrae."

That night, Dr. Northrop drove up to the house. On the table he set a small box. "Val, I stopped in the courthouse this morning. I'm following this every day. I sat near you. Are you getting any sleep at all?"

"Sometimes a little."

"Will you take one of these tablets every night? They are mild but they will help you relax and sleep."

She looked without interest at the little box. "How do you think it is going, Dr. Northrop?"

"I'm a doctor, not a lawyer."

"About Jessie? I felt faint and sick myself."

"No jury would believe Hal Martin traveled to California with that woman." Presently he added, "No matter which way it goes, I saw one person who will not survive this trial very long. Ezra Martin... He would not look like that if his son were innocent. He is a desperately sick man."

"Ben Loring has been wonderful. He has worked so hard but they have seemed to prove lie after lie. I don't understand everything but some days I feel that we have not only Ezra Martin with all his wealth and prestige but all the bank and all the city against us."

"Val, do you know that books have been written—in fact I own one—about innocent men who have served terms in prison for other men's crimes? There are probably men in our prisons today who are eating their hearts out in bitterness knowing their own innocence but also knowing it is impossible to prove it. Only a few months ago a man who had served fourteen years in the penitentiary was proved innocent and freed. The state gave him a large sum of money—as though money could compensate for that.

"For some reason this is a subject in which I am deeply interested. I like to ferret out the reasons why the innocent man became involved. If I were a preacher I might point out the danger of bad company."

"That went against Phil. Hal's friendship. Phil was known to need money and Hal swore he had never given him a dollar."

"If you walk in the mud or even near the mud you are bound to get spattered. To all appearances Hal and Phil were close friends." His fingers drummed on the table. "Phil swore he got the extra money he needed from Hal. He swore to that. So he needed money, more than his salary. Would it not follow that as he needed more and more he would take it from the bank? Where did it go? After his family were cared for, on women? On women like Jessie Macrae? Gambling? There was Phil's need of money and Hal's wealth."

"There is no way he can really prove the small amount he got from Hal. There were no checks, always cash." She was resting her head in her hands.

"Jessie's appearance was dramatic. She was trying to help Phil but I'm afraid her being one of the family means she was more nearly another nail in his coffin. Phil for years giving her money. She didn't succeed in pinning anything on Hal. He had reputable people swearing alibis for him. Hal Martin traveling to California with that woman? Living with her? You see how hard it would be for people to believe that. And she's a Macrae. She has sunk pretty low since she left here. I believe every word she spoke but still I think her testimony proved harmful."

Why had he come up here to talk to her like this? She took several audible breaths. "It helps to talk it over with you, Dr. Northrop. You have known us all so many years."

"I knew your mother. I brought most of you into the world. This is more than an exciting trial to me although, actually, it is getting to be a dull trial to the public. People are losing interest now they know their money is safe and feel the bank is sound."

There was a silence as he seemed lost in thought, then he went on. "Loring succeeded in pillorying Hal Martin. In spite of all the objections where I sometimes thought the judge unfair, he cleverly left a picture of a rake—but a rich rake. Not that plenty of people in town didn't know his life. Even though they save him, the Martin family name and pride has been dragged in the dirt. I feel nothing but pity for the old man. The bank is safe but he personally is ruined."

"I'm not sorry for him now. I think Phil really loved Ezra Martin. He looked up to him. I wouldn't have believed he would turn against Phil."

"To save his only son?"

"Perhaps I don't know what I'd do in such a case. There is one other point, Dr. Northrop. Phil has always said that Hal is not a fool or a 'sunny boy' but diabolically clever. I see now how sharp he is. He was so poised and handsome and dignified on the stand."

"The criminal mind is a fascinating study, Val. The majority of criminals are moronic, need drugs and liquor before they can act at all. But sometimes psychologists find a mind and ability that could have gained success, even distinction in other walks of life. That has always interested me."

Her dark eyes looked off thoughtfully into space as he continued slowly, "There is something important beyond all that. I want you to see it but it's hard to put into words."

A sad smile curved her lips as she looked up at him. "You came here tonight to try to prepare me for the worst."

"You are seeing only the Phil you know. There is another picture you do not see or understand. In all human beings—even in the animal world—there is a sadistic quality that crops up. Every living thing instinctively hates and turns on the abnormal." He smiled. "Once I had a chicken born without feathers. The normal chickens pecked and would have killed the creature if I hadn't taken it into the house. You remember those screaming headlines in the sensational papers? Can't you see in Sunny Boy, Hal Martin, surrounded with wealth and prestige, what the public loves? And then, Philip Macrae, the abnormal. . . Nervous, highstrung, his unusual eyes, his deformity. A scapegoat for the public's outraged conscience . . ."

She closed her eyes tightly; her lips twisted and she bit them before she answered, "I saw that from the beginning. I have always seen it. No one, not one of them, could even imagine what Phil is really like."

"I wanted you to see both pictures."

"I appreciate it, Dr. Northrop. Thank you for the tablets. Yes, I will take them but if this goes against Phil, I wish you could give me some that would make me sleep forever."

"No, Val. Remember what your mother so often said? There was something indestructible in her. You are in your mother's shoes now. Little Louise, Andy, Mark, they all need you. No matter what happens to Phil, *he* will need you more than he has ever needed anyone in his life before."

The haggard dark eyes looked up into his face. "You think it will go against Phil!"

"I felt the cards were stacked when Murphy and Smythe testified. Loring has put up a bitter fight but in the eyes of the law—and nothing else matters—I feel the case is nearly closed, although one never knows what a jury will do. That's why I came up to see you tonight. I want you to get some sleep. I want you to conserve your strength."

"Thank you."

Long after he left she sat with arms outstretched across the table, her lips pressed hard into the unyielding line, the dark eyes mirroring the suffering in her heart.

The case was closed. There were the tedious days of summing up, the tense moments when the jury brought in their verdict, "Guilty" with a request for clemency because of the youth of the accused, health—and most humiliating—the needy family. Words that cut deep. Valeria wanted to call out how little that judge knew the young man to whom he was droning out words. If she could flee forever from the sound of strange human voices, the sight of strange human faces! The sentence came—two years in State prison.

There was a day when she was allowed to say good bye and a day when Philip Macrae was taken between two officers aboard a train and Valeria drove home with Jake and Robert.

At the door of the empty house, Jake said, "You shouldn't be alone. Celia or Miriam will come down."

"No, thank you both for everything. Please don't come in. I want to be alone. What could I ever be afraid of—*now?*"

CHAPTER XXV

SEAR AND BROWN, the leaves fell from the branches of maple and elm to the earth where the frost was penetrating deeper day by day.

Marriage? The night of fathomless peace and happiness when she had promised Robert they would be married as soon as she "had caught her breath" seemed to have receded into some remote past when she had been some other Valeria. When she wakened in the morning she found this pain, like a stone heavy in her breast. Through the hours of the day, when she closed her eyes at night, it was still there. In those fall months, like Phil, she erected a wall of reserve, of silence, about herself— something no sensitive soul would venture trying to penetrate.

Once when Robert took her in his arms he pleaded, "Can't you let me take this burden on my shoulders, Val?"

With trembling lips and beseeching eyes she asked, "Can you be patient with me, Robert?"

He smiled a little sadly. "I can be patient."

Though she drew her pride about her like a cloak there was no fear in her heart. Every morning she arose early, prepared the breakfast and saw Louise in her little red coat get into the school bus that gathered the children from the hill and carried them to the central school. Every day she thanked God for the child with her gurgling laughter and her excitement in each moment of living.

She called Jake. "When you have time, Jake, will you teach me to drive this car?"

He brought down the Buick.

"No, Jake. I want to drive the old car. The mechanic came up, looked it over and said it was good for thousands of miles. I want to be a good driver."

He taught her and, after arranging with Miriam to have Louise left at the farm, she took a journey across the state to the penitentiary, staying at a small hotel overnight and driving home the next day.

Jake was hovering nervously about the house awaiting her return. She turned into the drive, to the barn. His relief was evident. "You have nerve, Val. No trouble?"

"At first the cities bothered me. I was afraid I wouldn't notice some sign but now I'm used to it. Nothing but a blizzard will keep me from going."

Sometimes in those hard weeks, to Robert's or Jake's anxious questions, she tried to describe her visits but who can visualize a prison who has not walked and lived behind the gates that lock out the world and all its busy, independent life? Once the warden, who was very kind to her, took her into the kitchen. Not once in the time she watched these convicts preparing food, not once as the long line passed her, filing into the bare hall for a meal, did her eyes look into another pair of eyes. If one, only one would look up at her as people in normal life were used to doing! The feet shuffled, the eyes were downcast or shifted quickly from hers.

The sad old faces! The fearful number of youthful faces— young in years only.

Each one had heard the words: "sentenced to hard labor." At that labor she learned that Phil had fainted, had twice collapsed, and now it was a comfort to know he was put to work in the office or library.

She was promised an interview with the doctor. She seized the opportunity to talk of Phil both to him and the warden. Earnestly she told them of his musical talents. Oh yes, she must take that hard trip as often as she could manage, step behind that grilled gate, walk through those frightful halls, smell the smell of human bodies, feel the despair, the anguish of human minds and sense the degradation of human souls. She was the one to go and go alone. There were faces she came to know and would never forget. There was a knowledge of vileness that sickened her. She came to know the stories of those who served sentences, went out into the world and committed more heinous crimes.

Sometimes as she drove alone over the long roads she multiplied the number of human beings behind these walls by all the men and women in prisons throughout the land. A world apart! Death in the midst of life! Even when men worked in the fields or marched in their exercise or played games, it was always under guard. Often she became physically sick as the faces became more deeply imprinted on her memory. Even in her own sweetly fresh bedroom she waked in the night finding herself living in that world of imprisoned men. What would it do to Phil?

It was on her second visit that she had found him in the hospital. He reluctantly told her of the faint, followed by a severe cold. Again and again he assured her, "I can take it, Val."

In spite of his pallor and weakness she felt sure there was no mental depression. He smiled as he talked and throughout her visit it was he who seemed to be trying to cheer her. Only once his lips twisted with bitterness. "If it were not for my family—for you and Miri and Mark and Andy—if I could forget you, I'd get through all right." Suddenly he raised himself, resting on an elbow. His eyes gleamed. "You know, Val, I wake in the night, not only hearing but seeing every note of music I want to write. Sometimes I feel as though everything had been cleared away and I am alone in the world and free to compose, to feel and hear nothing but music. If they would only allow me to have manuscript and pens and ink."

She told him how kind the warden had been to her, promising to do everything in her power to get him this privilege. However, it was many months before she was successful.

There were times through the following months when she

drove home fighting every mile of the way to keep tears from blinding her. Those were the days when she saw no vestige of light in his face, saw the hard lines deepening in the flesh, realized he was giving up the struggle to keep his back straight, was seemingly indifferent about his appearance. On such days she fought desperately, begging him to help them both keep what Mother had called "their integrity."

"The months are passing, Phil. There is all our life ahead of us."

"Never mind my life, Val. What about yours? I am keeping you from marrying Robert Loring. Or has he revised his opinion of the family?"

It was in such periods that she doubled the number of her visits and once, when she didn't dare brave the deep snow, allowed Jake to drive her.

Work! How she worked! She brought her writing materials to the kitchen table and, after Louise left for school, she began story after story but with no success.

She had become acquainted with a young woman who came every week to the prison, holding two children by the hand, patiently waiting for her half-hour visit with a husband sentenced to ten years. He had been drinking, got into a brawl and knocked down a man who died from the blow. She was a pretty creature with lovely blond hair. She could obtain a divorce and marry again. Instead she had taken a room, and a job in a factory to be near the young man because she loved him.

Valeria sat one morning thinking about her. Why did the girl's devotion, love and sacrifice link itself to Emerson in her mind? Was there here that divine spark, that part of the All Being? Was love the greatest thing in the world? This was what she wanted to write about, but couldn't.

She must talk to Robert. One afternoon he faced a bitter March wind to walk up the hill, smiling as he sat down beside her. "I am almost equally divided between envy of and thankfulness for Jake who is so near you and is privileged to come in morning, noon and night to help you."

"Jake can't help me with this." Well she knew the difference between Robert the lover and Robert the teacher. She could smile as she looked back at the time when she feared he was idolizing some false ideal of her, dreaded his overestimating her. Now his love had become the anchor that held amidst all the eddies and crosscurrents of her life. She was as sure of his love as of the warmth of the sun.

Her hands tightly clasped, lips quivering with earnestness, she told him of her trouble. "It isn't just the girl's story I want to write; it's what it means to me."

She went on with passionate intentness. "Once, I thought I didn't know enough about life. Now, I feel as though I know too much. Jessie Macrae, Hal Martin, Ezra Martin. . . Dr. Northrop tells me Ezra Martin has had a stroke and is lying in bed, slowly dying in his beautiful mansion. It isn't the facts of his life but what it means. About this girl—I want to write what her love means. I can't."

His hands held hers firmly. "Val, in writing, you have had what I would call a minor success. You wrote of what you knew, stories that were amusing, poured out with spontaneity and, unconsciously, filled with your deep love for the boys. You are trying now to do something that would give pause to the greatest writer.

"You have talent, originality and a passionate desire to write." He smiled. "There is all the difference in the world between the person who wants to write and the person who wants to be a writer. You want to write. You will be a writer. Let's face it. Think of a musician. For how many long, long years does he practice, sometimes six, seven hours a day before he is ready for a concert in Carnegie Hall? Through daily practice, with small successes and great failures, you acquire technique. When you sit down at your typewriter tomorrow morning, don't try to be an Emerson, just write simply that blond girl's story. Perhaps the reader will get more than you express in words.

"In my writing, I deal in facts and in the interpretation of those facts. You are creating life. You are arrogant where you must be humble."

Slowly she lifted her bent head and smiled into his eyes. "I see why you are a wonderful teacher, Robert. You humiliate a person at the same time that you inspire him. You will edit whatever I write? It was your editing that made the little book fit for publication."

"We'll work together. Always. Now, for the truth. Is it to earn money that you're working?"

"I want to be able to support both myself and Louise."

"I thought so. There is no lack of money. Our wants are simple and what I have is yours."

She murmured, "Until Phil is home again—sometimes I feel so bewildered."

Sometimes in the night she would waken as thoughts came racing through her mind, bringing in the dark some clarity that she had not acquired in the day. So often she had told herself that she knew poverty but was ignorant of wealth. Now she thought of Hal Martin and what money had meant to him. She thought also of Bobbie.

And what of Uncle William? He must be lonely. And what of his bad heart? He might die and she would never know. He had spent his life acquiring wealth and what had it given him in his old age, beyond every creature comfort that money could buy. The devotion of those who were paid for their devotion? She wondered.

One day she found herself thinking so much about him that she got out the road map. How many gallons of gasoline would it require to drive out to see him? Much cheaper than the train? No, it was too far, would require too many expensive stops. Perhaps he would be glad to send her the train fare. He might want to see her. She had always thought he liked her.

She would always remember this as an unique experience, something that showed there might be such a thing as mental telepathy, for one morning, even while she was thinking of him, the postman handed her a letter postmarked Cleveland.

She opened it eagerly.

What writing! Perhaps when a man has written only to sign his name for most of his life his handwriting *would* look like this. She worked over it.

Dear Valeria:

Are you teaching? If the doctors allow, next summer I shall come to see you. Write me fully of your condition. Your brother is not the first black sheep in the Macrae family. I should like to see you get away from them all. You will hear from me again. Write me.

                                            Your
                                                Uncle William.

Over and over, getting used to the scratched writing, she read the letter. Not a word about Bobbie. Not a word about his own lonely life.

Every week she wrote long letters to Mark and Andy. She could not write the kind of letters that her mother would have written. Sometimes her fingers dropped from the typewriter and she told herself, "No, I mustn't try to write like Mother. I must talk to them straight from my heart so they will know it is Val speaking." One morning she ended her letter, "We will stick to him as long as we live. He is so wonderful that he makes me feel ashamed. I have taken his manuscripts to him and they allow him to work on them. If it takes the three of us the rest of our lives we must somehow make this up to Phil."

On a cold, dreary November morning while she was deeply engrossed in her writing, she looked up at the sound of hail snapping against the window panes. Fearing the slippery roads, she had been hesitant about allowing Louise to go to school that morning. The storm seemed to be increasing. She remembered that Mark used to look out of the window when a football game was scheduled and there seemed to be a battle between clearing and raining, and exclaim impatiently, "I wish it would make up its mind." Now, after she had allowed Louise to take the bus, it had made up its mind to storm.

Only a few brown leaves clung to a single bough, shivering in the gale. She was deeply troubled, for two weeks more would bring Thanksgiving and before that would come Louise's birthday. What could she do for the child to make that a happy day? Perhaps Miri would have a party for her up at the farm. She would call Miri and talk that over.

Andy and Mark had both written they wished to come home for Thanksgiving. Had there been a deeply felt but unacknowledged hope that no one would come? Couldn't she be allowed just once to pass by this fateful time?

She would call her sister now and discuss the birthday. She was in the hall ready to telephone when, glancing through the window she saw a figure, a woman, head bent low as she buffeted the wind, coming up the path.

A stranger? She looked again and then there was a strange sensation, half fright and half pain, something that seemed like icy fingers clutching at her heart. She saw who it was. She had only a moment to close her eyes and think, "God give me strength to cope with this," and she opened the door.

Jessie Macrae. The woman stood there in a dripping black coat looking into her face. "I'd better go into the kitchen, Val, I'm soaking."

With unsteady fingers she fumbled at the buttons, got them opened and laid the coat and black felt hat near the stove. Her shoes and stockings and skirt were wet. Valeria's voice sounded strained as she said, "You ought to take off those wet stockings."

Jessie looked up at her and laughed and again icy fingers seemed to clutch at Valeria as she gazed down into that face.

She had seen her on the stand at the trial—but here in this house the evidences of dissipation seemed even more shocking.

"Got some of that 'medicinal' whiskey, Val?"

As Val walked across the room to the cupboard her feet and legs felt shaky. Yes, she was afraid. There was something she could be afraid of. There was Jessie Macrae.

She brought the bottle and a glass. There was not much but Jessie poured it all into the glass and drank it almost in one gulp. "I might catch cold!" She laughed again.

Valeria had no answer. She saw how the woman's thin hands shook as she smoothed the pale blond hair; saw how her eyes traveled about the room.

The jittery laugh again. "This kitchen's like the rock of Gibraltar, never changes, always here."

There was no answer to that.

"Why don't you *say* something, Val."

"Jessie, would you like something to eat?"

"I'd chew the heel off one of those loaves of bread you used to bake. Got an egg?"

"I'll get lunch. Would you like to lie down until it's ready?"

"No. I'm not taking care of myself, Cousin. I'd rather watch you. Used to watch you—used to try to figure you out—used to wonder what you were thinking of—used to—used to—"

Was it the whiskey? Or was Jessie really ill? Back and forth as fast as she could go, Valeria scrambled eggs in bacon, made coffee, cut slices of bread. She was setting the dishes on the table when the husky voice cried out, "Where's her chair? Where's the window? What have you done with her chair?"

"It's in the music room. We built on the new wing and made her room into a music room."

"Where? Show me where?" She staggered to her feet. Valeria went before her into the hall, into what had been the bedroom. Jessie walked through, looked at the new wing, came through the wide doors and held to the wall as she made her way back to the kitchen where she dropped heavily into a chair.

The muscles in her face were working spasmodically. "What did you do with her bed?"

Valeria explained.

"I slept in that bed. My baby was born in that bed. That was the only baby I ever had."

Valeria set the food on the table and tried not to watch the half-starved woman eat. When she had drunk the second cup of coffee, Valeria set cake and preserved peaches before her. She remembered peaches were Jessie's favorite dessert.

At last she leaned back, grinning. "I always licked the dishes clean. Got more coffee?"

She drained another cup. She looked at Valeria. "It's about her birthday, isn't it? Now you can tell me all about her. That's what I want to know—all about her."

Valeria began, "Louise is in school—" but she was interrupted, "What's that? You call her Louise? Like *her*?"

"Mother wished that." She went on, trying desperately to find words. "She is a very healthy, happy little girl."

"Where does she sleep?"

"When Miri was married we gave her that bedroom."

"My room?"

There was a long silence. Jessie's head dropped. She looked exhausted.

The old pain and fear and pity were almost choking Valeria. "Don't you want to lie down and rest, Jessie?"

The eyes with the deep black circles looked at her piercingly, the lips parted in a tremulous smile. "Sure, Val. I want to lie down and rest. How polite you always are. Just like her. She taught you that. You don't deserve any credit. She taught you. I went out to her grave. It was covered with snow. God, *she* needed to lie down and rest." Suddenly the whole wasted frame shook with hysterical sobs. Jessie made no effort to wipe away the tears that streamed down her face.

Valeria found a handkerchief and put it in her hands even as she glanced at the clock. It was half-past two. In a half hour the school bus would pass the door. What should she do? Why had Jessie come? What did she want?

Inexorably the hands of the clock moved on. It was twenty-five minutes of three.

Jessie had noticed. She was drying her face. "You're watching the clock, Val." She stood for a moment holding on to the table as if steadying herself. "She comes on the bus a little after three?"

"Yes. Perhaps if you would go up and sleep, you could freshen up and come down to supper."

For a moment she gazed into Valeria's dark eyes. "I know what I'm doing."

She went across the room and took down her coat and hat.

"Oh, Jessie, I can't let you go out again in this cold rain. You —you are ill! Where are you going?"

She was pulling on the coat, buttoning it clumsily, placing the hat on her blond hair, jerking it down about her ears. For a moment she hesitated, then walked toward the stove, holding out her hands. "I had to come back and see the house and see her. I'm going back to my father and Mexico. I'm stopping in New York to see Ben Loring to sign some papers. Then he'll send legal adoption papers to you." Again tears wet her face. "I never wanted that baby. I don't want her now. She's yours."

Valeria could find no words. Minutes ticked away before she cleared her throat and whispered, "Oh, Jessie."

"Cut it, Val. I hate dramatics."

Valeria following, she went into the hall, stood a moment looking into the parlor, the music room. "You always ran the whole show, Val. This is a lovely house for Louise to grow up in. You'll run it so that I'm pretty sure someday she'll be a bride and be married in that parlor. I don't know what you'll do about explaining me or her father. But you'll manage even that."

Valeria's heart ached with pity. "Jessie, don't go out in this rain. Oh, please tell me—have you a place to go?"

There was not much of her face to be seen between the pulled down hat and the collar of her coat but the eyes looked straight into Valeria's.

"Don't mention this visit to anyone. Good bye, Val. You'll never hear from me or see me again."

At the door, she turned. "I'll see Louise." She was out in the pouring rain and hail when she turned to add, "You have nothing to worry about. She won't see me."

The November days were short and with the heavy clouds low in the sky there was a semi-darkness like evening as Valeria slowly closed the door.

Now the gale was at her back, blowing the dark figure. Valeria stood at the window watching. She saw her reach the gate, then step behind a tree. The big maple hid her from view.

Valeria thought, "Mother would never have allowed her to go like this." And then, "She never spoke of Phil. She never spoke his name."

Her own hands icy cold, Valeria's eyes never wavered as she watched. The bus came into view, stopped. A little girl in a red coat alighted. She looked back to call to a school friend and Valeria saw the dark figure step out from behind the tree. She must have been able to look directly into the child's face.

The little girl came running fast against the wind but even as she held the door open Valeria hardly saw her for she was watching the thin figure hurrying down the road.

CHAPTER XXVI

LONG AFTER THE HOUR of the sun's setting the brilliant afterglow seemed to be mocking a silver crescent rising in the summer sky. Valeria waved to it. "Pale little moon. It's almost unnoticeable now but in a few hours it will be shining brightly."

She was walking in the garden with Robert Loring. "Sometimes I think the color of the flowers deepen just before the light fades; the blue of the larkspur, the purple of the heliotrope, and just look at that golden glow and the sunflowers by the barn."

He followed her down a grassy path to the center where the bird bath stood in a circular space. "At last you have a perfect garden, Val. I don't know how you ever find time to do all this work. Mother said she had never seen such bachelor's buttons, such a variety of zinnias, gladiolus, bluebells, your nasturtium, phlox, these borders of mignonette and pansies. How do you do it?"

She laughed. "She didn't see all the good cow manure Jake allows me to pilfer from the fields; but it isn't perfect, Robert. The wonderful thing about a garden is—it's always a dream of what one will do *next* summer; it's always leading you on."

She straightened up from pulling some weeds. "Besides, a garden must have walls. Thanks to you and Jake I have that wall of shrubs and evergreens started but it will take years to grow into the solid enclosure I visualize."

He knew that the happiness in her heart, the glow that lighted her eyes, was not caused but only enhanced by the splendor of her garden. Ben Loring had telephoned news that brought first tears, then laughter. There was a possibility that his persistent efforts to gain a commutation of Phil's sentence was to be successful. If the promises were fulfilled because of good behavior, illness and youth and because of all the arguments and pressure Ben had brought to bear on those in authority, Phil would be home in a matter of months, perhaps weeks.

There was also the question of Louise. Robert looked deep into the dark eyes as he held Valeria close in his arms. "A child needs walls as much as a garden, Val. A mother *and* father are needed to make that wall strong and complete. I know how you have felt about Phil. You belonged to him. You have always said, 'when Phil comes home.' He is coming. Must we wait longer? Don't you agree it is time for you to have a child of your own?"

He added "I practically live here now. I might as well be allowed to move in." He laughed, "The old women gossip, you know."

"I don't know the old women and they mean nothing to me. The cars don't stop as they used to while people stared at the house."

"Time heals all things. The public wearies of one sensation and wants something new."

"That has been the most trivial part of it. It never has bothered me as much as one might think it would."

"I know that."

"Andy wants to bring his girl up some week end. You say Ben really likes her?"

"They are delighted. I'm afraid they are preening themselves as successful matchmakers."

"It seems like a little boy marrying. I guess I've got to feeling like his mother. Sometimes I worry about Mark. He seems to have so many girls."

"Give him time and he'll find the right one. I knew the right one when I first saw her, even when she wore her hair in braids."

She stopped, wound her arms tight about his neck, her dark eyes holding a light that few had seen there. "There was something I always knew or felt when you came near me or spoke to me. So long you were sort of a god on a pedestal because I looked so far up to you. I needed all this time, Robert. There were so many things in the way—so many people, so much I was responsible for. Now I don't feel like a separate person. No one who has never known it would understand what I mean. We have done so much together. We have gone through so much, always together. There is no worst or best to be discovered. It was long before I could be sure that if you really knew me, you could still love me. Now I am sure."

"I am taking Mother to my brother. He is starting in his ministry and needs her."

"You will be alone?"

"All alone in that little house. Can't you feel sorry for me?" He was laughing.

"Not much. You have a contract for that book and can't get enough time to work on it. You need the time."

"Which I spend with you, keeping you from work."

"You are like Phil. You always win an argument."

"You mean I have won?"

She buried her face on his shoulder. "I'm not sure, dear. I must talk to you about something that troubles me. About Phil, I will be so thankful when I can start to build up his health. He needs good food and real rest. Sometimes, if it weren't for Louise I couldn't bear to see the food on our table and know his need of home cooking."

"Val, there is another question you evade. I don't want to press you but I worry too. Do you have money enough? It costs you plenty to make these trips and your last story hasn't sold yet."

She smiled. "Do I look so shabby in my old clothes? Mother always said I was too unconcerned about my looks. I even tried to cut my own hair but Miri almost wept about that so I go to the barber and begrudge every cent." She added thoughtfully, "Once I wanted pretty dresses and shoes—especially shoes—and coats and everything like that so badly. After that I never seemed to care. Please tell me if I look too dreadful, Robert."

"You are a fright. I have to remember my position and spruce up, myself. Let's get this straight. I expect to teach only long enough to save money to tide me over poor days when I am working on a book. With one published and doing fairly well and with this contract I want to give all my time to writing after this year. We will always be precariously balanced financially, dear."

She looked grave. "Where I would feel at home but where you need not be. Ben and your entire family are disappointed because you didn't accept that position at Princeton. They probably blame me."

"And you were unhappy about that. Tell me why. Tell the truth now."

"Let's go in."

They sat in the music room, she in the old armchair.

She looked across at him and answered. "Robert, if a woman marries a man she should love him so much that she would be willing to give up everything for him. She should be willing to follow him anywhere he goes, to any corner of the earth where his work takes him. I love you. I want to be your wife. I want to be with you, to love you and care for you as long as we both live but I can't honestly say that I could happily follow you anywhere you went in this world. I have lain awake nights trying so hard to think that out."

He walked up and down, watching her as she went on, "I want to be here when Phil comes home. That is why I am afraid to change anything now. It is worse than that. I can't understand it myself. I don't want to leave this place—even for you. It isn't the house entirely, though I love it; it's the woods, the fields, the garden, even the ravine."

He leaned over her, taking her hands in his. "What mountains you make out of molehills. Like a poor mendicant I beg you to allow me to come here. Don't you think you could let me have a corner? We would be poor perhaps, but we might find ourselves the richest people in the world, working together, suffering or rejoicing together. You make me beg."

She smiled. "There you go, winning an argument again."
He drew her up into his arms. "It is settled?"
"Yes. I'm happy."
"When am I to be wholly happy?"
"Robert, I'm afraid of your family. It is such a substantial big family. I have no one much here now. I wouldn't want a wedding. I wouldn't know what on earth to do about that. I would want just to get married. Your people wouldn't like that."
"Another molehill. We have been surfeited with weddings. I'd hate it. Let's have a minister or a proper authority say a few words and let it go at that."
She smoothed back the slightly graying hair from his temples, laughing. "I love how you look, Robert. You are so distinguished looking. You would be stunning standing at the altar before a crowd. What a pity to miss that. Instead, you will buy a new gray suit and I'll buy a new dress and we'll come home and put on our old clothes and go to work."
"May I come with you and choose the dress? It must be silk."
"And I want pretty shoes."

It was not quite so simple as they had planned. The words that made them man and wife were said before his brother in the parlor of the old house. Ben Loring insisted he was just passing through with his mother, so they were there. Andy came up with the young girl "to see again how it was done," Mark came on the night train. Miriam, Ned and Jake naturally came in. Mr. and Mrs. Waters and Mrs. Simms guessed there would be hungry people so they brought a wedding cake and arranged a fine supper.

Valeria had planned it on Louise's birthday so there was a little cake with candles and Louise thought the whole affair her birthday celebration and it was, for a few days later she was adopted legally by Robert Loring with the name Louise Macrae Loring.

If in every heart in that room there was a sad, deep consciousness of the one who was not there, no one spoke of it.

There were two cars now in the old barn and little Louise went off with Robert who left her at the central school, then went on to the high school. There was another winter of storms and the roads were treacherous with snow and ice and Valeria could not take those long drives but she wrote daily and successfully arranged the publication of some songs.

Laughingly she went to the hairdressers and kept her hair neatly trimmed and every evening she put on one of her good dresses for supper and every day Robert told her how he loved her and as the winter passed and the days lengthened a radiance came into her face that was to dwell there permanently.

There came a time for which she had never ceased to pray. Phil was coming home.

"I shall arrange for a substitute and drive you out there."

She looked across the table with love shining in her eyes. "No, Robert, nothing can happen to me. I'll have the mechanic look the car over. I know what Phil would want. I must go alone."

He looked worried. "I don't like it but I know how you feel. Would you be willing to let Jake go with you?"

"No. I must be alone with Phil."

She drove away from home when it was still dark one morning. It was late the following evening when the car turned into the drive. She stopped at the back door and they got out. There was a tired, drawn look in Valeria's face, for it had been an exhausting day.

One glanced at Phil and looked away. One's heart might cry out, "What has happened to him?" Thin almost to emaciation, pale as a sheet of one of his own manuscripts. Then one saw the brilliant dark eyes shining but often dropping quickly before another's gaze. Time. Over and over to herself, Valeria thought, "He must have time."

If Robert ever felt that he had slipped, even temporarily, into second place he gave no sign, and she blessed him for it. When she tried haltingly to explain that the one in greatest need must take precedence over the one who "has everything" as she said, until the need is over, he laughed at her tenderly. "Remember how Phil used to say, 'Why the worry?' "

Mornings, after Louise and Robert left, Phil walked about from room to room, back and forth, back and forth, first silently and then, as the days wore on, he talked. There was no subject, even to the details of Jessie's visit, that they did not discuss down to the minutest detail.

One Sunday Andy came home. On another Sunday, Mark came. Jake began to drop in, but as yet Phil had never taken a step toward the barn. His manuscripts were stacked on his bureau.

Knowing all his favorite dishes, Valeria produced them but he ate little. She asked, "Phil, would you be willing to have Dr. Northrop come up to see you? I think he might suggest a tonic."

"This air is tonic enough, Val. Give me time. I feel as though I will have to be born again and I miss Mother."

"I miss Mother." Again and again she heard those words until her heart ached; then, one day he added, "Long ago Mother and I used to discuss the lives of musicians, the great ones who had died in poverty, their days of hopelessness as they struggled for food enough to keep life in their bodies. Mother suggested that the government should subsidize those with talent. I knew she was wrong but it took eighteen months in prison to know why. I want to tell her—I want to tell the entire world what I learned."

Sometimes he paced up and down the floor, sometimes he would throw himself into a chair, stretch out his thin arms, his nervous hands clenched, the fingers digging into the palms as he talked. "Val, you remember how we read the philosophic theories of Marx, Engels and our own Dewey? They told us that the oldest and greatest fear in the world is the fear of want, hunger, and lack. They taught that if those fears could be removed there would be international peace and the primary cause of crime would be removed. Perhaps they would say that my case fits their theory perfectly. But the whole theory is false.

It's a black lie that could destroy all the advance of civilization."

He jumped up and walked rapidly back and forth. "Think, Val, what I had. I had food for my body of good quality and plenty of it. I wore a regulation uniform, always clean and fresh. I had a room to myself fairly large and airy. Economically speaking the State did a good job looking after my wants.

"I had no bills to pay. The barber came regularly to look after my hair. My laundry went out and came back with automatic regularity. If I became ill I was assured of medical attention. I was exempt from all forms of taxes. I had no home or family responsibilities. There were no civil or other obligations in my life."

He leaned over her. "Do you see, Val, I had perfect security in prison. 'Man shall not live by bread alone.' Those words beat through my brain day and night and some day I think I can set them to music. I learned that poverty is not the cause of crime nor is prosperity the cure of crime. The more prosperous our country grows, the more crime increases. That prison was not filled with typical paupers. If I had depended on my bodily securities and comfort for healing, I would not be healed. The peace I, like every other man, craves in his soul, the joy I hunger for in life, could not be governed by the amount of food I put into my stomach or by clean clothes or shelter."

As her mother had so many years ago, Valeria sat for minutes astonished and silenced by Phil's eloquence. Then she raised her head and asked thoughtfully, "Doesn't everybody crave and work for security? What about the insurance that Father left Mother? Wasn't that security?"

"Oh, Val, you are talking about something as different from what I mean as black is from white. While Father was working in the factory or in his office he scrimped and paid regularly some hundreds of dollars and at his death Mother received three thousand. Can't you see that it was hers? She was free to squander it, spend it wisely, hoard it. She made the decisions. Every father living is free to save, to dream of a home, buy it, engage in business, work or loaf. If he loves his wife or family, he plans for their protection, or not—he, a free man according to his circumstances." He stopped to laugh with something of his old sarcastic mischief. "Why if your great Uncle William should turn his generosity in our direction and leave us some of his hard-earned money—and I admit it probably was hard-earned—we would be free men still. We again would be free to spend or save. We would have to make our own decisions. That is freedom, exactly the opposite of security as exercised by an authority."

"I see the difference. I see exactly what you mean, Phil."

The nervous hands clasped and unclasped. "Not that I think for one minute that inherited wealth is a blessing. All the security produced by worldly means puts an end to growth. I can't put it into words but I know that struggle, the daily fight to live, to compete with other men in the world, to initiate, to dream and struggle to change the dreams into reality, to be endlessly *dis*satisfied, to be seeking and grasping for happiness, to know the joy of even minor achievements—all this means life and God's greatest gift is life.

"There are hundreds, I expect thousands of prison inmates who have adapted themselves to security, there are hundreds and thousands of dead souls in the security of those walls. God help them." He leaned back as though exhausted but there was a light in his eyes that spoke volumes to her.

"I understand, Phil. I can look back over my own little life and I wouldn't change one hour of work or struggle or suffering or any other anxiety."

"To face responsibility, decide something for yourself, regain your power of initiating something and accomplish it on your own. . . It was only after they allowed you to bring my manuscripts, give me a few hours to work on them, that I felt I might save my mind and not come out a dead man. You can't understand what I mean by having to be born again—to learn to walk about the house, to dress, to eat and sleep as *I* decide."

Sometimes it was the unexpected event that seemed to give him the greatest pleasure. Often, Miriam walked in carrying her fine baby boy. During the first visits, Phil's eyes merely rested on the child but there came a day when he took him in his arms. It was good to hear his laugh as he said, "The youngest of six children produces the first grandchild."

Miriam answered as gaily, "You wait a few years and you'll have more nieces and nephews than you bargain for."

Val saw the great relief it seemed to give him to "talk it out." "I am looking forward to the day when you will sit down at that piano and play for me. You have filled so many pages of manuscript and I long to hear what you have written. I have missed your playing!"

After almost a month there came a day when she heard him lift the cover, heard his fingers run over the keys and strike some chords. It was a school day, so they too were alone in the quiet house. Suddenly the doorbell rang sharply. She passed through the hall seeing a boy with a telegram. She signed for it and the boy ran down the steps. Phil, suddenly jerky with nervousness, watched her open it. She read quickly and handed it to him.

WILLIAM MACRAE DIED AT FOUR A.M. TODAY. HE WISHED YOU TO BE NOTIFIED.   SIGNED,
JOHN TRACY, ATTORNEY

They sat down in the kitchen, the telegram laid out on the table. Valeria looked sad and depressed. "I wanted to go out and see him but I didn't know how to manage it. Why should they notify me by telegram? Should I go to Cleveland now? What about Bobbie? Do you suppose there is anyone to take care of the funeral? We know nothing about him; haven't heard from him in all these months, not since that short letter. I can't see why they notify me unless there is something they expect me to do."

"He was methodical to the last degree. I am sure his lawyers know his wishes. Likely Bobbie is there. There is one thing that might be sensible. Why not telephone this John Tracy? Poor old Uncle. I'd telephone and find out what they expect of you."

She found the number in her mother's old book and Phil got the connection.

After many delays she heard a voice saying, "This is John Tracy. Valeria Macrae?"

To her questions about the telegram he asked, "This is Valeria Macrae? Mrs. Robert Loring?"

"Yes, sir."

In answer to her questions, he told her, "I will be on to see you within the week. All arrangements for your uncle's funeral have been made. Your sister is in Europe. No, there is no need of your coming here. I can tell you as I am your uncle's attorney that you are named sole heir to your uncle's estate."

And, "Your sister was provided for, also certain charities but you are the heir."

Phil had stood near listening but getting little idea of what the voice was saying. When Valeria hung up the receiver she told him.

He stared at her, following her into the kitchen where she sank weakly into a chair. "It is preposterous. I can't imagine what he was thinking of."

"He was evidently thinking of you, Val, when he made out that will."

Then, surprising him, shocking him, she began to cry. She spoke brokenly. "He has never tried to help me through all these black months. I would have given every cent he owned to save you from prison. Think what it would have meant over the years to have had some of this money, when you could have gone to college, when I could have gone to normal college, when Mother wouldn't call Dr. Northrop because of the fee, when Mark and Andy had to do every kind of menial work their hands could find to do for ten dollars or five dollars, when we sewed and mended and made over until Mother was exhausted, when you had to grind and grind in that bank and let your music go. I don't need his money now. I don't want it. I don't need it. I am so happy now. I'm sure that Robert and you and I can earn everything we are going to need. I was so happy thinking of our all working together. *I don't want his money.*"

For a few moments Phil watched her in consternation; then he began to laugh and there was something in that gay, spontaneous laughter that caused her to look up into his face. "What's so funny?"

"You, Val. I agree with you his timing was bad but I forgive the old fellow everything now. He knew you. He appreciated you. The great Uncle William has done something that even I call great at last. Perhaps the poor lonely old chap has always loved you. Perhaps leaving you money was one of his few ways of finding happiness. I forgive him everything because he appreciated you."

"I don't want my life changed, Phil. I love everything just as it is."

His face sobered. After a moment's thought he leaned over and laid his hand on her shoulder. "Who knows, Val? Perhaps this is to be the greatest test of your strength and character—the greatest in your life. You will be under no necessity to work, so you may choose whether to be a worker or idler. That's only one of many serious decisions you will have to make. Don't you see you are absolutely free? In some ways it is a great challenge. I think you have passed the test of poverty. Who knows? Perhaps the good Lord is planning to test you with riches. It could be. Your responsibility for Mark and Andy and Miri has passed. Now you're going to have the responsibility of spending this money. Don't you see what a challenge it is? And don't you see this is *not* administered by some authority but by you? Only your decisions will count."

She was gazing into his face, her eyes widening. "You are wonderful, Phil. I see what you mean." Then smiling at last, "I am glad Robert and I were married before this happened.

You understand?" A soft flush rose in her cheeks. "Our marriage is—is perfect without anything extraneous, like this."

"I understand. At least that timing was right."

With his old charm, with his ability to make any occasion a delightful one, he laughed again. "Val, will you lend me a few dollars when you get them? I'd like to fix that barn up. This is your house, and you can offer me a corner in it or—not, as you choose. Do you remember how Father planned to make that barn a real studio for Mother? Do you know what I used to dream about? I'd like to install a pipe organ, make it a workman's music studio. I drew plans once—just a crazy dream. Would you want to do that?"

She looked at him with wide-open eyes. Phil was soaring again! "Want to!" She felt almost dizzy with the surge of happiness. "We'll fix the barn up. We'll get a new car that won't rattle. I'll get some pretty dresses that Robert will like. We'll send Louise to a fine college. We'll just soar, Phil."

He laid his hand on her head as he rose. "We'll have a whale of a time."

She hardly realized he had left the room when the crashing chords of the concerto's finale echoed through the house. And it was as though neither the walls of the house nor her heart could contain the splendor of triumph expressed in the notes.

Some days later, John Tracy sat in the parlor with Val, Robert and Phil. She spoke soberly, "I want my husband and my brother to know all about the business."

Several calls followed the first, and endless papers and explanations. On the day when he left for Cleveland, Tracy turned at the door. "It has been very pleasant knowing you, Mrs. Loring. I don't wonder your uncle made you his heir. You are quite a rich woman, you know."

Her eyes were full of light as she said, "I expect I have always been a very rich woman, Mr. Tracy. Sometimes I didn't know it."